To Ron and Sue

From Teddy & Gloria

Thank you

May 1978

KING'S
VIEWS OF
NEW YORK
1896—1915
&
BROOKLYN
1905

KING'S VIEWS OF NEW YORK
1896—1915
&
BROOKLYN
1905

An Extraordinary Photographic Survey

Compiled by Moses King

New Introduction by A. E. Santaniello

ARNO PRESS NEW YORK 1977

The publisher wishes to acknowledge the courteous
cooperation of John H. Lindenbusch, Executive Director, and
the members of the staff of the Long Island Historical
Society in making the exceedingly rare original editions of
King's Views of New York available for reproduction.

First published Boston, 1896, 1903, 1905, 1908, 1911, 1915

Reprint Edition 1974 by Benjamin Blom, Inc.

Reprint Edition 1977 by Arno Press, Inc.

Copyright © 1974 by Benjamin Blom, Inc.

Manufactured in the United States of America

Library of Congress Cataloging in Publication Data

King, Moses, 1853-1909.
  King's views of New York, 1896-1915 & Brooklyn, 1905.

  Reprint of the ed. published by B. Blom, New York.
  Includes index.
  1.   New York (City)—Description—Views.   2.   Brooklyn
—Description—Views. I.   Title.

[F128.37.K52 1977]   974.7'1'040222   77-1779
ISBN 0-405-08710-1

INTRODUCTION

A. E. Santaniello

Confident that "at no far distant day New York will have erected a series of public buildings, founded an array of public institutions, beautified a number of thoroughfares, and added to her palatial homes, to her area, and to her population to such a degree that she will be freely accorded the pre-eminent position of the Chief City of the World," Moses King began a series of volumes at the turn of the century that would be one of the most complete photographic records of the city ever published. No record of the growth of New York City, and particularly a photographic record, remained definitive for even the shortest period, however, and *King's Views of New York* was continually updated.

Rare today, the volumes were issued almost annually and sold in the tens of thousands of copies—testimony to their popularity as well as to the unique quality of the subject matter—and were continued for decades after the death of the originator. An eloquent reminder of a vanishing world and a valuable source for much lost architecture, *King's Views* shows the many faces of the city as it embarked on one of its greatest periods of development.

The first volume reproduced in its entirety in this edition —originally published in 1896—appeared almost simultaneously with the beginning of the decade of spectacular growth that not only gave New York its celebrated skyline (the word itself actually seems to have been used for the first time in that same year) but set the tone and tempo for the city as we know it in the twentieth century.

What we have, then, in King's volumes is a kind of time exposure of the city breathlessly unfolding, filling out horizontally the outlines of its 1811 grid iron ground plan, lifting itself, not unexpectedly, to unheard-of heights, throwing down defiant new landmarks at what was only yesterday the rural outer limit, the very "Dakotas" beyond which urbanites were never meant to venture. Each new installment of King's photographic essay proved that today's frontier or this year's

fashionable enclave almost inevitably became tomorrow's settled, sometimes even slightly humdrum neighborhood. In New York, as in the other great and greatly expanding cities of the late nineteenth century, novelty was rapidly pressured into the commonplace: the new city dwellers prided themselves on their ability to take the astounding casually in stride, even while charting and proclaiming its exact dimensions.

The 1896 volume appeared at a most opportune time: the unparalleled growth of the new city matched by the extraordinary interest in photography and the perfection of techniques that made rapid and inexpensive reproduction possible. The books sold in the hundreds of thousands because they could be cheaply produced in that quantity. King's formula for success was followed throughout the series, in the same folio-size format: hundreds of photographs with full captions explaining the vital (i.e. financial) statistics of the building and its function, views of single buildings and monuments juxtaposed with more animated portraits of city street scenes, marketplaces, parks and areas of amusement, ships in the harbor, and waterfront activity. Occasionally the books stole a march on the future by including architects' renderings of proposed buildings; sometimes they included plans never put into execution.

The cover illustration for the 1905 volume, for example, shows the proposed design for a municipal office building and railroad terminal near City Hall which never reached fruition. Planned by the former bridge commissioner Gustav Lindenthal and architects Henry F. Hornbostel and George B. Post, the structure was to furnish "400,000 square feet of office room for the city departments . . . and have at its base a five-decked railroad station, with the subways in the basement."

Clearly, the emphasis in the new city under construction in 1905 was on its commercial growth. We have a perhaps unintentional reminder of this emphasis in the contrast between the 1905 cover and that of the 1903 book, for 1903 carries a splendid artist's rendering of what was "the noblest local edifice in construction at this time," the cathedral of St. John the Divine. (The cathedral, of course, remains incomplete, the original plan in part abandoned or radically altered by later architects.)

By the 1908/09 double volume King's portrait of New York included not merely conjecture but actual fantasy: the first plate, entitled "King's Dream of New York," is a vision of a multi-leveled "cosmopolis of the future" with a fervid if indeed somewhat overheated proclamation. "A weird thought of the frenzied heart of the world in later times, incessantly crowding the possibilities of aerial and inter-terrestrial construction, when the wonders of 1908—the Singer Bldg., 612 ft. high, with offices on 41st floor, and the Metropolitan Life tower, 658 ft. high—will be far outdone, and the 1,000-ft. structure realized; now nearly a million people do business here each day; by 1930 it is estimated the number will be doubled, necessitating tiers of sidewalks, with elevated lines and new creations to supplement subway and surface cars, with bridges between the structural heights. Airships, too, may connect us with all the world. What will posterity develop?"

A fervid peek into the future, but the question certainly does not suggest timidity. By the time the 1911/12 volume appeared King's same visionary panorama became more elaborately detailed, more immense, more girded by suspended sky-walks and tram-lines. The even more assertive commercial towers troubled a sky dense with flying machines of baroque (or perhaps just late Victorian) complexity. And if the artist has stretched his fancy, he has left the copy-writer far behind: the ingenious title of 1908/09 is gone, these things are no longer just "King's Dream of New York," and such present realities as the "pyramidal Woolworth Building" rob the dreams of 1911 of any value as prophecy. The caption for 1911/12 proclaims with awe: ". . . the limit is not yet. Plans have been drawn for an hundred story building, 1,260 feet high, which would have 45 acres of rentable area." The city is now "of five million"; it is "rapidly over-hauling London" in rate of population growth; it "maintains 700 hotels capable of entertaining 300,000 people without crowding."

In some ways the 1915 volume represents the fulfillment of many prophecies. New York is now preeminently the city of skyscrapers; the canyons of the financial district are deeper, darker than ever before; more and more photographs show the stately buildings of a past time and style being edged out by the imposing new vogue of classicism. The city's mighty new Municipal Building straddles its uncomfortable site, a brilliant design and engineering response to a formidable problem of irregular plot and the need for carefully channeled traffic flow. King's comment on the building hails it as the "largest structure" of its kind in the world, one reared on the "most difficult foundations ever constructed." By this time the city itself could be described in the same terms: a massive social organism evolving and developing on the difficult foundations of a highly competitive economy, constantly escalating real estate values, and an unprecedented influx of new citizens. New York seemed to

be in a state of constant growing pains, and the results were always spectacular in one way or another.

But Manhattan is not all of New York. All the King volumes did contain sections devoted to Brooklyn, but that was not enough to satisfy those who, just as many still do today, complained that the cares and concerns of Manhattan are always given priority. Thus in 1904 King devoted a single volume to the borough that was even then called the "dormitory" for Manhattan. King's introductory remarks put the case for a separate volume on Brooklyn: "The vastly important position which Brooklyn has attained in the earlier years of the twentieth century is unknown to a large number of its own people. The significance of current events in its growth is not realized by many of those concerned." Although the book tends to emphasize the new commercial activity in the borough—perhaps just to remind Manhattanites that people do walk the streets there during the day—the predominant image is of a surviving green refuge, quite unlike its perpetually busy neighbor across the river. Some of Brooklyn's new office buildings can compete with Manhattan's, but more important are the views of quiet streets and squares, small neighborhoods, the pleasures of sea bathing, the wonders of amusement parks. Brooklyn has its stately homes, but even they seem more relaxed than the showcases that march up Fifth Avenue. The Brooklyn of 1904 has a style all its own; King's photographs capture it.

King's Views of New York & Brooklyn, 1896-1915 bears all the authority that the unflinching camera alone can convey. Add to the more than 1300 photographs thousands of captions giving the most explicit details of land costs, construction techniques and materials, building use, capsule histories of all kinds of commercial establishments, educational institutions, charitable and philanthropic organizations: add to this a series of long introductions that describe the history of the city and its latest achievements—the result is a guidebook as constantly varied as the city of a thousand faces it so accurately mirrors.

The brief intervals that separated the original editions of *King's Views* resulted, of course, in some duplication. In preparing this volume four editions—1896, 1908/09, 1915 and Brooklyn 1905—were selected because duplication is minimal, and these are reproduced in their entirety here. In three others—1903, 1905 and 1911—duplication is significant, and photographs not appearing elsewhere were selected as representative of the period and are reproduced at the end of this volume. We have also included five of the original paper covers, despite the imperfections of years of use.

It would be a disservice to the indefatigable editor of such a valuable contemporary record to end without some comment on Moses King's background and his other books about New York and the United States. King was born in England in 1853 and died in Boston in 1909. As compiler and publisher he was widely known for his handbooks and guides to American cities and to the country as a whole. Among his most important books are the massive volumes in two editions, 1891 and 1893, of the *Handbook of New York City* recently reissued by Benjamin Blom, Inc. It is in many ways a model of this kind of practical, precise, and exceptionally readable guidebook. Few if any American cities have ever received such a thorough scrutiny. The more than 1000 photographs are an extraordinary visual record of the way things actually looked at the beginning of the last decade of the century. But it is the 24-page triple-column index that gives a clue to the book's scope—more than 5000 items and about 20,000 references are given, ranging from waterways and underground transport to sewers, reservoirs, hotels and inns, city administration, taxation and finance, charitable and benevolent institutions, final resting places, theatres and places of amusement, publishing, manufacturing and retailing, and social life in all its varied aspects. The two volumes of the *Handbook* are so full of fact and observation, statistics and anecdotes that they provide not just historical background to an era but fascinating reading in their own right—the saga of New York recounted here is as compelling a tale as any fiction ever written about it.

King also excelled in his major publication on the history and present-day reality of the United States as a whole. New York may supply the glamor and the grandeur, but what about Des Moines and Minneapolis, the Colorado River and the 80,000,000 bushels of corn produced in Tennessee? The answers are supplied in *King's Handbook of the United States,* edited by Moses King and published with a comprehensive text by M. F. Sweetser. These two volumes, complete with 2,500 illustrations and 51 maps, were issued in 1891, a fit summary to a century of development that saw the fledgling nation stretch across a full continent, expand its industrial and agricultural capacity to undreamed-of results. *King's Handbook of the United States* is a state by state, city by city review but not merely a compilation of statistics and charts; it is rather a history of the life behind the figures, the human realities that have produced the impressive profit reports. Thus when King's *Handbook* centers on the vital industry of Hartford, Connecticut, the Hartford Insurance Company, we learn more than the facts that there are buildings devoted to insurance in Hartford and that they employ many people in the city. We also learn the early history of the company, how it met the crisis of the New York fire of 1835 and how it learned from that calamity to be prepared for such eventualities—among which, of course, was the terrible Chicago conflagration of 1871. We can stay with Hartford for another illuminating insight into how King planned his *Handbook:* Hartford had a cloth industry, but King wants us to know that its first major achievement was to weave Washington's inaugural suit.

Through cities and states, from end to end of the nation, King recorded and commented on the life of America at the turn of the century and created a book that is at once an encyclopaedia, an almost trail-by-trail guide, and a history of manners and customs in an era of good will and grand vision. Taken together, *King's Views of New York,* the *Handbook of New York City* and the *Handbook of the United States* (also reissued by Benjamin Blom, Inc.) is a vital contemporary record of life in America at the turn of the twentieth century.

New York 1974

INTERIOR OF THE MAIN FLOOR OF THE NEW YORK STOCK EXCHANGE IN 1897

VIEW LOOKING TOWARD THE SOUTHEAST

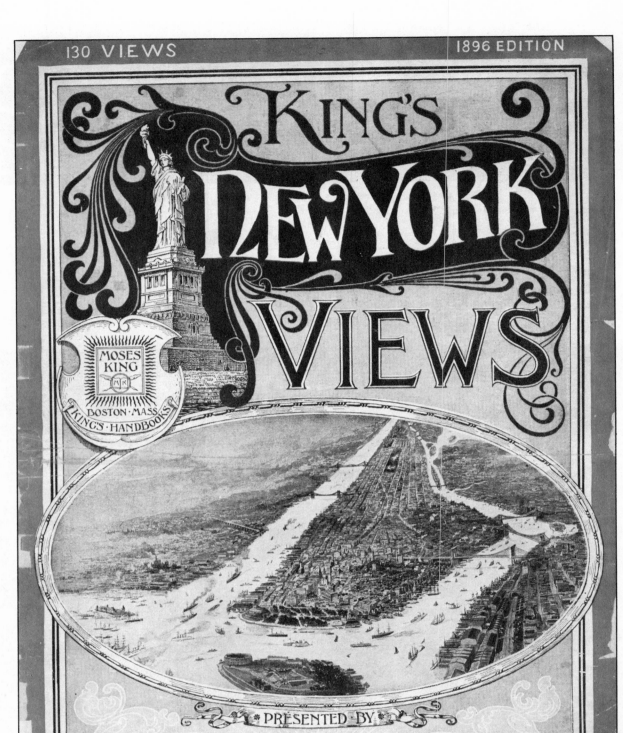

Original paper cover

NEW YORK

A GLANCE AT NEW YORK'S RECENT DEVELOPMENT.

Edited and Published by
MOSES KING

Supplementary to "King's Handbook of New York City."

NEW YORK is the foremost city of the Western Hemisphere, and in some respects the foremost city of the world, ranking with London and Paris. In great lofty structures; in commercial activity; in financial affairs; in international relations; in polyglotical representation; in gigantic enterprises; in notable scientific and engineering achievements; in colossal individual aggrandizements; in mammoth corporate wealth; in maritime commerce; in absolute freedom of citizens; and in the aggregation of civil, social, philanthropic, and religious associations, New York stands unsurpassed anywhere on the globe. There is as yet a lack of noble public structures, and perhaps a needed symmetry of outlines in external construction; there is still quasi-crudeness in forms of development attained by cities of the Old World, but even in these no city ever before reached such a thorough development in a few centuries after its settlement.

At no far distant day New York will have erected a series of public buildings, founded an array of public institutions, beautified a number of thoroughfares, and added to her palatial homes, to her area, and to her population to such a degree that she will be freely accorded the pre-eminent position of the Chief City of the World.

The "Views" merely give a glance at a part of the city. For a detailed knowledge of the whole city and its thousands of institutions, get "King's Handbook of New York City," an elaborate and thoroughly made book, containing more than one thousand solidly packed pages of text, including upward of a thousand original photographic illustrations, obtainable at two dollars a copy at any leading bookstore throughout the world.

Less than a century ago New York was only a quaint little provincial city, covering the lower part of Manhattan Island. The hundred and forty pictures in this paper tell an unmistakable story of her present gigantic magnitude.

SUB-TREASURY.   ASSAY OFFICE.   CUSTOM HOUSE.
THE WASHINGTON STATUE IN FRONT OF UNITED STATES SUB-TREASURY.
WALL ST., NORTHEAST CORNER OF NASSAU ST.   ON THIS SPOT GEORGE WASHINGTON WAS INAUGURATED PRESIDENT.

WASHINGTON MEMORIAL ARCH.
WASHINGTON SQUARE, BEGINNING OF FIFTH AVENUE.

THE AMERICAN LINER "ST. LOUIS" AND HER SISTER SHIP "ST. PAUL,"—INTERNATIONAL NAVIGATION CO.
THE GREATEST STEAMSHIPS CARRYING THE AMERICAN FLAG.

STEAMSHIPS "LUCANIA," AND "CAMPANIA," OF THE CUNARD LINE.
THE GREATEST STEAMSHIPS CARRYING THE BRITISH FLAG.

THE UNITED STATES WAR SHIP "NEW YORK," UNITED STATES NAVY.
THE GREATEST WAR SHIP OF ITS TYPE CARRYING THE AMERICAN FLAG.

TWIN SCREW EXPRESS STEAMSHIP "FUERST BISMARCK," OF THE HAMBURG-AMERICAN LINE.
THE GREATEST STEAMSHIP CARRYING THE GERMAN FLAG.

MALLORY STEAMSHIP LINES—NEW YORK AND TEXAS STEAMSHIP COMPANY.

PIER 20, EAST RIVER, NEAR FULTON FERRY.

McCOMB'S DAM BRIDGE AND THE HARLEM RIVER.

THE NEW YORK BASE BALL GROUNDS IN THE FRONT AT THE LEFT.

THE NORTH RIVER, ALSO CALLED "THE HUDSON." STEAMSHIP "NEW YORK" STARTING FOR SOUTHAMPTON.

JERSEY CITY AND THE PENNSYLVANIA RAILROAD STATION IN THE DISTANCE, AND BABBITT'S GREAT SOAP WORKS IN THE FOREGROUND.

THE EAST RIVER, OR NEW YORK AND BROOKLYN, SUSPENSION BRIDGE.

ACROSS THE EAST RIVER FROM CITY HALL PARK, NEW YORK, TO BROOKLYN.

THE BOWLING GREEN BUILDING:
BOWLING GREEN, THE BEGINNING OF BROADWAY.

AMERICAN SURETY BUILDING—21 STORIES HIGH.
BROADWAY, SOUTHEAST CORNER OF PINE STREET.

THE MANHATTAN LIFE BUILDING—19 STORIES HIGH, 350 FEET TO TOP OF DOME.
64 AND 66 BROADWAY, EAST SIDE, BETWEEN WALL STREET AND EXCHANGE PLACE.

THE NEW YORK LIFE INSURANCE COMPANY.
BROADWAY, SOUTHEAST CORNER OF LEONARD STREET, EXTENDING TO ELM STREET.

R. H. ROBERTSON, ARCHT.   GEO. R. READ, AGENT.

THE AMERICAN TRACT SOCIETY BUILDING—23 STORIES HIGH.
NASSAU STREET, SOUTHEAST CORNER OF SPRUCE STREET.

GEO. B. POST, ARCHT.   H. O. HAVEMEYER, OWNER.

ST. PAUL BUILDING—25 STORIES HIGH.
BROADWAY AND ANN STREET, OPPOSITE ST. PAUL'S CHAPEL.   SITE OF "NEW YORK HERALD" AND "BARNUM'S THEATRE."

WASHINGTON BUILDING.
BROADWAY, BATTERY PLACE AND BATTERY PARK.   BEGINNING OF BROADWAY.

GEO. EDW. HARDING & GOOCH, ARCHTS.   FREDERICK GERKEN, OWNER.

THE GERKEN BUILDING.
CHAMBERS STREET, SOUTHWEST CORNER OF COLLEGE PLACE.

GOLDING & WHITEHOUSE, REAL ESTATE AGENTS.   LAMB & RICH, ARCHTS.

THE SYNDICATE BUILDING.

NASSAU STREET, SOUTHWEST CORNER OF LIBERTY STREET, OPPOSITE "MUTUAL LIFE" BUILDING.

GOLDING & WHITEHOUSE, REAL ESTATE AGENTS.   JAMES B. BAKER, ARCHT.

THE JOHNSTON BUILDING.

BROAD STREET, EXCHANGE PLACE, AND NEW STREET.

U. S. SUB-TREASURY.   HANOVER BANK.   MARTYRS' MONUMENT.

THE HANOVER NATIONAL BANK OF NEW YORK.

HANOVER BANK BUILDING, NASSAU AND PINE STREETS, OPPOSITE U. S. SUB-TREASURY.

BROADWAY, FROM THE UNION TRUST COMPANY TO THE AMERICAN SURETY BUILDING.

FROM RECTOR STREET TO CEDAR STREET.

THE MILLS BUILDING AND BROAD STREET.
VIEW OF EAST SIDE OF BROAD STREET FROM EXCHANGE PLACE TO WALL STREET.

COMMERCIAL CABLE BUILDING—21 STORIES HIGH,—COMMERCIAL CABLE BUILDING CO.
BROAD STREET, WEST SIDE, BETWEEN WALL STREET AND EXCHANGE PLACE.

THE SAMPSON BUILDING.
NOS. 63 AND 65 WALL STREET, SOUTH SIDE, JUST BELOW THE CUSTOM HOUSE.

POSTAL TELEGRAPH BUILDING—POSTAL TELEGRAPH-CABLE CO.
BROADWAY, NORTHWEST CORNER OF MURRAY STREET, WEST SIDE OF CITY HALL PARK.

8

BROAD STREET. CUSTOM HOUSE. ASSAY OFFICE. SUB-TREASURY. NASSAU STREET.

THE UNITED STATES SUB-TREASURY AND THE UNITED STATES ASSAY OFFICE.

WALL STREET, LOOKING EAST FROM NASSAU AND BROAD STREETS.

POSTAL TEL. HOME LIFE. SHOE AND LEATHER BANK. NEW YORK LIFE. STEWART BLDG. COURT HOUSE. CITY HALL.

BROADWAY, AT THE NORTHWEST CORNER OF THE CITY HALL PARK.

VIEW FROM THE MURRAY STREET PATH, LOOKING NORTHWARD.

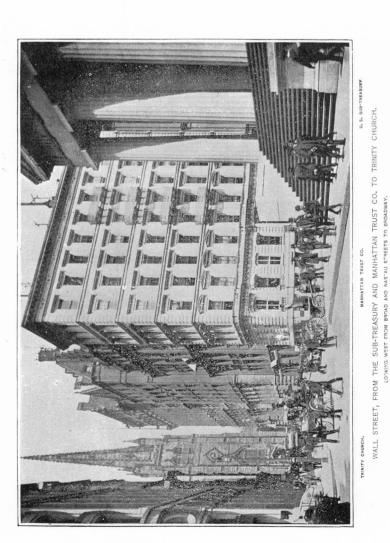

TRINITY CHURCH. MANHATTAN TRUST CO. U. S. SUB-TREASURY.

WALL STREET, FROM THE SUB-TREASURY AND MANHATTAN TRUST CO. TO TRINITY CHURCH.

LOOKING WEST FROM BROAD AND NASSAU STREETS TO BROADWAY.

THE BOWLING GREEN. BROADWAY. PRODUCE EXCHANGE.

BOWLING GREEN AND THE BOWLING GREEN BUILDING—THE BEGINNING OF BROADWAY.

THE SOUTHERN END, OR STARTING POINT, OF THE WORLD'S GREATEST THOROUGHFARE.

CITY HALL. "WORLD." "SUN." "JOURNAL." "TRIBUNE." AMERICAN (MAIL BLDG.) "TIMES." POTTER BLDG. "PRESS."

CITY HALL AND CITY HALL PARK FROM BROADWAY TO PARK ROW.

THE DAILY PAPERS AND PROMINENT BUILDINGS OF "NEWSPAPER ROW."

DREXEL BUILDING: J. PIERPONT MORGAN & CO.

WALL STREET, SOUTHEAST CORNER OF BROAD STREET.

WORLD. SUN. TIMES. POST OFFICE.

PRINTING HOUSE SQUARE; "TIMES" AND POST OFFICE.

JUNCTION OF PARK ROW AND NASSAU STREET.

BRADSTREETS. BROADWAY. MUTUAL RESERVE. STEWART BUILDING.

BROADWAY, LOOKING NORTH FROM "BRADSTREETS," JUST BEYOND THE UPPER END OF THE CITY HALL PARK.

VIEW SHOWING NORTHWARD FROM CHAMBERS STREET.

UNITED STATES POST OFFICE IN NEW YORK.
BROADWAY, AT ITS JUNCTION WITH PARK ROW.

BROADWAY.   STEWART BUILDING.   POST OFFICE.   "STAATS ZEITUNG."   PARK ROW.

THE TOMBS: THE PLACE OF DETENTION FOR CRIMINALS AWAITING TRIAL.
FRANKLIN, CENTRE, LEONARD, AND ELM STREETS.

THE TOMBS.   CRIMINAL LAW COURTS.

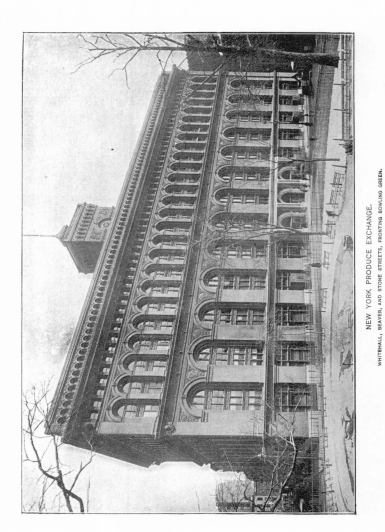

NEW YORK PRODUCE EXCHANGE.
WHITEHALL, BEAVER, AND STONE STREETS, FRONTING BOWLING GREEN.

CITY HALL, CITY HALL PARK AND BROADWAY.
VIEW TAKEN FROM THE "TIMES" BUILDING.

POSTAL TELEGRAPH.   HOME LIFE.   SHOE & LEATHER BANK.   CITY HALL.

THE COUNTY COURT HOUSE.

BROADWAY AND CHAMBERS STREET, IN NORTHWEST CORNER OF CITY HALL PARK.

HILTON, HUGHES & CO., SUCCESSORS OF A. T. STEWART & CO., AMERICA'S GRANDEST RETAIL ESTABLISHMENT.

OCCUPYING ENTIRE SQUARE, BROADWAY, FOURTH AVENUE, 9TH AND 10TH STREETS.

THE EQUITABLE LIFE BUILDING.

BROADWAY, EAST SIDE, FROM PINE TO CEDAR STREET.—VIEW LOOKING NORTH ON BROADWAY.

MUTUAL LIFE BUILDING: THE MUTUAL LIFE INSURANCE COMPANY OF NEW YORK.

NASSAU, LIBERTY AND CEDAR STREETS.

CLINTON & RUSSELL, ARCHTS.

BROAD STREET.   STOCK EXCHANGE.   WILKS BUILDING.

THE NEW YORK STOCK EXCHANGE.
MAIN FACADE ON BROAD STREET, WEST SIDE, NEAR WALL STREET.

ROBERT W. GIBSON, ARCHT.

THE NEW YORK CLEARING HOUSE.
CEDAR STREET, NORTH SIDE, BETWEEN BROADWAY AND NASSAU STREET.

FARMERS' LOAN AND TRUST COMPANY OF NEW YORK.
WILLIAM STREET, NORTHEAST CORNER OF BEAVER STREET.

NINTH NATIONAL BANK OF NEW YORK.
NOS. 407, 409 AND 411 BROADWAY, BETWEEN WALKER AND LISPENARD STREETS.

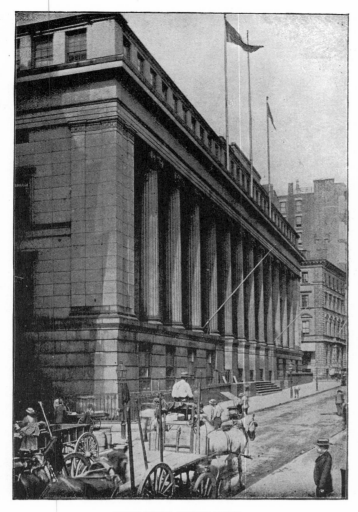

UNITED STATES CUSTOM HOUSE.
WALL STREET, SOUTH SIDE, BETWEEN WILLIAM AND HANOVER STREETS.

THE NEW YORK COTTON EXCHANGE.
BEAVER, WILLIAM AND PEARL STREETS. HANOVER SQUARE.

THE METROPOLITAN TRUST COMPANY OF NEW YORK.
NOS. 37 AND 39 WALL STREET, BETWEEN BROAD AND WILLIAM STREETS, SHOWING PROPOSED ADDITIONAL FOUR STORIES

WILKS BUILDING.   STOCK EXCHANGE.   TRINITY.   WASHINGTON.

THE WILKS BUILDING—N. W. HARRIS & CO., BANKERS.
NO. 18 WALL STREET, SOUTHWEST CORNER OF BROAD, ADJOINING STOCK EXCHANGE.

TRINITY CHURCH.   NEW YORK LIFE INSURANCE & TRUST CO.

WALL STREET, FROM NEW YORK LIFE INSURANCE & TRUST CO. TO TRINITY CHURCH.

VIEW LOOKING WESTWARD FROM 52 WALL STREET TO BROADWAY.

NEW YORK LIFE INSURANCE & TRUST CO.   WALL STREET FERRY.

WALL STREET, FROM NEW YORK LIFE INSURANCE & TRUST CO. TO WALL STREET FERRY.

VIEW LOOKING EASTWARD FROM 52 WALL STREET TO EAST RIVER.

WALL STREET, FROM THE CUSTOM HOUSE TO TRINITY CHURCH.

VIEW LOOKING WESTWARD.

WALL STREET, FROM THE CUSTOM HOUSE TO EAST RIVER.

VIEW LOOKING EASTWARD.

ROBERT W. GIBSON, ARCHT.

UNITED STATES TRUST COMPANY OF NEW YORK.

45 AND 47 WALL STREET, SOUTH SIDE, BETWEEN BROAD AND WILLIAM STREETS.

TRINITY.   SUB-TREASURY. GALLATIN BANK. THOMPSON BUILDING.

THE MERCHANTS' NATIONAL BANK.

42 AND 44 WALL STREET, NORTH SIDE, BETWEEN WILLIAM AND NASSAU STREETS.

TRINITY.   SUB-TREASURY.   BANK OF AMERICA.

THE BANK OF AMERICA.

WALL STREET, NORTHWEST CORNER OF WILLIAM STREET.

WILLIAM STREET.   WALL STREET.

THE BANK OF NEW YORK.

WALL STREET, NORTHEAST CORNER OF WILLIAM STREET.

JERSEY SHORE. HUDSON RIVER. GOVERNOR'S ISLAND. BATTERY PARK. BARGE OFFICE. EAST RIVER. BROOKLYN BRIDGE. BROOKLYN.

BIRD'S EYE VIEW OF NEW YORK CITY.

SHOWING CONTEMPLATED BRIDGES ACROSS THE EAST AND NORTH RIVERS.

MADISON SQUARE PARK AND THE MADISON SQUARE GARDEN TOWER.

VIEW OF THE NORTHERN SIDE OF MADISON SQUARE AND VICINITY.

UNION SQUARE AND WASHINGTON EQUESTRIAN STATUE.

VIEW SHOWING NORTHWEST PART OF UNION SQUARE AND BROADWAY FROM 15TH TO 17TH STREET.

DECKER BLDG.   BROADWAY.   "THE CENTURY."   EVERETT HOUSE.   FOURTH AVE.

(COPYRIGHT 1895, LOEFFLER.)

METROPOLITAN LIFE BLDG.   DR. PARKHURST'S CHURCH.   MADISON SQUARE TOWER.   MADISON SQUARE PARK.   SEWARD STATUE.   FIFTH AVENUE.   BROADWAY.   FIFTH AVENUE HOTEL.   SECOND NAT'L BANK.   TWENTY-THIRD STREET.

THE FIFTH AVENUE HOTEL AND MADISON SQUARE; THE MADISON SQUARE GARDEN TOWER AND VICINITY.

JUNCTION OF FIFTH AVENUE AND BROADWAY, BETWEEN TWENTY-THIRD AND TWENTY-SIXTH STREETS.

AMERICAN MUSEUM OF NATURAL HISTORY.
CENTRAL PARK WEST, BETWEEN WEST 77TH AND WEST 81ST STREETS.

GENERAL U. S. GRANT'S MONUMENT.
RIVERSIDE PARK, MORNINGSIDE HEIGHTS.
*PRESENT PLACE OF BURIAL.
VIEW IN APRIL, 1896.

METROPOLITAN MUSEUM OF ART.
CENTRAL PARK, NEAR FIFTH AVENUE AND 82D STREET.

METROPOLITAN OPERA HOUSE.
BROADWAY, WEST 39TH AND WEST 40TH STREETS, AND SEVENTH AVENUE.

"THE TEACHERS' COLLEGE.
MORNINGSIDE HEIGHTS: WEST 120TH STREET, NEAR AMSTERDAM AVENUE.

ERNEST FLAGG, ARCHT.

ST. LUKE'S HOSPITAL.
MORNINGSIDE HEIGHTS: MORNINGSIDE AND AMSTERDAM AVENUES, BETWEEN WEST 113TH AND 114TH STREETS.

McKIM, MEAD & WHITE, ARCHTS.

COLUMBIA COLLEGE LIBRARY AND SURROUNDING COLUMBIA COLLEGE BUILDINGS.
MORNINGSIDE HEIGHTS: MORNINGSIDE AND AMSTERDAM AVENUES, BETWEEN 116TH AND 120TH STREETS.

HEINS & LA FARGE, ARCHT.

CATHEDRAL OF ST. JOHN THE DIVINE—PROTESTANT EPISCOPAL.
MORNINGSIDE PARK, MORNINGSIDE HEIGHTS.

THE BOWERY.
LOOKING NORTH FROM CANAL STREET.

LORD & TAYLOR'S DRY GOODS ESTABLISHMENT ON BROADWAY.
BROADWAY, SOUTHWEST CORNER OF 20TH STREET. VIEW LOOKING SOUTH ON BROADWAY AND WEST ON 20TH STREET.

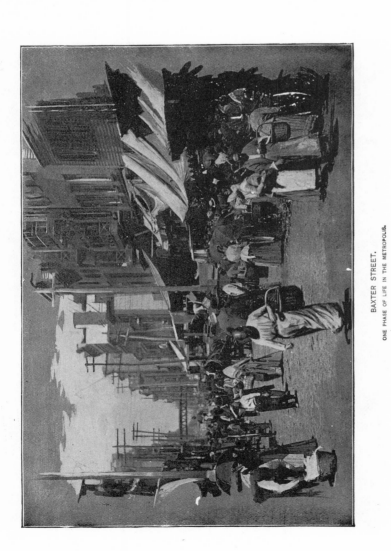

BAXTER STREET.
ONE PHASE OF LIFE IN THE METROPOLIS.

LORD & TAYLOR'S ESTABLISHMENT ON GRAND STREET.
GRAND STREET, SOUTHEAST CORNER OF CHRISTIE STREET.

THE PARK AVENUE HOTEL.

PARK AVENUE (FOURTH AVENUE), BETWEEN 32D AND 33D STREETS, MIDWAY BETWEEN MADISON SQUARE AND GRAND CENTRAL STATION.

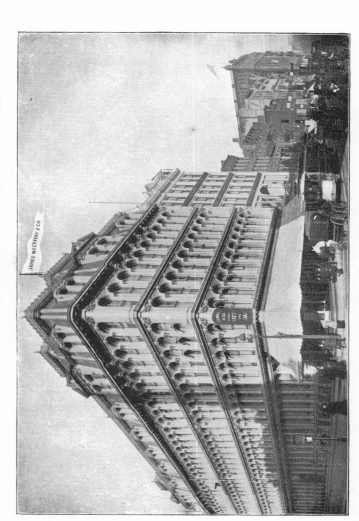

TWENTY-THIRD STREET AND SIXTH AVENUE; JAMES McCREERY & CO.'S NEW ESTABLISHMENT.

VIEW SHOWS THE McCREERY BLOCK OF BUILDINGS, PARTLY ON SITE OF BOOTH'S THEATRE.

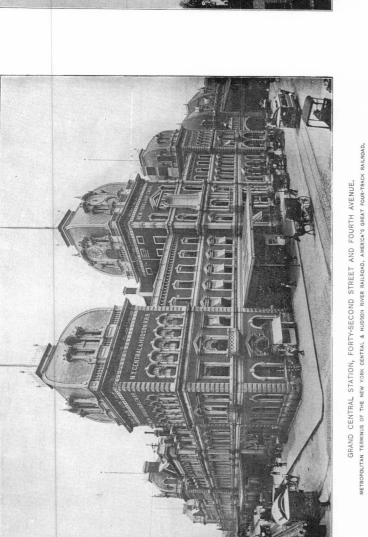

GRAND CENTRAL STATION, FORTY-SECOND STREET AND FOURTH AVENUE.

METROPOLITAN TERMINUS OF THE NEW YORK CENTRAL & HUDSON RIVER RAILROAD, AMERICA'S GREAT FOUR-TRACK RAILROAD.

BROADWAY, AT ELEVENTH STREET; JAMES McCREERY & CO., DRY GOODS ESTABLISHMENT.

VIEW OF BROADWAY, LOOKING WEST FROM McCREERY'S, CORNER OF 11TH STREET.

H. O. HAVEMEYER'S NEW BUILDING; SITE OF METROPOLITAN HOTEL.

BROADWAY, NORTHEAST CORNER OF PRINCE STREET. ON THIS SITE STOOD NIBLO'S GARDEN.

N LE BRUN & SONS, ARCHTS.   GEO. R. READ, AGENT.

HOME LIFE INSURANCE COMPANY OF NEW YORK.

BROADWAY, WEST SIDE, BETWEEN MURRAY AND WARREN STREETS, OPPOSITE CITY HALL PARK.

LAWYERS' TITLE BUILDING.

MAIDEN LANE AND BUILDING OF LAWYERS' TITLE INSURANCE CO.

VIEW OF MAIDEN LANE, LOOKING WEST TOWARD BROADWAY FROM WILLIAM STREET.

WILLIAMSBURGH CITY FIRE INSURANCE COMPANY.

BROADWAY, NORTHEAST CORNER OF LIBERTY STREET.

THE PRESBYTERIAN BUILDING.

FIFTH AVENUE, NORTHWEST CORNER OF TWENTIETH STREET.

ARNOLD, CONSTABLE & CO. 18TH STREET.

THE CONSTABLE BUILDING.

FIFTH AVENUE, NORTHEAST CORNER OF EIGHTEENTH STREET; ADJOINS ARNOLD, CONSTABLE & CO.

GERMANIA LIFE. U. S. SUB-TREASURY.

THE GERMANIA LIFE INSURANCE COMPANY OF NEW YORK.

NASSAU STREET, EAST SIDE, BETWEEN CEDAR AND PINE STREETS.

DR. PARKHURST'S CHURCH. N. LE BRUN & SON, ARCHTS. GEO. R. READ, AGENT.

METROPOLITAN LIFE BUILDING.

MADISON SQUARE: MADISON AVENUE, NORTHEAST CORNER OF 23D STREET.

ORPHAN ASYLUM.   CARDINAL'S RESIDENCE.

ST. PATRICK'S CATHEDRAL—ROMAN CATHOLIC.

FIFTH AVENUE, EAST SIDE, FROM 50TH TO 51ST STREET.

THE BUCKINGHAM HOTEL ON FIFTH AVENUE.

FIFTH AVENUE, SOUTHEAST CORNER OF 50TH STREET, IMMEDIATELY OPPOSITE THE CATHEDRAL.

BROADWAY CENTRAL.   GRACE CHURCH.

BROADWAY, FROM THE BROADWAY CENTRAL HOTEL TO GRACE CHURCH.

VIEW LOOKING NORTHWARD FROM THE BROADWAY CENTRAL, AT BOND STREET.

NETHERLAND.   ARION SOCIETY.   SAVOY.

FIFTH AVENUE AND FIFTY-NINTH STREET: NETHERLAND AND SAVOY HOTELS.

VIEW LOOKING EASTWARD IN FIFTY-NINTH STREET.

MADISON SQUARE GARDEN—THEATRE, AMPHITHEATRE, AND ROOF GARDEN.
MADISON AND FOURTH AVENUES, EAST 26TH AND EAST 27TH STREETS.

THE HOTELS WALDORF AND SCHERMERHORN.
FIFTH AVENUE, FROM THIRTY-THIRD TO THIRTY-FOURTH STREETS. NOW IN PROCESS OF ERECTION.

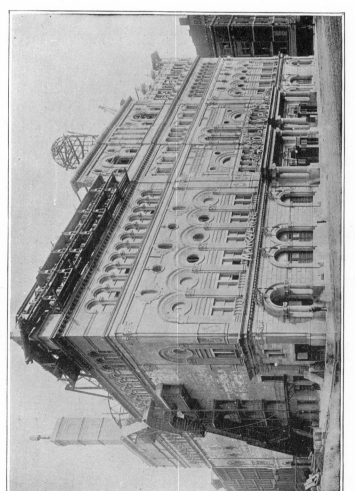

THE GERARD: A FIREPROOF APARTMENT HOTEL.
FORTY-FOURTH STREET, NORTH SIDE, BETWEEN BROADWAY AND SIXTH AVENUE.

HAMMERSTEIN'S OLYMPIA—THEATRE, CONCERT HALL, MUSIC HALL, AND ROOF GARDEN,
BROADWAY, FROM FORTY-FOURTH TO FORTY-FIFTH STREETS. IN PROCESS OF COMPLETION.

FOURTH AVENUE, NORTHEAST CORNER OF TWENTY-THIRD STREET.

THE HORTON BUILDING, OCCUPIED BY PACKARD'S BUSINESS COLLEGE AND THE J. M. HORTON ICE CREAM CO.

HERALD SQUARE AND THE "NEW YORK HERALD" BUILDING.

HERALD SQUARE: BROADWAY, WEST 35TH AND WEST 36TH STREETS, AND SIXTH AVENUE.

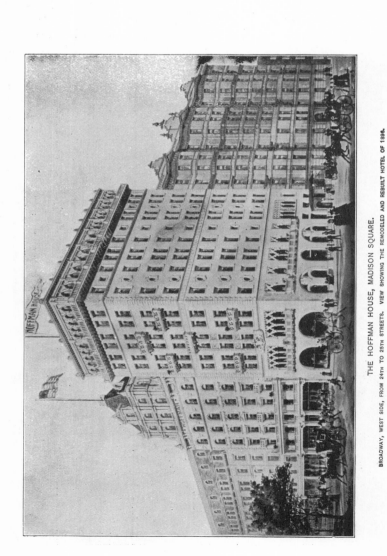

THE HOFFMAN HOUSE, MADISON SQUARE.

BROADWAY, WEST SIDE, FROM 24TH TO 25TH STREETS. VIEW SHOWING THE REMODELED AND REBUILT HOTEL OF 1898.

GREELEY SQUARE: THE GREELEY STATUE, THE 33D ST. ELEVATED STATION, AND THE UNION DIME SAVINGS INSTITUTION.

VIEW OF GREELEY SQUARE, AT JUNCTION OF BROADWAY, SIXTH AVENUE, AND 32D AND 33D STREETS.

CENTRAL PARK: THE BOAT HOUSE AND LAKE.
VIEW TAKEN BY LOEFFLER IN 1895.

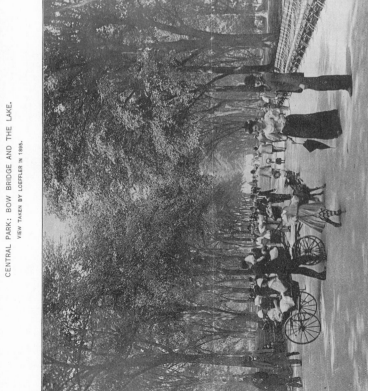

THE PLAZA: THE PLAZA HOTEL AND ENTRANCE TO CENTRAL PARK.
FIFTH AVENUE, WEST SIDE, FROM 58TH STREET TO 59TH STREET, AT FIFTH AVENUE ENTRANCE TO CENTRAL PARK.

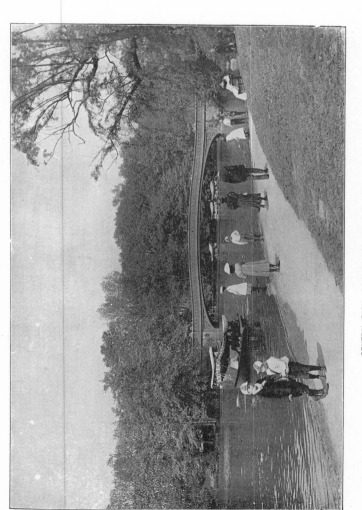

CENTRAL PARK: BOW BRIDGE AND THE LAKE.
VIEW TAKEN BY LOEFFLER IN 1895.

CENTRAL PARK: THE GOAT WAGONS ON THE MALL.
VIEW TAKEN BY LOEFFLER IN 1895.

HARVARD HOUSE OF THE HARVARD CLUB.

FORTY-FOURTH STREET, NORTH SIDE, BETWEEN FIFTH AND SIXTH AVENUES.

THE BERKELEY SCHOOL FOR BOYS.

No. 20 WEST 44TH STREET, SOUTH SIDE, NEAR FIFTH AVENUE.

EPISCOPAL CHURCH MISSIONS HOUSE.

FOURTH AVENUE, SOUTHEAST CORNER OF 22D STREET.

WEBB'S ACADEMY AND HOME FOR SHIP BUILDERS.

SEDGWICK AVENUE AND ACADEMY STREET, HARLEM.

TRINITY CHURCH—PROTESTANT EPISCOPAL.

BROADWAY, BETWEEN RECTOR AND THAMES STREETS, AT THE HEAD OF WALL STREET.

MARBLE COLLEGIATE CHURCH. GEO. EDW. HARDING & GOOCH, ARCHTS.

HOLLAND HOUSE, ON FIFTH AVENUE.

FIFTH AVENUE, SOUTHWEST CORNER OF THIRTIETH STREET.

WESTERN UNION TEL. MAIL AND EXPRESS. ST. PAUL'S. ASTOR HOUSE. POSTAL TEL.

BROADWAY, LOOKING NORTH FROM DEY STREET.

VIEW SHOWING WEST SIDE OF BROADWAY FROM DEY TO CHAMBERS STREET.

"STAATS ZEITUNG." BRIDGE APPROACH. "WORLD." "SUN." "TRIBUNE." "TIMES."

PARK ROW, EAST SIDE OF CITY HALL PARK, PRINTING HOUSE SQUARE.

VIEW LOOKING WEST FROM THE POST OFFICE.

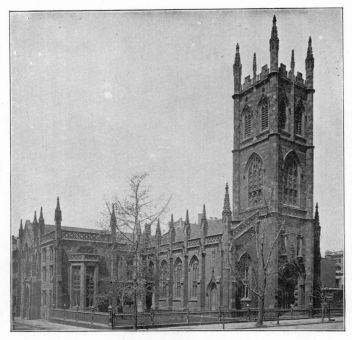

FIRST PRESBYTERIAN CHURCH.
FIFTH AVENUE, NORTHWEST CORNER OF ELEVENTH STREET.

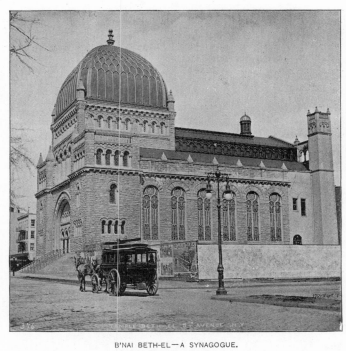

B'NAI BETH-EL—A SYNAGOGUE.
FIFTH AVENUE, SOUTHEAST CORNER OF SEVENTY-SIXTH STREET.

BOWERY SAVINGS BANK.
GRAND STREET AND THE BOWERY.

BANK FOR SAVINGS.
FOURTH AVENUE AND TWENTY-SECOND STREET.

METROPOLITAN CLUB—ALSO CALLED THE MILLIONAIRES' CLUB.
FIFTH AVENUE, NORTHEAST CORNER OF SIXTIETH STREET.

THE NEW YORK BAR ASSOCIATION.
FORTY-FOURTH STREET, SOUTH SIDE, BETWEEN FIFTH AND SIXTH AVENUES.

MRS. WILLIAM H. VANDERBILT.   W. D. SLOANE.   MRS. ELLIOTT F. SHEPARD.   W. K. VANDERBILT.

FIFTH AVENUE, WEST SIDE, NORTH FROM FIFTY-FIRST STREET.
SHOWING VANDERBILT RESIDENCES AND ST. THOMAS' EPISCOPAL AND THE FIFTH AVENUE PRESBYTERIAN CHURCHES.

THE CORNELIUS VANDERBILT MANSION.
FIFTH AVENUE, WEST SIDE, FROM 57TH TO 58TH STREET, AT ENTRANCE TO CENTRAL PARK.

COLLIS P. HUNTINGTON RESIDENCE.
FIFTH AVENUE, SOUTHEAST CORNER OF FIFTY-SEVENTH STREET.

JOHN JACOB ASTOR RESIDENCE.
FIFTH AVENUE, NORTHEAST CORNER OF SIXTY-FIFTH STREET.

SOC. PREV. CRUELTY TO CHILDREN.   CHARITIES.   EP. CHURCH MISSIONS.   CHRIST CHURCH.

FOURTH AVENUE, EAST SIDE, TWENTY-FIRST TO TWENTY-THIRD STREET.
AN INTERESTING GROUP OF PHILANTHROPIC INSTITUTIONS.

THE NEW YORK EYE AND EAR INFIRMARY.
SECOND AVENUE AND THIRTEENTH STREET.

MANHATTAN CLUB.
FIFTH AVENUE, NORTHWEST CORNER OF 34TH STREET.   FORMERLY RESIDENCE OF A. T. STEWART.

THE UNION LEAGUE CLUB.
FIFTH AVENUE, NORTHEAST CORNER OF 39TH STREET.

NINTH REGIMENT ARMORY.

FOURTEENTH STREET, NORTH SIDE, BETWEEN SIXTH AND SEVENTH AVENUES.

TROOP A ARMORY.

MADISON AVENUE, BETWEEN 94TH AND 95TH STREETS.

EIGHTH REGIMENT ARMORY.

PARK AVENUE AND 94TH STREET.

SEVENTY-FIRST REGIMENT ARMORY.

PARK AVENUE, FROM 33D TO 34TH STREETS.

TWELFTH REGIMENT ARMORY.

COLUMBUS AVENUE, SOUTHWEST CORNER OF 61ST STREET.

SEVENTH REGIMENT ARMORY.

66TH AND 67TH STREETS, PARK AND LEXINGTON AVENUES.

THE TOMBS.   "BRIDGE OF SIGHS."   CENTRE STREET FAÇADE.

THE CRIMINAL LAW COURTS.

CENTRE, WHITE, FRANKLIN, AND ELM STREETS.

| Sub-Treasury | Assay Office | Row of Banks | National City Bank | Drexel Bldg. | J. P. Morgan & Co. |

WALL STREET, from Nassau toward East River; banking center of New York; on north side of street, Gallatin National Bank, founded 1829; Bank of Manhattan Co., 1799; Merchants' National, 1803; Bank of America, 1812; Bank of New York, N. E. cor. William St., 1797, oldest in state; N. Y. Life Insurance & Trust Co., 1830; Central Trust Co., 1875; International Bank; Seamen's Bank for Savings, 1829, at Pearl St. South side, J. P. Morgan & Co., greatest banking house in world; Mechanics' & Metals Nat'l Bank, 1810; Trust Co. of America, 1899; U. S. Trust Co., 1853; Metropolitan Trust Co., 1881; Atlantic Mutual Ins. Co., 1842; National City Bank, 1812. Deposits in these banks exceed $640,000 000.

1908/09

Sub-Treasury   Assay Office   Row of Banks   National City Bank   Drexel Bldg.   J. P. Morgan & Co.

WALL STREET, from Nassau toward East River; banking center of New York; on north side of street, Gallatin National Bank, founded 1829; Bank of Manhattan Co., 1799; Merchants' National, 1803; Bank of America, 1812; Bank of New York, N. E. cor. William St., 1797, oldest in state; N. Y. Life Insurance & Trust Co., 1830; Central Trust Co., 1875; International Bank; Seamen's Bank for Savings, 1829, at Pearl St. South side, J. P. Morgan & Co., greatest banking house in world; Mechanics' & Metals Nat'l Bank, 1810; Trust Co. of America, 1899; U. S Trust Co., 1853; Metropolitan Trust Co , 1881; Atlantic Mutual Ins. Co., 1842; National City Bank, 1812. Deposits in these banks exceed $640,000 000.

KING'S VIEWS

NEW YORK

1908   **1909**

FOUR
HUNDRED
ILLUS-
TRATIONS

THE MOST VALUABLE REAL ESTATE IN THE WORLD

RISING grandly from the water's edge on the tapering end of Manhattan Island are the great, towering buildings in which are centered the business interests of the New World. In imposing array they proclaim the commercial might of the Metropolis. Impressive as architectural piles by day, scintillating with myriad lights by night, Manhattan challenges admiration and wonder. The site of this throbbing heart of the world less than three centuries ago was purchased from the Indians for the equivalent of twenty-four dollars. Now the portion of the island below Grand Street is assessed as having a land value of $507,156,350, and the buildings thereon are estimated as worth $219,472,360—a total of $726,628,710. But real-estate experts calculate that the properties fronting on the half mile of Broadway from Bowling Green to St. Paul's Chapel would bring $500,000,000 and that the Skyscrapers of Manhattan, with the plots on which they stand, are worth $2,000,000,000. The land of Manhattan alone, exclusive of buildings and streets, was assessed at $3,312,261,571 in 1907; land of the entire city, $4,363,293,224; total realty value, 1908, $8,000,000,000.

Hall of Records   City Hall Park   Centre St. Front   Chambers St. through Arcade   Park Row   McKim, Mead & White, Architects   Third Ave. "L"   "World"

MUNICIPAL BUILDING, imposing $7,000,000 city office bldg., being erected on triangle bounded by Centre and Duane Sts. and Park Row, in connection with new $2,000,000 Brooklyn Bridge Terminal. Largest municipal bldg. in world, housing all city departments except Police, Fire, Docks and Ferries, and Health ; subway in basement ; entrances Chambers St. arcade on street level ; 34 stories ; height of tower, 210 ft. 8 in., including 24-ft. figure ; total height of bldg., 539 ft. 10 in.; height above subway tracks, 559 ft.   Diameter of clock face, 25 ft.

NEW YORK CITY---THE WORLD'S COMMERCIAL CENTRE

WILLIAM WIRT MILLS, Journalist

GREATEST in commerce and manufactures, New York City in 1908 outranks every metropolis of the world in these determining factors of supremacy, and has wrested from London the laurels of primacy, save only in respect to population.

The capital of the British Empire has been growing great these 2,000 years. The site of New York was a virgin forest in 1609, when Hendrick Hudson's discovery paved the way for the first colonists, who arrived nearly a score of years later.

Now the most gigantic office buildings in the world seem fairly to jostle each other in this new World Centre. Five of them, standing within the space of a bow-shot, covering less than four acres of land, have 60 acres of office space and room for 36,000 tenants on their 145 floors.

This massing of business energy is an effect rather than a cause. It is the result of the most stupendous manufacturing, commercial and financial development in the history of the world. The material fabric of the city is the translation into steel and stone of the statistics of its vast business.

In 1907 vessels in foreign trade entering the port of New York aggregated 11,383,345 tons, 202,119 more than those whose destination was London, while the clearances showed a tonnage of 10,472,000 tons, 789,340 in excess of the British capital. Vessels under American register belonging to New York aggregated 2,000,-000 tons, equivalent to the entire merchant-fleet of Germany.

It was estimated in June, 1908, that a vessel left London every 28 minutes carrying a cargo averaging $60,000 in value, making shipments to foreign and domestic ports at the rate of $1,200,000,000 a year, while New York City sent out a vessel every 36 minutes, with merchandise averaging in value $92,000 to a ship, an indicated total of $1,350,000,000 a year.

Exports of the port in the year ended June 30, 1908, were valued at $734,000,000, or $230,000,000 in excess of London; the imports, $714,000,000, or $100,000,000 less than London; a total foreign commerce of $1,448,000,000—10% greater than London. Duties collected at the port of New York in the year ended June 30, 1908, were $186,747,429.

The city's annual water-borne commerce including shipments to and from domestic ports and over inland waterways, was estimated at 155,000,000 tons, its aggregate value, $10,150,000,000.

New York in 1908 has a population of 4,442,685; London, 5,070,952; estimates based on present rates of growth indicate for the American metropolis a population of 6,200,000 in 1920, with 6,085,-000 for London. New York's population is nearly 5% of that of the entire United States, twice that of Chicago, and nearly equals the combined populations of Chicago, Philadelphia, St. Louis and Boston.

Of the city's inhabitants 1,590,000 are foreign-born, 325,000 being Germans, 278,000 Irish and 300,000 foreign-born Jews. The Hebrew population of New York is 900,000, or more than half of the entire number of Jews in the United States.

The furthermost point in the city is 19 miles from the City Hall. Taking this radius, the circle includes portions of New Jersey, Westchester County and Long Island that are essentially parts of the Metropolis. This Greatest New York now includes 5,962,247 inhabitants as compared with 6,881,372 within the 25-mile radius of Metropolitan London. It is estimated that this "largest New York" will have 8,036,400 people in 1920 against 7,675,969 for Metropolitan London, and that by 1950 there will be 19,250,000 inhabitants in this area.

In manufactures New York far exceeds every producing centre of the earth. In 1908 it had 23,816 factories, representing nearly 300 lines of industry and $1,390,595,316 of capital with 619,621 wage-earners receiving $347,379,462 and 78,586 salaried employees to whom $100,703,540 was paid. The output of these factories represented the conversion of $1,208,029,267 of materials into products having a wholesale value of $2,289,784,509, 10% of the entire output of all the factories of the United States.

About 20% of the city's manufactured products were in the clothing line and the output of its 2,000 printing and publishing houses was valued at $150,000,000, its newspapers and periodicals having an aggregate circulation of 40,000,000 copies. In three other lines the products exceeded $50,000,000 in value; six industries each produced over $25,000,000 of goods; seventeen others over $10,000,000 each.

The banks of the city, with resources aggregating $5,000,000,000 in June, 1908, had $3,200,000,000 in deposits, and the actual currency in circulation in the city was estimated at $747,128,000. In silver dollars this would make 12,500 piles as high as the Singer

Tower. The interest and dividend payments in June, 1908, were $176,967,371.

The value of the taxable real-estate according to the 1907 assessment was $5,704,009,652, twice the combined assessments of Philadelphia, Boston and Pittsburg, and the exempt realty was valued at $1,156,346,803. The average value of land per acre in Manhattan was put at $194,247; the record price paid for No. 1 Wall Street, corner of Broadway, was $25,000,000 per acre.

New buildings were erected in 1907 at a cost of $178,230,429, or three times as much as Chicago spent. In 25 months ended April 1, 1908, $500,000,000 was spent in rebuilding the city. In the last six years 19,739 apartment-houses were erected, with accommodations for 230,036 families, making room for an increase of a million in population. In this period living-room for half a million additional people was provided in Manhattan alone, where the population, in 1908, averaged 157 to the acre and 100,492 to the square mile. Rebuilt on this scale, the entire city can accommodate 32,837,226.

In Manhattan in 1905 there were 312,048 people living in 122 blocks covering 332 acres, 15% of the population of Manhattan being housed on 2% of the area.

The skyscrapers' part in the development of New York is illustrated by the fact that there are 76 square miles of floor space in the buildings of Manhattan, or four times the area of the Island.

There are 11 railroad terminals, including the Pennsylvania and the New York Central, two largest in the world, and 114 steamship-terminals. Trans-Atlantic lines alone in 1907 carried 2,957,328 passengers, and 1,300 tons of freight for export were loaded every hour.

Four bridges and 14 tunnels, to be completed by 1909, at a cost of $300,000,000, will furnish 38 tracks connecting Manhattan with New Jersey and Long Island, and their combined passenger-capacity will be 400,000 passengers per hour. The north and south lines in Manhattan carry 150,000 passengers per hour during rush periods. There are in the entire city 1,267 miles of railways carrying 1,400,000,000 passengers a year, and operated at an annual cost of $30,000,000, while 110 miles of new subways have been planned.

Engineering works to cost $600,000,000 are now under way and others to the extent of an additional billion have been planned. The bringing to the city of 200,000,000 gallons of water a day from the Catskill Mountains involves building 12 reservoirs and a conduit 60 miles long at a cost of $161,000,000. This will give a daily supply of 500,000,000 gallons. For fighting fires the city is installing a high-pressure service by which water will be delivered through 85 miles of special mains to the hydrants at a pressure up to 300 pounds per square inch, which would force a stream up, through stand pipes, 700 feet without the use of fire engines.

The city government is costing $143,572,266 in 1908, including $66,000,000 for salaries, there being an office-holder for every 70 people. The chief items in the budget are $27,514,363 for education, $14,350,499 for police, $7,483,485 for fire department, $6,632,-856 for street cleaning, $3,214,146 for charity.

The city owns parks valued at $429,724,000; public schools, $78,000,000; docks and ferries, $58,200,000; bridges, $47,375,000; penal and charitable institutions, $32,474,000; armories, $10,588,000; rapid-transit subway, $46,074,000. The churches of the city are valued at $150,719,000; humanitarian institutions, $128,300,000.

It is estimated that $50,000,000 a year is spent in the theatre district, of which $6,000,000 is for music alone. There are 100 play-houses and two opera-houses, seating about 120,000 people with an average attendance of 80,000. About 4,000 actors are employed and some 700 plays are given in a season.

In New York the average workingman spends $837 a year as compared with $397 for the London wage-earner. The annual food-bill of the city is estimated at $1,250,000,000, of which $150,000,000 is for meat. Some of the items are 370,000,000 pounds of sugar, 5,360,000 pounds of tea and 5,000,000 tons of ice.

In the city 26,000,000 matches are lighted every day; the street lamps have 180,000,000 candle power.

The city's annual postage bill is $22,000,000; it spends $52,-000,000 for telegrams and cable messages, and holds 350,000,000 telephone conversations in a year.

In 1907 there were 51,097 marriages in New York: 120,722 births, and 79,205 deaths.

These figures, many of which are beyond the power of the mind adequately to grasp, give some conception of the magnitude of this greatest city of the new world and future metropolis of the globe, while the pictures in this book show graphically its present physical pre-eminence.

W. 62d Street   Façade and Main Entrance on Central Park West   Carrère & Hastings, Architects   W. 63d St.

NEW THEATRE, Central Park West, 62d to 63d St., most complete and magnificent playhouse in the world; erected and maintained by corporation of wealthy New Yorkers for elevation of dramatic art; spacious Colonial structure, seating 2,318; two tiers of boxes; finest stage ever constructed, 100 ft. wide, 68 ft. deep, 112 ft. high; 40 dressing rooms all connected with stage by elevators; exits arranged for emptying house in 100 seconds.   New Theatre Co., Wm. K. Vanderbilt, Pres.; H. R. Winthrop, Sec.; Otto H. Kahn, Treas.   To be opened Fall, 1909.

W. 23d St.   Site of Fifth Avenue Hotel, 1858-1908   Fifth Avenue and Broadway   Opposite Madison Square   Broadway   Albemarle

FIFTH AVENUE BUILDING, $4,000,000 office structure, with stores on street level, facing Madison Sq. where Broadway crosses Fifth Ave. diagonally, with 197.5 ft. frontage, extending 259.8 ft. along 23d St., 264.7 ft. along 24th St., 18 full city lots.   Built of steel, granite, limestone and brick; 14 stories high; Maynicke & Franke, Archts.; Fifth Avenue Building Co., Dr. Henry C. Eno, Pres.; Henry Lane Eno, Treas.   In heart of shopping district, on historic site of Corporal Thompson's Inn, 1830; Franconi's Hippodrome, 1853.

Barge Office   Produce Exchange   Governor's Island Ferry   Staten Island Ferry   Hamilton Ave. Ferry   Atlantic Ave. Ferry   South Brooklyn (39th St.) Ferry   Brooklyn Bridge   East River

MUNICIPAL FERRY TERMINAL, East River from Whitehall to near Broad St.; 700 ft. long; main cornice 64 ft. above mean tide; turrets, 100 ft. high; $3,000,000 steel, copper and glass structure, with seven slips for the boats plying to Staten Island and on three Brooklyn lines; waiting rooms, each 150 by 65 ft.; concourse, 30 ft. wide, and exterior loggia, 15 ft. along South St.; offices of Dock Department, 700 by 70 ft., above waiting rooms; glass-covered playground on roof.   Walker & Morris, Architects.   A. N. Spooner, Commissioner of Docks and Ferries.

INDEX TO VIEWS AND TEXT

Black face numerals indicate titles of pictures or prominent features of views.

Escalators and Stairways in City Hall Park   Bridge over Park Row   Trolley and Train Terminal   Roadway   "World"

BROOKLYN BRIDGE TERMINAL, Park Row, imposing granite and limestone structure to replace unsightly iron shed now used for Manhattan terminal of Brooklyn Bridge. Immense trolley car terminal on mezzanine floor at level of bridge over Park Row; elevated train terminal on floor above, with six platforms each long enough for a seven car train. Structure to cost $2,000,000. Hoppin & Koen, Architects. Designed to accommodate 100,000 passengers an hour. James W. Stevenson, Commissioner of Bridges.

SUPPLEMENTARY FACTS

Additional information pertaining to the Views on pages 1 to 96, with changes that have occurred since printing.

Page 7. Steel Work on Blackwell's Island Bridge completed June 11, 1908.

Page 8. Assessment rolls for 1908 increase value of taxable realty to $6,722,415,789. Estimates of property owned by city make actual value $2,000,000,000.

Page 11. July 1908, Cunard liner Lusitania averaged 25.01 knots (28 76 miles) an hour in voyage of 2,890 knots ; Mauretania, in June, 24.86 knots. Best day's runs, Lusitania, 643 knots (740 miles) ; Mauretania, 636 knots.

Page 14. Whitehall Building being enlarged and raised to 34 stories.

Page 17. Welding Ring succeeded W. H. Douglas as president of the Produce Exchange.

Page 19. George Brennecke succeeded Dr. J. H. Parker as president of the Cotton Exchange.

Page 19. Charles H. Badeau succeeded Ogden D. Budd as president of the Consolidated Stock Exchange.

Page 20. Rev. Dr. Wm. T. Manning succeeds the late Dr. Dix as rector of Trinity Church.

Pages 35 and 60. Fifth Avenue Hotel torn down to make room for 14-story office building.

Page 49. Receipts New York Post Office, year ended June 30, 1908, $18,563,709.

Page 55. Everett House vacated ; to be replaced by 20-story office building.

Page 59. Alexander S. Webb, Jr. made president of Lincoln Trust Co.

Page 63. Metropolitan Life Tower raised to 52 stories ; 700 feet high.

Page 78. Giulio Gatti-Casazza made Manager Metropolitan Opera.

The Makers of This Book.

Copyright, 1908, by MOSES KING, Editor and Publisher.

Paper supplied by Henry Lindenmeyr & Sons. Engravings by Walker Engraving Company.

The 1908-1909 Edition of 135,000 copies was printed by The Charles Francis Press.

Binding in cloth by J. J. Little & Ives Company. Binding in leather by "Bradstreet's" and "Ives." Dies by Becker Brothers.

Drawings by Richard W. Rummell, H. M. Pettit and others. Page groupings by Charles E. Sickels. Covers and titles by Becker Brothers and E. Stetson Crawford.

Photographs by Irving Underhill, George P. Hall & Son, Brown Brothers, Pach Brothers, William H. Kirk, et al.

Descriptions and index by Wm. Wirt Mills. Supervised by Miss Annie M. Buckminster.

THE COSMOPOLIS OF THE FUTURE. A weird thought of the frenzied heart of the world in later times, incessantly crowding the possibilities of aerial and inter-terrestrial construction, when the wonders of 1908—the Singer Bldg., 612 ft. high, with offices on 41st floor, and the Metropolitan Life tower, 658 ft. high—will be far outdone, and the 1,000-ft. structure realized; now nearly a million people do business here each day; by 1930 it is estimated the number will be doubled, necessitating tiers of sidewalks, with elevated lines and new creations to supplement subway and surface cars, with bridges between the structural heights. Airships, too, may connect us with all the world. What will posterity develop?

Park Row Bldg.   Fulton Bldg.   Fulton St.   Dey St.   Hudson Terminals, River View   Cortlandt St.   Penna. R. R. Ferries   Geo. A. Fuller Co.   Cortlandt Bldg.   Cortlandt St.   Cortlandt Bldg.   "McAdoo Terminals" from projector, Wm. G. McAdoo; view from river and Church St.   HUDSON AND MANHATTAN R.R. CO.   Hudson Terminal Bldgs., known as "McAdoo Terminals" from projector, Wm. G. McAdoo; view from river and Church St.; FULTON BUILDING, Dey to Fulton St.; twin structures, 22 stories, 275 ft. high, largest offices in world, 18,110,000 cu. ft.; heaviest, 200,000 tons, resting on biggest coffer-dam ever made, 400 by 178 ft., 75 to 98 ft. deep.   Trains from Hudson and Manhattan Co. twin tubes from New Jersey, under Hudson River, enter station in basement 30 ft. below surface; passage under Dey St. to Subway under Broadway.   Office space for 20,000 people; 39 elevators.   Tunnels connected under Jersey City with twin tunnels crossing to Morton St., up 6th Ave. to 33d St. and across 9th St. to Fourth Ave.

"World"   "Tribune"   Am. Tract.   Park Row Bldg., 382 ft.   St. Paul   Hudson Companies' Church St. Terminal   City Investing   Singer, 612 ft.

SKYLINE OF LOWER MANHATTAN from Jersey City, showing first great sky-scraper, Pulitzer ("World") Building, erected '89, 309 ft. high; the Park Row Bldg., 382 ft., first structural wonder of the 20th century; three marvels of 1908; 200,000-ton twin Hudson Companies' Buildings, 34-story City Investing Bldg., and 612-ft. Singer tower, the three accommodating 41,000 tenants. Manhattan Island, 19.65 sq. miles, purchased in 1626 from Indians for about $24, land value now $3,430,261,571 exclusive of area occupied by streets, total realty value, with improvements, is $5,099,956,321, average $405,215 per acre. The island has 2,292,894 inhabitants; lower end has office population of 250,000; land here is worth from $200 to $600 a sq. ft. and office space rents at from $1 to $40 a sq. ft., making profitable the erection of costly skyscrapers.

"Evening Post"   Federal Bldg.   Park Row Bldg.   N. Y. Telephone   Site City Invest Bldg.   Singer   Washington Life   Am. Exch. Bk.   U. S. Realty   Trinity Bldg.   Am. Surety   Gillender Trust Co. Am.   Union Tr. Co   Manhattan Life   U. S. Express, 330 ft. high   Standard Oil

Washington Life   West St. Bldg.   Am. Surety   Trinity   U. S. Express   Empire   Manhattan Life   Exchange Court

Hudson Terminal   St. Paul's   Electrical Exchange   Liberty St.   Beard B'dg.   Fid. & Casualty Co.   Cedar St.   Thames St.   Albany St.   Hamilton Bldg.   Trinity   Am. Bank Note Co.   Empire Bldg.

LOWER WEST SIDE, from Vesey St. to Bowling Green, where the skyline is being changed from month to month by the erection of new skyscrapers; the 539 buildings over 10 stories high have a total of 6,553 floors, and their office population could not be massed upon a plot four times the area of the ground these buildings occupy. Here, in the streets west of Broadway, are the headquarters of the machinery and electrical-supply business; in each of these narrow streets from 3,000 to 5,000 people pass in an hour during the business day, while 165 "L" and Subway trains traverse the district each hour and at the Hudson Companies' tunnel-terminal 600,000 will come and go daily. The twin Trinity buildings north of Trinity Spire present beautiful façades; in the gap appear the steel columns of the City Investing and Singer Bldgs.

Albany St.   Cedar St.   Cortlandt St.   Thames St.   Rector St.

Castle William   Parade   Officers' Row Whitehall West St. Bldg.   Fort Columbus   Singer   Financial Dist.   60 Wall St.   Municipal Ferryboat "Brooklyn"   Buttermilk Channel   Brooklyn Bridge

GOVERNOR'S ISLAND, from Red Hook, with skyscrapers of Manhattan in the background; an island of 65 acres, separated from Manhattan by East River, from Brooklyn by Buttermilk Channel. U. S. Army Headquarters, Atlantic Division and Department of the East.   Bought from Indians by Gov. Van Twiller, 1634; Army Post since 1802; being enlarged to 120 acres by filling in; to be made one of the most important military depots in world, with piers for transports and ordnance ships.   Castle William, built 1812, now military prison.   Ferry to Whitehall St.

STATEN ISLAND, RICHMOND BOROUGH, 57.19 sq. mi., bet. N. Y. Bay and Lower Bay, separated from N. J. by Kill von Kull, S. I. Sound and Arthur Kill; population, 79,801, least densely populated of the five boroughs; value of taxable land, $35,471,922, an increase of 24 per cent. in one year; total realty value, $60,574,222; desirable residence-section, brought within 20 minutes of Whitehall St., Manhattan, by swift municipal ferryboats; 325 miles of streets and roads; 13 miles frontage on ocean; Toad Hill, 413 ft. above sea level, is highest point in city.

Upper East Side, Manhattan   Metropolitan Hospital   Workhouse   Bridge, under construction Almshouse   East River   Penitentiary   City Hospital   Power House   Training School for Nurses

BLACKWELL'S ISLAND, 120 acres, in East River, from 50th to 86th Sts.; $25,000,000 property devoted to charitable and correctional purposes at expense of $1,500,000 annually to city; Metropolitan Hospital, at north end, 1,200 patients; Workhouse, 1,200 inmates; City Home for Aged and Infirm, just above bridge, 5,400 inmates; Penitentiary, just below bridge, 600 prisoners; City Hospital, 702 beds, 7,000 patients a year; N. Y. City Training School for Female Nurses, 100 pupils; total of 1,100 employees; ferries to island from E. 52d, E. 26th, and E. 70th Sts.

Long Island Sound   Belden Point   Marine Observatory   Pelham Bay   Church of St. Mary, Star of the Sea   Hofbauer's Boat House   Dixon's Boat House

CITY ISLAND, famous yachting rendezvous, in Long Island Sound, off Pelham Bay Park, connected by bridge with Rodman's Neck section of Park; with horse-car line to Bartow Station, N. Y., New Haven & Hartford R. R.; 1½ miles long.   Pelham Bay, to the north, shut in by Hart's Island, and Eastchester Bay, to the east, form admirable anchorages for pleasure craft, and City Island is a centre of boat building and repairing, the chief yards being those of Purdy & Collison, the H. Bocker Co., A. Hansen and B. F. Wood.

Isolation Hospital   Transfer Boats   Physicians' Residence   Hospital   Slip for Ferry to Barge Office   Immigration Depot

ELLIS ISLAND, the Gateway of the New World, in New York Bay off the Battery. All immigrants are taken from the steamers in barges and are examined here by officers of the Department of Commerce and Labor before being permitted to enter America. The criminals, paupers, diseased and contract-laborers are deported at the expense of the steamship companies and the rest are landed at the Barge Office. Of 1,330,624 passengers arriving in 1907 in trans-Atlantic steamships, 1,013,199 were aliens, and 12,000 were deported. All buildings of modern construction.

SWINBURNE ISLAND, in Lower Bay, two miles from the Narrows; Hospital Ship "Illinois," at anchor; physician's residence; pest houses; crematory; place of detention for persons suffering from contagious diseases arriving in the port on ships; chiefly used for cases of cholera, bubonic plague and yellow fever; burying ground at Seguin's, S. I.; under control of Commissioners of Quarantine of the State of N. Y., office, 62 William St.; Dr. Alvin H. Doty, Health Officer of the Port, Clifton, S. I.; no large number of patients here since Asiatic-cholera epidemic of 1892.

HOFFMAN ISLAND, in Lower Bay, one mile from Narrows, place for detention of well persons arriving on infected vessels; all ships report to Health Officer of the Port at Quarantine, the boarding-station at Quarantine, S. I., just within the Narrows, in New York Bay; if cases of contagious diseases are discovered, patients are removed to Swinburne Island, those exposed to infection are held for observation on Hoffman Island, and the ship is disinfected; vessels arriving from infected ports are thoroughly disinfected; quarantine remarkably thorough and efficient.

Harlem River   Children's Home   "Maryland" ferrying Colonial Express train from New Haven tracks at Mott Haven to Penna. R. R., Jersey City   Little Hell Gate

RANDALL'S ISLAND, 100 acres, at mouth of Harlem River, separated from the Bronx on the north by the Bronx Kills and from Ward's Island on the south by Little Hell Gate, with the Sunken Meadow and the East River on the east. Main part of island devoted to children's hospital, home and schools, where 1,700 waifs are cared for by the Charities Department; famous for Nathan Straus' demonstration of the life-saving effects of pasteurized milk. Thirty acres at south end occupied by House of Refuge, where manual training is provided for 900 juvenile delinquents.

Dredge at Work   Liberty Statue, 151 ft., by Bartholdi;   Pedestal, 155 ft., R. M. Hunt, Arch.   Steamer "Liberty" plying to Battery   U. S. Signal Corps School

STATUE OF LIBERTY, Bedloe's Island, New York Bay, 1¼ miles from the Battery; colossal figure of Liberty Enlightening the World, largest made in modern times, designed by Auguste Bartholdi, constructed by Eiffel, presented to America by the French, lights the harbor with an electric torch held 306 ft. above the water, the highest beacon in the world.   Pedestal rests on largest concrete monolith ever made, 91 ft. square at bottom, tapering to 67 ft., 65 ft. high.   War Department Signal Corps School teaches wireless telegraphy and handling of military balloons.

Lower end of Manhattan   Fulton Ferry   Brooklyn Bridge   Empire Stores   Brooklyn Factories   Tower Manhattan Bridge   East River   Battleship "Connecticut"   Pike Street, Manhattan

MANHATTAN BRIDGE, enormous wire-cable, double-decked suspension bridge, part of a great thoroughfare being constructed from the Bowery at Canal St. to the extension of Flatbush Ave., Brooklyn; $16,000,000 structure, begun 1901, to be completed 1909; length, 6,854 ft.; width, 120 ft.; height, 135 ft.; to carry four trolley-tracks, four "L" lines, 35-ft. roadway, and two promenades; tenements housing 7,200 people condemned for Manhattan approach.   Ryan-Parker Construction Co., contractors.   Will have greatest traffic-capacity of any bridge in world.

Royal Bldg.   St. Paul   Park Row   Am. Tract   "Tribune" "World" B'way Chamb.   Manhattan Tower   Roosevelt St. Ferry   L. I. R. R. Freight Piers   Brooklyn Tower, 278 ft. high

BROOKLYN BRIDGE, over East River, from City Hall, Manhattan, to Sands St., Brooklyn; opened May 24, '83; cost to date, $21,000,000; $12,000,000 Manhattan terminal under construction.   Suspended on four cables, each of 5,296 wires, capable of sustaining weight of 48,000 tons, river span, 1,595 ft. long, weighs 14,680 tons, total length, 5,989 ft.; width 85 ft.   Crossed daily by 300,000 people, 4,000 trolley cars, 6,000 "L" cars, 3,000 vehicles.   Built by John A. Roebling, Engineer.   Unsurpassed in beauty.   Capacity to be doubled.

Manhattan　　Astoria in the distance　　　Avenue A　　Almshouse, Blackwell's Island　　Sound Liner　　　Ravenswood Park　　Penitentiary　　　City Hospital　　　Long Island City

BLACKWELL'S ISLAND BRIDGE, over the East River from East 59th St. and 2d Ave., Manhattan, to Jane and Academy Sts., Long Island City; great cantilever structure costing with approaches $25,000,000; rests on six masonry piers; 7,636 ft. long; west span, 1,182 ft.; clear height over channels, 135 ft.; height of island towers, 324 ft.; width 86 ft.; two decks with 53-ft. roadway, four trolley lines, two railroad tracks and two promenades; will open short, direct route to Queens Borough; designed by Gustav Lindenthal, Bridge Commissioner, 1901-3; to be opened 1908.

Grand St. Ferry　　Manhattan Tower　　　　　East River　　　　　　Greenpoint　　　　　Havemeyer Sugar Refineries　　　Approach to Broadway, Brooklyn

WILLIAMSBURG BRIDGE, crossing East River from Delancey and Clinton Sts., Manhattan, to Broadway, Brooklyn; combined cantilever and suspension bridge, opened Dec. 19, 1903; approach extended 1904 to the Bowery by demolishing ten half-blocks of tenements. Length, 7,200 ft.; river span, 1,600 ft.; height, 135 ft. clear; width, 118 ft.; two roadways, two "L" tracks, four trolley tracks; two promenades; cost, $10,000,000; contains 41,634 tons of steel; crossed daily by 120,000 people; through trolley-cars between Manhattan shopping district and Brooklyn.

Washington Bridge Park　　The Bronx　　N. Y. Central R.R.　　　Harlem River　　High Bridge Station　　McComb's Dam Park　　　Speedway　　　Water Tower High B'ge Pk. Wash'ton Heights

HARLEM RIVER, from Fort George, with the Bronx on the left, Washington Heights on right. Washington Bridge, in foreground, at 181st St., beautiful steel and granite structure, 2384 ft. long, 80 ft. wide. High Bridge, at 175th St., 1460 ft. long, carries old Croton Aqueduct over river at height of 116 ft. to pumping station and high-service reservoir; aqueduct completed 1842; capacity 90,000,000 gallons a day. Second aqueduct, completed 1890, carries 290,000,000 gallons a day under Harlem at 135th St. At 158th St. is Putnam R. R. drawbridge.

THE CITY OF NEW YORK, within dotted lines, 326.9 square miles, including Boroughs of Manhattan, Brooklyn, The Bronx, Queens and Richmond, consolidated 1898.   Population, 1908, 4,422,685; subur
$1,156,346,803; including $814,833,200 owned by city; grand total, $8,500,000,000 increase in real-estate assessments in 1908, $472,000,000.   Cost of city government, 1908, $143,572,266; largest items
including $50,000,000 worth of piers built by the city.   Shipped by water in 1907 $1,200,000,000 worth of goods, two-thirds going to foreign ports.   City owns $46,000,000 subway; street railways, inclu

Vashington Heights · Spuyten Duyvil · Harlem River · Bronx River · Westchester · Throggs Neck · City Island · Larchmont · Great Neck · Sands Point · Manhasset Harbor · Long Island

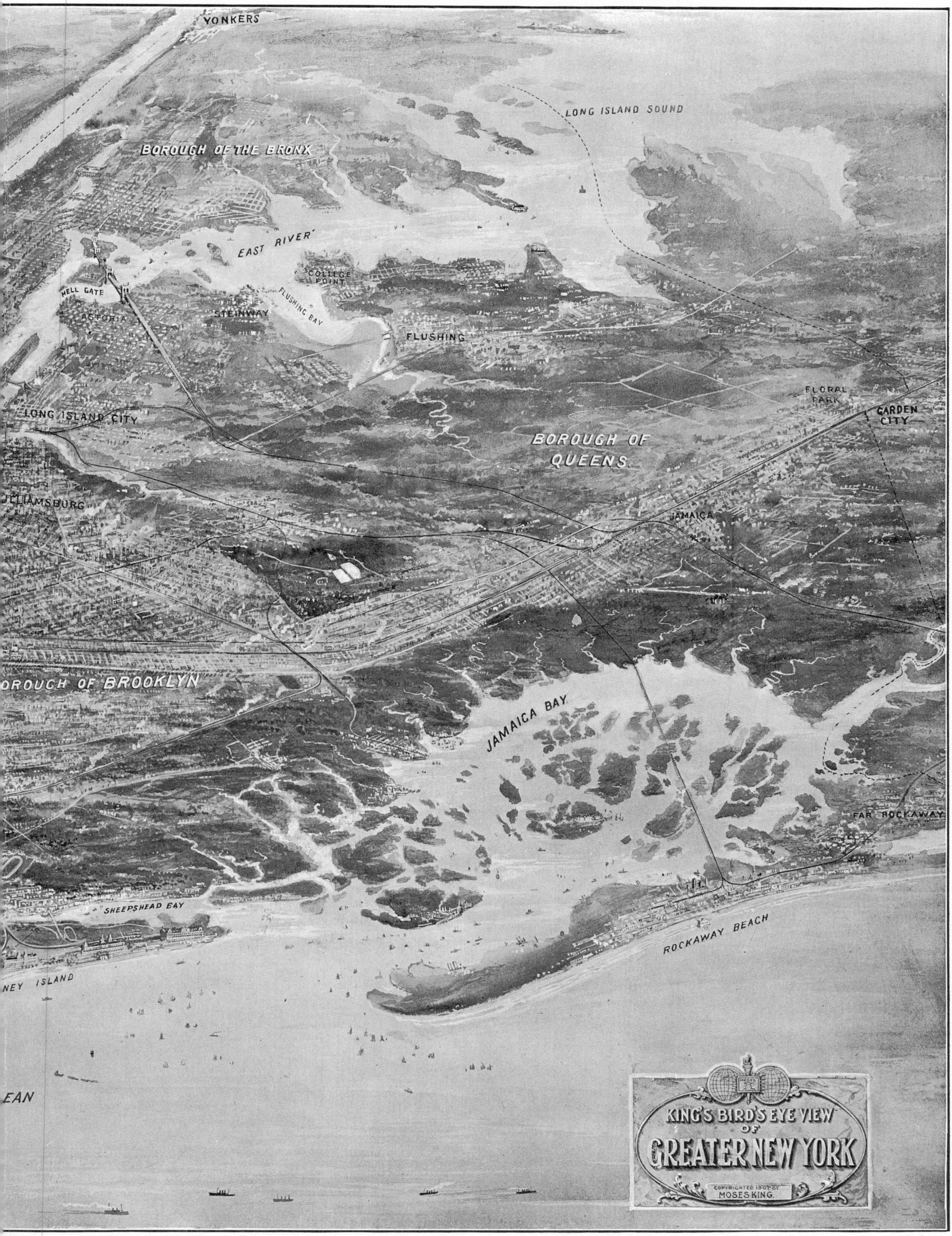
YONKERS
BOROUGH OF THE BRONX
LONG ISLAND SOUND
EAST RIVER
COLLEGE POINT
HELL GATE
ASTORIA
STEINWAY
FLUSHING BAY
FLUSHING
FLORAL PARK
GARDEN CITY
LONG ISLAND CITY
BOROUGH OF QUEENS
ILLIAMSBURG
JAMAICA
OROUGH OF BROOKLYN
JAMAICA BAY
FAR ROCKAWAY
SHEEPSHEAD BAY
ROCKAWAY BEACH
NEY ISLAND
EAN
KING'S BIRD'S EYE VIEW OF GREATER NEW YORK
COPYRIGHTED 1907 BY MOSES KING.

ighton Beach · Manhattan Beach · Oriental Hotel · Bergen Beach · Rockaway Inlet · Barren Island · Rockaway Park · Duck Marshes · Arverne · Edgemere · Rockaway

population, 1,300,000. Taxable property, land and improvements, $6,176,009,652 franchises, etc., $536,470,950; personalty, $554,889,871; total, $7,267,370,473; real estate exempt from taxation ools, $27,514,363; interest on debt, $24,576,522. Parks, 7,071 acres; cemeteries, 2,155 acres; miles of streets, 4,720. Water-front, 353 miles; piers and bulkheads have a total wharfage space of 404 miles, Subway and "L" lines, have 1,276 miles of tracks and carried 1,425,000,000 passengers in 1907. Public improvements to cost $1,600,000,000 planned; 56 buildings completed daily, costing $750,000.

ENRIQUE MULLER PHOTOGRAPHER

Corlears Hook, Manhattan   Coaling Cruiser "Brooklyn," 9,215 tons, 43 guns   Floating Derrick   Battleship "Iowa," 11,346 tons, 48 guns, going into Dry Dock No. 3   "Brooklyn"   Cruiser "Yankee"   Battleship "Kentucky"   Battleship "Illinois," 11,520 tons, 42 guns

NEW YORK NAVY YARD, Wallabout Bay, East River, between Brooklyn and Williamsburg Bridges, Brooklyn; established 1803; built first steam war-vessel "Fulton," 1815; 17,666-ton steel battle-ship "Connecticut," 1903-6; most important and best equipped of the nine American Navy Yards; 2½ miles water-front; 144 acres; four dry-docks—No. 3, 657 by 90 ft. at top and 29 ft. deep; granite, cost $2,000,000; No. 4, being built, slightly wider; $55,000,000 construction and repair plant, covering 45 acres, employing an average of 2,572 mechanics; chief naval base, with vast storehouses filled with war supplies.   U. S. Naval Lyceum, founded by officers in 1833.   Marine barracks east of Navy Yard.   Naval Y. M. C. A., 167 Sands St., built by Miss Helen M. Gould.   U. S. Naval Hospital, Flushing Ave., 21 acres, 500 beds.

HAMBURG-AMERICAN LINE'S STEAMER "KAISERIN AUGUSTE VICTORIA," fitted like a palatial hotel, with elevators, telephones and every comfort to be had ashore, including an a la carte restaurant.   Length, 700 ft.; beam 78 ft.; displacement, 43,000 tons.   This company has contracted with Harland and Wolff, Belfast, for the largest steamer in the world, the "Europa," 800 ft. long, 50,000 tons.

HAMBURG-AMERICAN LINE'S STEAMER "DEUTSCHLAND," six years holder of record for fastest day's run, 601 knots or 24.19 knots an hour.   Record voyage, Sept. 1900, New York to Plymouth, 5 days, 7 hours, 38 min.   Length, 686 ft.; beam, 67 ft.; 23,620 tons; built by Vulcan Co., Germany, 1900.   Emil L. Boas, Resdt. Dir. and Gen. Mgr., 45 B'way; piers in Hoboken.

CUNARD LINE'S STEAMER "LUSITANIA," biggest and swiftest in world, having broken all trans-Atlantic records Nov. 3–8, '07, crossing from Daunt's Rock, Ireland, to Sandy Hook, 2,781 knots, in 4 days, 18 hours, 40 minutes; average 24.25 knots, or 27.88 land miles per hour. Best day's run, 618 knots, averaging 24.80 knots, or 28.52 miles an hour. Length 790 ft.; beam, 88 ft.; depth from boat deck 80 ft.; draught (loaded), 37 ft. 6 in.; displacement, 45,000 tons; height to mastheads, 216 ft.; to funnel tops, 155 ft.; to mastheads, 216 ft.; to funnel tops, 155 ft.; carries 2,650 passengers, 900 crew; driven by four screws rotated by turbine engines of 68,000 h. p. Built, 1907, by J. Brown & Co., Clydebank, Scotland. Sister ship, "Mauretania," record day's run, 624 knots (25.12 per hour) Nov., '07. Vernon H. Brown, 24 State St., Agent.

THE HUDSON RIVER DAY LINE STEAMER "HENDRICK HUDSON," licensed to carry 5,000 passengers, the largest license ever issued. The most commodious and sumptuous craft ever operated in inland waters; all boilers and machinery below decks; length 400 feet, beam 82 feet; 6,000 horse power, compound engines; speed 25 miles per hour; plate glass used exclusively for windows; all interiors furnished in richest hard woods; dining room on main deck; large luncheon rooms forward below; grand promenade one-seventh of a mile in circuit; orchestra arranged so as to be heard on four decks. Cost nearly $1,000,000; every available safety-appliance in construction and equipment. Built by the W. & A. Fletcher Co. Day Line established 1863; Eben E. Olcott, President. Fleet includes "New York," "Albany," and "Mary Powell."

NORTH GERMAN LLOYD LINE'S STEAMER "KAISER WILHELM II," for over three years holder of record for fastest average speed, 23.58 knots per hour, made June, '04, Sandy Hook to Eddystone, off Plymouth, in 5 days, 11 hours, 58 min. Length, 706 ft.; beam, 72 ft.; depth from main deck, 52 ft.; height of funnels, 130 ft.; 26,500 tons; 38,000 horse power; built in 1902 by Vulcan Co., Stettin, Germany. "Kronprinzessin Cecilie," put in service '07, most powerful steamship of reciprocating type, 50,000 horse power. Oelrichs & Co., 5 B'way, Agents.

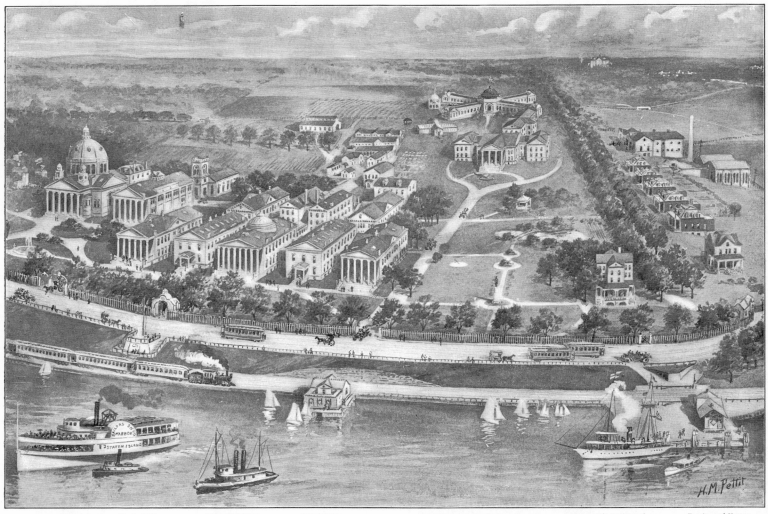

| Chapel | Music Hall | Main Buildings | Storehouses | Sanitarium and Hospital | Governor's Residence | Employees' Homes |

SAILORS' SNUG HARBOR, Richmond Terrace, New Brighton, Staten Island, facing Kill von Kull; largest and wealthiest charitable institution in the world; founded 1801 by Capt. Robt. Richard Randall, who bequeathed a farm worth $4,600 for the care of aged and infirm American merchant-marine sailors; which property, along Broadway below 14th St., has become so valuable that it yields an income of over $700,000 a year. Institution opened 1831; grounds cover 196 acres; 931 inmates; 300 employees. J. Edw. Simmons, Pres. of Trustees. A. J. Newbury, Governor.

PEOPLE'S LINE STEAMER C. W. MORSE, first steel-hull river-steamer, which inaugurated a radical departure in inland navigation; night boat to Albany; 430 feet long; largest craft of the kind in the world; 452 staterooms, including many suites with baths; carries 2,000 passengers; with companion boat Adirondack maintains nightly service between Pier 32, Hudson River, and Albany, where connections are made with trains North, East and West; gorgeous scenery of the American Rhine illuminated by powerful searchlights. Built by W. & A. Fletcher Co., Hoboken.

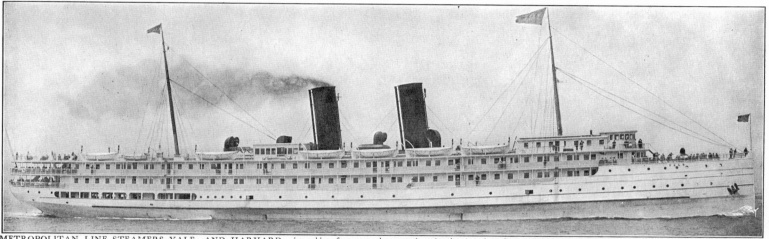

METROPOLITAN LINE STEAMERS YALE, AND HARVARD, sister ships, fastest merchant-vessels under the American flag, attaining a speed of 25 knots an hour; commissioned 1907; driven by triple screws, rotated by turbine engines; 407 ft. long, 63 ft. beam, 16 ft. draught; fireproof; practically unsinkable; plying nightly between Pier 45, North River, and India Wharf, Boston; luxuriously appointed, with daintily furnished suites with baths; café on hurricane deck; service inaugurated 1907; built at the W. & A. Fletcher Co.'s North River Iron Works, Hoboken.

ROYAL MAIL STEAM PACKET COMPANY'S STEAMER "TAGUS," luxurious steel liner; 5,545 tons; 410 ft. long; 50 ft. beam; 23.3 ft. draught; built 1899 by R. Napier & Son, Ltd., Glasgow. Line, chartered 1839, maintains a fortnightly service over the triangular route between New York and Southampton, via Jamaica, Colon, Savanilla, La Guayra, Trinidad, Barbados and Cherbourg, with connections for Mexico, South America, North and South Pacific, Brazil and Argentina. Pier 50, W. 12th St. Sanderson & Son, Agents, 22 State St.

Clyde Steamship Co.   Metropolitan Line Turbine Steamers "Yale" and "Harvard"   Floating Derrick   Hoboken

W & A. FLETCHER COMPANY'S WORKS, 12th to 14th St., Hoboken, N. J. Foremost shipbuilders on the Hudson. Contractors for the Hudson River Day Liner "Hendrick Hudson," the largest, finest and swiftest river-steamer afloat. The 25-knot Metropolitan turbine liners "Yale" and "Harvard," the celebrated river-steamers "Mary Powell," "Albany," "New York," "C. W. Morse," and Fall River Liners "Priscilla," "Puritan," and "Plymouth" are products of these works; builders of Parsons Marine Turbines, which are revolutionizing navigation.

Whitehall Bldg., 254 ft. high   Bowling Green Offices   Columbia Bldg.   Standard Oil   44 Broadway   Manhattan Life, 350 ft. high   Broad Exchange   Bank N. America   Atlantic Mutual   St. Paul Bldg.   60 Wall St., 362 ft. high   Am. Tract Soc.   "World"

Battery Park   Barge Office   Staten Island Ferry   Maritime Bldg.   Custom House   Brooklyn Ferries   Produce Ex.   39th St. Ferry   Imp. and Traders Bldg.   N. Y. Cent. Pier   Corn Exch.   Cotton Exch.   Coffee Exch.   Beaver Bldg.   Erie Pier   Enterprise Line

MANHATTAN, as seen from South Brooklyn; imposing array of skyscrapers from the Whitehall Building, 254 ft. high, overlooking the Hudson, or North River, to the "World" dome, 309 ft. high, at the Manhattan terminal of the Brooklyn Bridge; geographical centre of the Port of New York, where the Hudson and East Rivers form New York Bay, stretching for seven miles from the Battery to the Narrows, with broad channel for ocean liners and 14 square miles of anchorages; trans-Atlantic steamers berth in the North River, while the East River, centre of coast-wise trade, is the most congested waterway in the world, traversed daily by 6,000 craft. At the Barge Office, the gateway of the New World, 3,300 immigrants are landed each day; at the Custom House, the imports of merchandise average nearly $3,000,000 each business day.

COPYRIGHT 1907 BY GEO. P. HALL & SON

Hoboken   Hudson River   Red Star Liner in Berth   Starin and D., L. & W. Pier   Fall River Liners   West St.

WEST STREET, looking north from Cortlandt St., with 200 ft. wide marginal street, giving access to piers and ferries; throughfare constantly congested with trucks hauling merchandise; view shows Pennsylvania R. R. ferry-house jutting into street, Lackawanna and Starin Terminal, American Line piers, N. Y. Central pier, Providence and Fall River Lines, Erie Ferry and Terminal.

Williamsburg   Mollenhauer Sugar Refineries   Wallabout Bay   N. Y. Navy Yard   Brooklyn

BROADWAY FERRIES, Brooklyn, heart of manufacturing section of Williamsburg district, with ferry lines running across the East River to East 42d St., East 23d St., Grand St., and Roosevelt St., Manhattan, carrying daily over 4,000 trucks and in the rush hours being jammed with thousands of workers who live in the great Brooklyn residence-districts back from the river.

NORTH GERMAN LLOYD PIERS, on North River, 2d to 4th Sts., Hoboken; largest and most modern steamship-terminal occupied by a single company in New York Harbor; stone piers with steel superstructures erected 1901-'2 in place of wooden piers burned June 30, 1900. Norddeutscher Lloyd fleet consists of 48 fast steamships. Sailings Tuesdays and Thursdays to Plymouth, Cherbourg and Bremen; Saturdays to Gibraltar, Naples and Genoa; connecting lines to Mediterranean ports, Australia, China, Japan. Oelrichs & Co., Agents, 5 Broadway.

Anchor Line   Penna. R. R. Ferry   Union Ferry Terminal, Erie, Lackawanna and Jersey Central   Cunard Liner "Lusitania"

CHELSEA IMPROVEMENT, from W. 23rd St. to Gansevoort Market at Little W. 12th St.; most important development of the city's water-front; up-town terminal of the ferry lines of the railroads running into Jersey City and Hoboken; $15,000,000 granite steamship-terminal for trans-Atlantic liners, with nine piers and sixteen berths each 750 ft. long; swift Cunard liner "Lusitania" first vessel to land its passengers here; piers to be covered with ornamental steel superstructures; White Star, French and American lines to have piers in this section, as well as the Cunard

Bowl. Green Offices   Washington Bldg.   Corn Exch. Bk.   Produce Exch.   6th & 9th Ave. "L"   Custom House   P. O. Br.   Bridge St.   Battery Park Bldg.   Pearl St. Chesebrough Bldg. Aquarium

BATTERY PARK, from Dock Dept. Pier; Naval Landing in foreground; Washington Building, first skyscraper, on site of Kennedy Mansion, once Washington's headquarters; Bowling Green, in front of Custom House; imposing façade of new $7,200,000 Custom House on State St., the early thoroughfare of fashion; Battery Park, 21.2 acres, has a fine sea-wall commanding an unobstructed view of the harbor; the "L" skirts the inner side of the park and the Municipal Subway passes underneath to South Ferry and through twin tunnels under the East River to Brooklyn.

Battery Sea Wall   New York Bay   Battery Park   The Aquarium   Liberty   Fire Boat Dock   New Jersey Shore   Naval Landing   Ellis Island   Dock Dept. Pier

THE AQUARIUM, on the Battery sea wall, containing in 122 glass tanks the finest collection of living fishes ever displayed. The building was erected in 1807 on a small island and was called Fort Clinton; in 1822, joined to the mainland by filling in, it became a place of amusement known as Castle Garden and Jenny Lind sang there in 1850; from 1855 to 1892 it was the immigration depot, which was moved to Ellis Island, and in 1896 the old Fort was converted into an aquarium; visited annually by 2,000,000 people; 2,500,000 food fish hatched and distributed each year.

CASS GILBERT, ARCHITECT

Produce Exchange Roof   Whitehall Street   Produce Exch. Branch P. O. in basement, at Bridge St. end.   Custom House, Cass Gilbert, Arch.; John Peirce, Builder   Bowling Green   Battery Park
Produce Exchange Roof   Produce Exch. Branch P. O. in basement, at Bridge St. end.   Emblematic Groups — Asia, America, Europe, Africa — by Daniel C. French
U. S. CUSTOM HOUSE, facing Bowling Green at foot of Broadway, occupying entire block between Whitehall and State Sts., to Bridge St., magnificent carved granite structure, finest of the sort in the world, erected 1901-7, at cost of $7,200,000, including ground, on site of Fort Amsterdam (1626) and Government House (1787) and later headquarters of steamship lines.   Embellished with stately Doric colonnades; cartouche emblematic of America, by Carl Bitter, crowning attic; great commercial nations represented on the cornice, in this order—Greece and Rome, by F. E. Elwell; Phœnicia, by F. W. Ruckstuhl; Genoa, by Augustus Lukeman; Venice and Spain, by F. M. L. Tonetti; Holland and Portugal, by Louis St. Gaudens; Scandinavia, by Johannes Gelert; Germany, by Albert Jaegers; France and England, by Charles Grafly.

Beaver St.   Produce Exchange, George B. Post, Architect   Whitehall St.   Bowling Green   Stone St.   Kemble Bldg.

NEW YORK PRODUCE EXCHANGE, fronting on Bowling Green; organized 1861; $3,000,000 building, 307 by 150 ft., occupied 1884; clock tower, 40 by 70 and 240 ft. high; trading room, second floor, 220 by 144 ft. and 60 ft. high, daily scene of the largest volume of trading in grain and provisions of any exchange in the world; 2,493 members, representing every important shipping centre in America. Important factor in improvement of the waterfront and the building of $101,000,000 barge-canal across New York State. William H. Douglas, President.

Hamburg-American Building, Formerly Aldrich Court

HAMBURG-AMERICAN LINE, 45 Broadway, site of first bldg. erected (1613) on Man. Isl.; purchased 1907; remodeled, forming finest steamship-offices in America; has 376 steamships. Emil L. Boas, Res. Dir. and Gen'l Mgr.

Columbia Bldg.   Broadway   Seaboard Bank   Produce Exchange Bank   Beaver Street   Produce Ex.

NEW YORK PRODUCE EXCHANGE BANK, 10-12 Broadway, N. E. cor. Beaver St., opp. Produce Ex. one of the large and strong state banks, seven branches in various parts of city; capital and surplus, $1,656,000; deposits, $8,000,000; assets, $10,000,000; new bldg. erected for bank 1905. Forrest H. Parker, Pres.

Beaver St. Corn Exchange Bank, 270 ft. high   William St.   Lord's Court
CORN EXCHANGE BANK, N. W. cor. William and Beaver Sts.; largest State bank; 21 branches; capital and surplus $8,500,000; deposits, $51,500,000; assets $66,000,000.   William A. Nash, Pres.

IRVING UNDERHILL PHOTO.

Farmers' Loan   Cotton Exchange   Stone St.   S. William St.   Corn Exchange Bk.
J. & W. SELIGMAN & CO., BANKERS, S. William, William and Stone Sts.; new $1,000,000 home of famous international banking-house, erected 1907; 11 stories, Francis H. Kimball and Julian C. Levi, architects; near all exchanges and new Custom House; overlooking Hanover Square, East River and Bay; one of the strongest and oldest American banking-houses

Mills Bldg.   Wall Street Exchange, Clinton & Russell, Arch.   Atlantic Bldg.
WALL STREET EXCHANGE, 43-49 Exchange Place; one of the tallest office-buildings in the heart of the financial district; 25 stories, 327 feet high; built for the National Bank of North America.

Coffee Exch.   Beaver St.   Cotton Exch.   William St.   Hanover Sq.   Seligman Bldg.

COTTON EXCHANGE, Beaver and William Sts.; organized 1870; $1,000,000 building occupied 1885; 450 members; Dr. James H. Parker, President. America produced in 1907 13,540,000 bales out of world's supply of 19,000,000; exported 8,365,000.

William St.   The Farmers' Loan and Trust Co.   Beaver St.

FARMERS' LOAN AND TRUST CO., N. E. cor. William and Beaver Streets; Fifth Avenue Branch, No. 475 Fifth Avenue, between 40th and 41st Streets. First trust company in America, chartered 1822. Edwin Sprague Marston, President.

Seligman Bldg.   Beaver St.   Consolidated Exchange, Clinton & Russell, Architects   Broad St.

CONSOLIDATED STOCK EXCHANGE, S. E. cor. Broad and Beaver Sts.; the centre of seven exchanges; formed '85 by union of the Mining Stock Exchange (founded '75) and five other boards; from April, '88, to Aug., '07, occupied building at Broadway and Exchange Pl.; Aug. 26, '07, moved into new $300,000 home erected on $870,000 site; trading room, 95 by 82 ft., contains 12 trading posts for railroad and industrial stocks, mining-stock department and wheat pit; 132,000,000 shares dealt in year ended June 30, '07; 1,250 members; Ogden D. Budd, President.

Trinity Bldg.   Am. Exch. Bk.   Equitable   Bk. Commerce   Am. Surety Co.   Trinity, 284 ft. high   United Bank Bldg   Gillender Bldg.   No. 7 Wall St
TRINITY CHURCH, head of Wall St.; wealthiest parish in America; finest, pure Gothic architecture; erected 1846 on site of original church (1697); churchyard, 391.5 ft. front on B'way, average depth to Trinity Pl., 243 ft.; land now worth $40,000,000, contains tombs of Alexander Hamilton, Robert Fulton, Martyrs' Monument, etc.   Morgan Dix, Rector; Wm. T. Manning, Assistant.

Empire Bldg., 20 stories, 293 ft.; Marc Eidlitz & Son, Bldrs.   Trinity Churchyard   Hamilton's Grave   6th Ave. "L"   U. S. Express   Trinity Spire
EMPIRE BUILDING, 71 Broadway, cor. Rector St., through to Trinity Place, with arcade to "L" station; Kimball & Thompson, Architects; owned by Orlando B. Potter Estate, Frederick Potter and Clarence H. Kelsey, Trustees, Executive offices of U. S. Steel Corporation, biggest industrial concern in world; organized by J. Pierpont Morgan; W. E. Corey, Pres.; E. H. Gary, Chairman.

Rector St.   6th Ave. "L"   Fulton's and Hamilton's Graves   U. S. Express, 320 ft.   North River   West St. Bldg.

UNITED STATES EXPRESS CO., N. W. cor. Rector St. and Trinity Pl.; erected 1907; overlooking the harbor and the North River. Has more modern conveniences and is the best lighted office-building in the world.   U. S. Senator Thomas C. Platt, President.

Am. Bank Note Co.   Trinity Parochial School   Trinity Church, 284 ft.   Trinity Bldg. 308 ft.

TRINITY CHURCH, Broadway at head of Wall St.; founded 1697; church, third on site, completed 1846; $40,000 bronze doors and $100,000 white marble altar and reredos gifts of Astor family; wealthiest parish in America, real-estate income $775,000; eight chapels, hospital and schools.

United Bank Bldg.   No. 1 Wall St.   Trinity Church   74 Broadway   Manhattan Life
ONE WALL STREET, S. E. cor. Broadway, occupying the most expensive plot in New York, costing $598.21 a square foot, ground floor and basement rents for $37,500 a year; 18 stories; 217 ft. high; profitable utilization of costly plot, only 29 ft. 10 in. front on Broadway, and 39 ft. 10 in. on Wall Street, made possible by steel-frame construction and especially compact elevators.

N. German Lloyd   Bowling Green Offices   Int. Mer. Marine   Stevens House   Hamb.-Am.   Empire Bldg.   Standard Oil   Seaboard Bk.   Produce Ex. Bk.
BROADWAY, from beginning of 15-mile thoroughfare to Trinity Building, viewed from new Custom House; 12 trans-Atlantic steamship lines on left, Hamburg-American on site of first dwelling of white men on island.   Petroleum industry of world centres in 17-story Standard Oil Bldg.   Bowling Green Offices, 229 ft. high, largest in city when built by Spencer Trask.

Manhattan Life   Tower Bldg.   44 Broadway, Geo. A. Fuller Co., Bldrs.   Standard Oil
FORTY-TWO BROADWAY, through to New St; fifth largest office-building in world;
21 stories; 270 ft. high; 286,000 sq. ft. office room; Henry Ives Cobb, Architect
J. S. Bache & Co., Bankers; and Empire Trust Co., LeRoy W. Baldwin, Pres.

Union Trust Co.   74 Broadway   Manhattan Life, Kimball & Thompson, Arch.   Empire Bldg.
MANHATTAN LIFE INSURANCE CO., 66 Broadway; founded 1850; 350 ft. high; one
of finest façades on B'way; insurance in force, $70,300,000; contingent reserve fund,
$1,750,000; real estate, $6,000,000; assets, $20,300,000; H. B. Stokes, Pres.

Pine St.   Am.Surety Bldg., 306 ft. high; Bruce Price, Arch.   Schermerhorn Bldg.   United Bank Bldg.
AMERICAN SURETY COMPANY, 100 Broadway, S. E cor. Pine St., organized
1884; capital and surplus, $5,000,000; general bonding-business; accepted as surety by
U. S. Government; Henry D. Lyman, Pres.   U. S. Weather Bureau Station on roof.

| N. Y. Life Building | Tombs Prison | Blackwell's Island Bridge | Singer Tower | Park Row Building | Edison Electric Light Co. | Consolidated Gas Co. | Long Island City | Robert Hoe & Co. | Standard Oil Refineries | Williamsburg Bridge | American Sugar Refineries |

COPYRIGHT 1907 BY MOSES KING.

| Hudson Term. | West St. Bldg. | City Investing | Twin Trinity Bldgs. | U. S. Express | Empire | Hanover | Whitehall | Bowling Green Bldg. | 42 Broadway | 60 Wall Street | Broad Ex |

SKYSCRAPERS OF LOWER MANHATTAN, where the business interests of 90,000,000 people centre in enormous steel, fireproof buildings that have risen, most of them within the decade, to accommodate of $14,000,000,000 worth of railroads, of manufacturing concerns with a capital of $25,000,000,000, of business enterprises of all sorts that represent investments aggregating $200,000,000,000. The city $2,855,713,391 resources. The post offices handle 7,000 pieces of mail a minute and the city spends $70,000 a day on postage. $6,000,000 worth of goods are manufactured in the city every worki

R.W. Rummell

se rapidly increasing demands for office room in the new world centre; $73,000,000 are now being spent on buildings from 12 to 48 stories high that are under construction. Here are the headquarters or agencies

banks and trust companies in 1907 had resources totaling $4,072,460,598 and here centered the business of 162 fire-insurance companies with $418,093,727 assets, and 223 life-insurance corporations with

v and the imports amount to nearly $3,000.000 a day. There are about 14,000 telephone conversations every minute and 12,000 fares a minute are paid to the traction companies during the rush hours.

Blair Bldg.   Commercial Cable Bldg.   Stock Exchange, Broad St. facade.
COMMERCIAL CABLE BUILDING, 20 Broad St., through to New St., 21 stories, 275 ft. high; headquarters Commercial Cable system, organized 1884 by John W. Mackay and James Gordon Bennett; 26,000 nautical miles of cables; C. H. Mackay, Pres.

Sub-Treasury   J. P. Morgan & Co.   Broad Street   Mills Bldg.   German-American Bank   Exchange Pl.
MILLS BUILDING, N. E. cor. of Broad Street and Exchange Place, extension to 35 Wall St.; one of first great office-buildings, erected for Darius O. Mills, before the day of steel-frame construction; tenanted by famous financial and legal firms; opposite Stock Exchange and U. S. Sub Treasury.

Old Custom House   Lord's Court   William St.   Atlantic Bldg., Clinton & Russell, Arch.   U. S. Tr. Co.
ATLANTIC MUTUAL INSURANCE CO., 49 Wall St. to Exchange Pl.; since 1842 has insured vessels and cargoes to value of over $22,000,000,000; received $230,000,000 in premiums; paid $130,000,000 losses; assets, $13,000,000.   Anton A. Raven, Pres.

Central Tr. Co.   Centre of Wall St.   No. 60 Wall St., Clinton & Russell, Arch.   Trust Co. of America, Francis H. Kimball, Arch. Mills Building   Mechanics' Nat'l Bank

SIXTY WALL ST., through to Pine St.; 362 ft. high; conspicuous landmark; visible from the ocean; contains Wall St. Branch P. O., second only to General P. O. in receipts. International Banking Corp., branches in 17 foreign cities; capital, $9,500,000; Gen. Thos. H. Hubbard, Pres.

TRUST CO. OF AMERICA, 37-43 Wall Street; 327 ft. high; erected 1907. Tallest building in Wall Street. Trust Co. main floor; capital and surplus, $9,000,000; deposits, $20,000,000; assets, $48,000,000; Oakleigh Thorne, President; John E. Borne, Chairman Board.

Kuhn, Loeb & Co.   William St.   Bank of N. Y., N. B. A., founded 1784   Wall St.

THE BANK OF NEW YORK, NATIONAL BANKING ASSOCIATION, 48 Wall Street, N. E. corner William Street.   Occupied this corner since 1797.   Oldest bank in the State.   Capital and surplus, $5,000,000; Herbert L. Griggs, President.

Manhattan Trust Co. Merch. Bk.   Bank of America   Cor. Wall & William Sts

BANK OF AMERICA, in block occupied by Sub-Treasury, and Assay Office; founded 1812 on present site; Oliver Wolcott, first president; capital and surplus, $6,131,900; deposits, $21,863,335; assets, $34,822,418.   William H. Perkins, President.

William St.   Bank of N. Y.   City Bank   60 Wall St.   Wall St. Ferry   Sampson Bldg.   Hanover St.   Façade of old Custom House, built 1841; Ionic monoliths 38 ft high, 4½ ft diam.   William St.

WALL STREET, from William to the East River, crossed by "L" at Pearl Street, where the Seaman's Savings Bank, fourth largest in city, stands at N. W. corner; deposits, $70,000,000. Opposite, at S. W. corner, is the Eagle Building; adjoining are two properties secured 1907 by the U. S. Realty Co. for the erection of a new skyscraper; next is the Sampson Building, and at the S. E. cor. of Hanover and Wall Streets is the international banking-house of Brown Brothers & Co.   The Custom House is being remodeled for occupancy by the National City Bank.

Trinity Manhattan Tr. Co. Hanover Bk.   Manhattan Bank Merchants' Bank Bank of America

MERCHANTS' NATIONAL BANK, 42 Wall Street, founded, 1803, with Oliver Wolcott, President; capital and surplus, $3,650,000; deposits, $24,279,000; assets, $30,000,000; R. M. Gallaway, President. View westward to Trinity Church.

Atlantic Bldg. Tr. Co. Am. Wall St.   J. P. Morgan & Co., Drexel Bldg. Broad St. Mills Bldg.

J. P. MORGAN & CO., S. E. cor. Wall and Broad Sts.; offices of America's greatest banker, who has twice averted panics by his resources and his vigorous action; organizer of U. S. Steel Corp., International Mercantile Marine, etc.; philanthropist, art patron.

Old Custom House, to be remodeled for Nat'l City Bank, by McKim, Mead & White   Atlantic Mutual Tr. Co. of Am.   No. 1 Wall St. Trinity Bk. of Am.   Bank of N. Y. Nat. City Bk.   Cent. Tr. Co.

WALL STREET, from Old Custom House to Trinity Church on Broadway; financial heart of America; occupied entirely by banks, financial institutions and allied interests. The National City Bank, the greatest financial institution in America, founded 1812, on present site, is about to move into the remodeled Custom House, built 1841, bought for $3,000,000; four stories to be added; banking room in rotunda to be the largest in the world; deposits average $180,000,000; actual cash in vaults averages $40,000,000; James Stillman, Pres. since 1891.

Cedar St.   Mercantile Safe Deposit Co.   Broadway   Equitable Building   Mercantile Tr. Co.   Am. Surety Co.
EQUITABLE LIFE ASSURANCE SOCIETY, 120 B'way; Cedar to Pine Sts.; Nassau St., Cedar to Pine Sts.; founded 1859 by H. B. Hyde; re-organized 1905, Grover Cleveland, Morgan J. O'Brien and Geo. Westinghouse trustees of majority stock owned by Thos. F. Ryan; one of largest life-insurance companies; policies in force, $1,500,000,000; surplus, $65,000,000; assets, $430,000,000. Paul Morton, Pres.

Old Mutual Life Bldg.   Broadway   Am. Ex. Nat'l Bank, 235 ft. high; Marc Eidlitz & Son, Bldrs.   Cedar St.   Clearing House   Chase Nat'l Bank
AMERICAN EXCHANGE NATIONAL BANK, 128 B'way, cor. Cedar St.; fd. 1838; banking house and office bldg., erected 1901; Clinton & Russell, Arch.; 47,440 sq. ft. office room on plot of 4,508 sq. ft.; 25 ft. lot adjoining bought for extension; capital and surplus, $10,000,000; deposits, $39,000,000; assets, $54,000,000; circulation, $4,976,747; Dumont Clarke, Pres.

Trinity   Empire   Martyrs' Monument   Trinity Bldg., F. H. Kimball, Arch.   Carnegie Tr. Co.   Broadway   Cedar St.   U. S. Realty Bldg., Francis H. Kimball, Architect   Trinity Pl.

TRINITY BUILDING, 111 Broadway, and UNITED STATES REALTY BUILDING, 115 Broadway; perfect application of English Gothic architecture; combined frontage of 129.5 ft. depth, 260 to 275 ft; 21 stories and cupola, 308 ft. high; 552,873 sq. ft. floor-space, 7 times area Madison Square Garden; each building rests on 70 pneumatic caissons, sunk 75 ft., capable of bearing 60,000 tons; steel-frame Realty Bldg., erected by Geo. A. Fuller Co. in 63 days, stone-work, 146; trim, 45 days; United States Realty Co., Owner; Harry S. Black, President.

American Exchange National Bank, 16 stories, 235 ft. high   Chase National Bank   N. Y. Clearing House, built 1896; R. W. Gibson, Arch., Marc Eidlitz & Son, Bldrs.   National Bank of Commerce, 20 stories, 274 ft.

NEW YORK CLEARING HOUSE, 77-83 Cedar St., the conservator of sound banking; an association of 32 national and 20 state banks of $129,100,000 capital and $163,396,900 surplus, formed Oct. 11, 1853; average daily clearings, 1907, $313,000,000; total, 60 years, $1,856,000,000,000; record day, Jan. 3, 1906, clearings, $686,844,890; Alexander Gilbert, President Market and Fulton Bank, Pres.; A. H. Wiggin, Secy.; William Sherer, Manager; Wm. J. Gilpin, Ass't. Mgr.; James T. Woodward, Chairman.   The Chase National Bank, founded '77, occupies ground floor and basement; deposits, $72,000,000; Hon. Alonzo B. Hepburn, President; Albert H. Wiggin, Vice-Prest.; H. W. Cannon, Chairman.

Commercial Cable Bldg., 275 ft. high   Stock Exchange, George B. Post, Architect; cost $3,000,000   Wilks Bldg.   Stock Exchange Entrance   Wall St.   Trinity

NEW YORK STOCK EXCHANGE, Broad St., through to New, with entrance on Wall St., founded May 17, 1792; carved white-marble building, occupied May, 1903; board room, 138 by 112 ft. and 80 ft. high, with ceiling in gold relief; façade of Corinthian columns each 52 ft. high.   Trading 10 a. m. to 3 p. m.; daily sales average 700,000 shares of stock and $1,700,000 in bonds; biggest year in stocks, 1906, 288,000,000 shares; in bonds, 1905, $1,024,000,000.   1,100 members; seats have sold as high as $97,000.   R. H. Thomas, President.

Central Bldg. Cedar Street   The West Street Building, Cass Gilbert, Arch.; John Peirce Co., Builder   Albany Street   Singer Bldg.   Washington Life

THE WEST STREET BUILDING, West St., Albany to Cedar; most imposing structure on water front; 24 stories; 324 ft. high; erected by West St. Improvement Co., Gen. Howard Carroll, Pres.: built of steel, granite and terra cotta, heated to 2,000 degrees; ornamented with architectural terra cotta and copper; cost $4,000,000; one of handsomest and most absolutely fire-proof buildings in world; facing 250 ft. marginal street, Jersey Central ferry, B. & O. and Penn. R. R. ferries. etc.   Club rooms top floor.   Offices of Lackawanna R. R., Dupont Powder Co., Bell Telephone Co., etc.

BROADWAY, from Post Office north, with Postal-Telegraph, Home Life, Rogers, Peet & Co., Smith, Gray & Co. and Broadway Chambers facing City Hall Park. On right, Dun Bldg., rising above Stewart Bldg. In Park, near Mail St., MacMonnies' statue of Nathan Hale.
BROADWAY at Canal St., beginning of dry-goods and millinery jobbing-district, extending a mile to the north; formerly Lispenard meadows.

BROADWAY at Chambers St; Broadway Chambers and Barclay Buildings on left, Stewart Building, occupied by city's financial department, East facing City Hall Park. Here begins wholesale dry-goods district, extending a mile to the north. River Savings Inst., and Hope men's furnishing-store, on the right.
BROADWAY at Bond St., with the B'way Central Hotel on the left, centre of millinery and men's furnishing—jobbing and manufacturing district.

BROADWAY, with Trinity Ch. at head of Wall St., Martyrs' Monument, façade of Trinity Building; on right First Nat. Bank and No. 1 Wall St.
CITY HALL PARK, from Broadway, with skyline formed by Emigrant Industrial Savings Bank, Hall of Records, City Hall cupola, Rhinelander Building, Pulitzer ("World") Building, with dome; "Tribune," 41 Park Row, and Potter Building. Mail St. end of Post Office at right.

BOWLING GREEN, beginning of Broadway, entrance to skyscraper canyon, north from Custom House; Produce Exch. and Beaver St. on right.
BROADWAY & PARK ROW, from St. Paul's Chapel, looking north; Astor House on left, Dun Building in distance; Federal Building (P. O. and U. S. Courts) between two thoroughfares; Brooklyn Bridge terminal projects across Park Row, beyond Printing House Square.

BROADWAY at Tenth Street, looking toward Union Square, with the Hotel St. Denis on the left and Grace Episcopal Church (built 1845) and Chantry on the right, adjoining the Fleischmann Bakery, where the "bread line" forms every night for free loaves given away at midnight.
BROADWAY looking north from Fourteenth Street, Lincoln Bldg. and Bank of Metropolis on left, facing Union Square, and Lincoln Monument.

BROADWAY, looking from Union Square south to Wanamaker's. Here the Broadway trolley cars describe an "S" and in the days of cable cars it became known as "dead man's curve," "from the number of accidents. Fourteenth St., crossing here, is a busy shopping-thoroughfare.
FIFTH AVENUE, looking north, the Flat-Iron Building and Madison Square on the right, with the Brunswick Building; Fifth Ave. Hotel on left.

BROADWAY AND FIFTH AVENUE, looking south from the Worth Monument, with the Metropolitan Life Building across Madison Square, vista of fashionable stores reaching to Union Square, "Flat-Iron" Bldg., Scribner's, Fifth Ave. Hotel and the Albemarle.
BROADWAY at 54th Street, looking north to Circle, the automobile-centre of America, where all motor-car makers of the world are represented.

FIFTH AVENUE at Broadway, looking north from 23d St., with the Fifth Avenue Hotel on the left, the Brunswick Building on the right, Madison Square Garden tower looming up across Madison Square, and Metropolitan Annex and Metropolitan Life Building at extreme right.
COLUMBUS CIRCLE AND MONUMENT, Broadway at the left, Eighth Ave., Reisenweber's, Pabst's, Majestic Theatre, and W. 59th St.

Clinton & Russell, Architects   Liberty St.   Mutual Life Building   Morton Trust Co.   Nassau St.   Guaranty Trust Co.   Cedar St.   Columbia Tr. Co.

THE MUTUAL LIFE INSURANCE CO. OF NEW YORK, Nassau to William Sts., Liberty to Cedar; imposing granite bldg. with marble corridors, on site of Middle Dutch Church, erected 1729, used for worship 115 years, occupied by Post Office 1844-75, taken down 1882, made way for Mutual Life Bldg. Company org'd 1843, richest in world, assets $500,000,000, including $30,000,000 in real estate producing $1,700,000 a year in rents; insurance in force, $1,500,000,000; paid policy holders in 65 years nearly $800,000,000. Charles A. Peabody, President.

Liberty St.   Morton Trust Co.   Nassau St.

MORTON TRUST COMPANY, No. 38 Nassau Street, New York City. Incorporated 1889. Capital, surplus and undivided profits, $9,000,000. Transacts a general trust-company business. Hon. Levi P. Morton, President.

Pine St.   Redmond & Co., Banking House   Commonwealth Trust Co.   Sub-Treasury

REDMOND & CO., BANKERS, 31-33 Pine St., leading international banking house and dealers in high-grade investment securities; exquisite white marble bank-building, finished in beautifully wrought bronze; unique five-story steel vault, 15 feet square.

Singer   William St.   German-American Bldg., Hill & Stout, Arch.   Maiden Lane   Silversmith's Bldg.
GERMAN AMERICAN INSURANCE CO., Liberty St. and Maiden Lane; 21 stories, 282 ft. high, rests on largest caissons, 42 ft. below cellar.   Org. 1872; cap., $1,500,000; reserve, $7,168,303; surplus, $5,130,426; assets, $13,798,729; W. N. Kremer, Pres.

Maiden Lane Bldg.   Lawyers Title Ins. & Trust Co. Bldg., Clinton & Russell, Arch.; erected 1908
LAWYERS TITLE INSURANCE AND TRUST CO., 160 B'way; 16 stories; 8-story L on Maiden Lane; Banking Dept. now 59 Liberty St., first floor; main offices, 37 Liberty and 46 Maiden Lane; capital and surplus, $9,500,000.   E. W. Coggeshall, Pres.

Washington Life   Bourne Annex   Liberty Street   A. B. Leach & Co.   Singer Building, Ernest Flagg, Arch.   City Investing Bldg.   Wessels Bldg.   Telephone Bldg.   Cortlandt St.

SINGER BUILDING, N. W. cor. Broadway and Liberty St.; tallest building in world; 47 stories, including 6 in cupola; 612 ft. high, surmounted by flag pole 59 ft. high; tower, resting on 36 caissons sunk to bed rock, 92 ft. below curb, rising 421 ft. above main building, 65 ft. sq., weighing 18,365 tons, anchored with eye-bars imbedded in concrete, so braced as to withstand a wind-pressure of 30 lbs. pounds to the square foot or of 330 tons against any face; tower, 5,000 tenants; six Otis traction elevators; entire building, 9½ acres floor space.   Built by The Singer Mfg. Co.

Broadway Entrance, City Investing Bldg. Wessels Bldg. Cortlandt St. Façade City Investing Bldg., Francis H. Kimball, Architect; Hedden Construction Co., Builders Church St.

CITY INVESTING BUILDING, Broadway, Cortlandt and Church Sts.; largest office-building in the world; 34 stories; 486 ft. high; covering plot of 27,000 sq. ft., with 13 acres floor-space and room for 6,000 tenants; corridor 38 feet wide from Broadway to Church Street, 315 feet; on line of subway, with entrances direct to Sixth Avenue elevated road; 21 elevators; light and air protected by control of adjoining properties; unsurpassed in all its details by any office-building in the world. City Investing Company, Owners; Robert E. Dowling, Pres.

South Brooklyn	Governor's Island	Produce Exchange	Narrows		Staten Island	Manhattan Life	Whitehall	Empire	Trinity Church	U. S. Express	Trinity and	Liberty	L
Buttermilk Channel	East River	240 ft. high	Harbor		Battery	350 ft.	254 ft.	293 ft.	284 ft.	308 ft.	U. S. Realty	306 ft.	

COPYRIGHT BY MOSES KING - 1908

Tr. Co. Am., 318 ft. Broad Exch., 279 ft. Mutual Life Stock Exchange Hanover Bk., 329 ft. Provdt. Savgs. Life Nassau St. Am. Surety, 306 ft. Chamber Commerce Am. Exch. Bank Trin. & U. S. Realty, 308 ft. Lawyer

FINANCIAL DISTRICT, where two billion dollars' worth of skyscrapers and other business-buildings cluster on the lower end of Manhattan Island, with an office population of 250,000, with nearly a million pe
stories; 200, 12 to 14; 101, 11; and 164 10 stories; two are over 600 ft. high; two over 400 ft.; 14 over 300 ft.; the block bounded by Broadway and Church St. and Cortlandt and Liberty provides office
structures, built of steel, protected and enclosed with imperishable brick, with partitions and floors fire-proofed with hollow tiles, with window frames, fittings and doors of metal, with wire-glass windows, are

nia   Washington Life   Hudson River   Singer   Communipaw   City Investing Bldg.   Jersey City   West Street Bldg.   Penna. Terminal
        273 ft.   612 ft.   Terminal   486 ft.   Population 250,000   324 ft.   Jersey City

Richard Rummell '07

e   Maiden Lane Bldg.   Singer Building   Broadway   Cortlandt Street   City Investing Bldg., B'way to Church St.   West St. Bldg.   N. Y. Telephone Co.   Hudson Terminal

assing to and fro each day, 20,000 an hour through Broadway alone; of 539 skyscrapers erected in the city since 1890, the three tallest have 34, 47 and 48 stories, 20 have from 20 to 26 stories; 51, 15 to 19
for 20,000 people, and if the hundred small blocks below Fulton St. are similarly built up there will be room for 2,000,000 to work daily in this financial and commercial clearing-house of the world; these
safest in the world, as proved by the Baltimore fire and the San Francisco earthquake; they rest on bed-rock, pneumatic caissons being sunk to the required depth, 92 ft. in case of the Singer Building.

Broadway   The Importers' and Traders' National Bank, J. H. Freedlander, Arch.; Marc Eidlitz & Son, Builders   Murray St.
THE IMPORTERS' AND TRADERS' NATIONAL BANK, 247 Broadway, S. W. cor. Murray St.; fd. 1855; capital and surplus, $8,643,000; deposits, $27,000,000. Erected 1907-1908, for exclusive use of bank; South Dover marble; receiving and note teller on 1st, paying teller on 2d, officers' quarters on 3d floor. Special elevator connections, all floors. Edward Townsend, President.

Singer Tower   Iron Worker 540 ft. above street   Broadway   Dun Bldg.   P. O.   St. Paul Bldg.   Park Row Bldg., 382 ft.
BROADWAY, looking north from Singer Tower. Photo by Brown Bros. from height of 540 ft., showing main thoroughfare of New York, congested East Side with East River beyond. Park Row Bldg. with twin cupolas, long the highest in the world, St. Paul Bldg., 317 ft., and massive Federal Bldg., appear dwarfed from this elevation, and the people in the streets are mere specks.

Park Bank, Donn Barber, Arch.   Marc Eidlitz & Son, Builders   Liberty St.   Chamber of Commerce   Lawyers' Title, Banking Dept.   Liberty Pl.   Chem. Bank, Trowbridge & Livingston, Arch.   Marc Eidlitz & Son, Bld.

NAT. PARK BANK, 214 B'way; Ann and Fulton Sts.; f'd '56; capital and surplus, $12,337,500; deposits, $82,783,600; ass., $100,000,000; R. Delafield, Pres.

CHAMBER OF COMMERCE, 65 Liberty St.; org. in Fraunces' Tavern, April 5, 1768; $1,500,000 white marble bldg. dedicated Nov. 11, 1902, by Pres. Roosevelt; J. Edward Simmons, Pres.   J. B. Baker, Arch.

CHEMICAL NATIONAL BANK, 270 Broadway; banking room in domed "L" on Chambers St.; f'd 1824; Capt. and sur., $8,708,700; dep. $44,795,800; W. H. Porter, Pres.

Broadway   Liberty National Bank   Liberty St

LIBERTY NATIONAL BANK, 139 Broadway; org. 1891; classic marble banking-house, erected 1903; Capital and surp., $3,424,700; dep., $14,035,000; assets, $19,272,000. Frederick B. Schenck, Pres.; Dan'l G. Reid and Chas. W. Riecks, Vice-Prest's.

Fulton St.   Market & Fulton National Bank.   Gold St.   Leather District

MARKET AND FULTON NATIONAL BANK, 81 Fulton St., N. W. cor. Gold; Fulton Bank (org. '24), and Market Bank ('52); consolidated '87; capital and surplus, $2,586,200; deposits, $8,550,000; assets, $12,000,000.   Alexander Gilbert, Pres.

East River Am. Exch. Nat'l Bk. Equitable Am. Surety Man. Life U. S. Realty & Trinity Bldgs. Empire N. Y. Bay Singer Tower
BROADWAY, south from Singer tower; view taken 350 ft. above St.; East River beyond dome of Commercial Cable Bldg. on Broad St.;
canyon formed by skyscrapers ends with square tower of Standard Oil Bldg. at Bowling Green; beyond Battery Park is the Bay;
Am. Exchange Nat'l Bank in foreground, at left, 225 ft. high; Washington Life on right, 237 ft.; Trinity Bldg. 308 ft.

Bethune St. Western Electric Co., 13-story steel frame building West St., overlooking North River
WESTERN ELECTRIC CO., 436 West St., occupying greater part of block, through to Washington and Bank Sts.; for thirty years
largest manufacturers of telephonic apparatus in the world; makers of famous Western Electric motors and of complete electric
equipments; salesrooms, warehouses and factories in eighteen cities; 16,000 employees, including 5,000 in this building.

"Chelsea"

"Audubon"

"Gramercy"

"Franklin"

GENERAL OFFICES

"38th"

"Broad"

"Orchard"

"Spring"

"Chelsea," "Franklin" and "Broad St." Centrals   General Offices, 15 Dey St., through to Cortlandt; "Audubon" and "Orchard" Centrals   "Gramercy," "38th St." and "Spring" Centrals

NEW YORK TELEPHONE COMPANY, General Offices 15 Dey St., 18 Cortlandt St. Has 29 central offices in Manhattan and The Bronx, with 240,000 telephones, 545,000 miles of wire in underground cables, 10,000 employees and an average of 1,000,000 originating calls a day. Officers: Theodore N. Vail, President; Union N. Bethell, 1st Vice-President; John H. Cahill, 2d Vice-President and Secretary; H. F. Thurber, General Manager; Ford Huntington, Treasurer; Walter Brown, Auditor; J. S. McCulloh, General Contract Agent.

"Evening Post" Bldg, Robert D. Kohn, Arch.; Marc Eidlitz & Son, Builders.   St. Paul's Graveyard and Chapel   Post Office   Am. Tract   Park Row Bldg.   St. Paul Bldg.   National Park Bank   Fulton St.

"EVENING POST," 20-24 Vesey St.; founded Nov. 16, 1801, at 40 Pine St., by Alexander   ST. PAUL'S CHAPEL, Trinity Parish, occupying valuable block on Broadway, from Fulton to
Hamilton and other prominent Federalists ; most widely known evening newspaper in America;   Vesey St.; Clergy House and offices of Trinity Corporation on Church St. end.   Erected 1766;
new building, 1906-7, 13 stories; Oswald Garrison Villard, President; Rollo Ogden, Editor.   oldest church edifice in city; contains pew in which Gen. Washington worshipped.

St. Paul's Churchyard   Vesey St.   Astor House   Broadway, looking North   Barclay Street   Postal Telegraph Bldg.

ASTOR HOUSE, Broadway, Vesey to Barclay Sts., opposite beginning of Park Row and Federal Building.   Oldest hotel in the city; opened in 1836, for a generation it had for guests the most emi-
nent people of the Nation; scene of banquet to Congressman John Bell, Nov. 28, 1837, when Daniel Webster spoke from 2 to 4 a. m.; reception to Henry Clay, August '39; dinner to Lord
Ashburton, Sept. '42; headquarters of James K. Polk, presidential campaign of '44.   Only big downtown hotel.   The large rotunda is one of the most famous lunch-rooms in the city.

City Hall   "The Tribune" Am. Tract., 300 ft. high   No. 41 Park Row   Potter Bldg. Temple Court Mail St. end of Federal Bldg. Broadway   Park Row Bldg., 382 ft.   St. Paul Bldg., 317 ft.

CITY HALL PARK, from Chambers St. and Broadway, looking toward Park Row; showing 250-ft. platform along the 279-ft. façade of General Post Office, where 3,300 mails are received and dispatched each day.   City Hall Park, 8¼ acres, scene of official ceremonies, from celebration of Perry's victory on Lake Erie the year City Hall was completed (1812) to opening of the Municipal Rapid Transit Subway, which has a loop under Park, on Oct. 27, 1904.   Departments of City Government occupy ten buildings in and around Park.   Col. Geo. B. McClellan, Mayor.

Nassau St.   Provident Life Bldg.   Liberty St.

PROVIDENT SAVINGS LIFE ASSURANCE SOCIETY, S. W. cor. Nassau and Liberty Streets; an imposing, substantial, modern office building, immediately opposite the Mutual Life Building, in New York's financial district.

Stock Exchange Man. Trust Co. Hanover Bk.   Bk. of Com.   Mutual Life Am. Tract Sub-Treasury

NASSAU STREET CANYON, from U. S. Sub-Treasury, on Wall St., in heart of financial district, through banking-section and jewelry district, to Printing House Square; most congested thoroughfare in the world, 8,000 people passing in an hour.

"Tribune," founded '41   Greeley Statue   Spruce St.   Am. Tract, 300 ft. high   41 Park Row, Geo. A. Fuller Co., Bldrs., City Hall Park.
PRINTING HOUSE SQUARE, Park Row, Nassau and Spruce Sts.; newspaper centre 60 years.   "TRIBUNE," Bldg, erected '73;
enlarged '06.   "Sun," founded '33, adjoining; "World" in next block; "Press," "Commercial" and "Staats Zeitung," on Spruce
St.; "American," "Evening Mail," "Evening Post," and "Globe" within 500 yards.   41 Park Row formerly "Times" Bldg.

Manhattan Terminal, Brooklyn Bridge   Pulitzer Bldg., 309 ft. high; 375 ft. basement to dome   Frankfort St.   "The Sun"   "The Tribune"
"THE WORLD," PULITZER BUILDING, Park Row, opposite City Hall Park; founded 1883 by Joseph Pulitzer;
largest newspaper office-building, tallest in city when erected in 1889; enlarged 1907; Horace Trumbauer, Architect; D. C.
Weeks & Son, Builders.   Site, formerly French's Hotel, purchased 1888 for $630,000.   Morning and evening editions.

Dun and Stewart Bldgs.   Broadway, looking north   General Post Office and U. S. Courts   Park Row   "World"   Potter Bldg.   Park Row Bldg.

FEDERAL BUILDING, one of the finest granite buildings in the world, 144-ft. façade at intersection of Broadway and Park Row, with 262½ ft. on each thoroughfare and 279 ft. on Mail St. Commanding and central location for U. S. District and Circuit Courts and General Post Office, which has 41 branches, 234 sub-stations; 38 post offices, 70 branches, 367 sub-stations in entire city. 1,600 mails dispatched daily, 1,700 received; receipts, year ended June 30, '07, $18,552,207; entire city, $22,000,000; 6,472 clerks and carriers. Edward M. Morgan, Postmaster.

Broadway   Dun Bldg. Stewart Bldg. City Hall Park Emigrant Savings Bk. Edison Co. County Court House Hall of Records   City Hall   Tryon Row Brooklyn Bridge   "American"   "World"

CITY HALL, $500,000 white marble structure erected 1803-12; 216 by 105 ft.; seat of city government, chambers of the Board of Estimate and Board of Aldermen and offices of Mayor, President of Manhattan and City Clerk. Stands in park of 8¼ acres, facing Federal Building. Tweed's $10,000,000 job, the County Court House, in rear of City Hall, fronts on Chambers St.; Stewart Building, occupied by City's Financial Department, at Broadway end of block; new Hall of Records at Centre St. end. Dun Building (R. G. Dun & Co.) overlooks the Park.

Am. News Co.   Dun Bldg.   Chambers St.   Main Entrance, Hall of Records, flanked by Philip Martiny's groups of Indians and early settlers   Centre St.   Shot Tower

HALL OF RECORDS, Chambers St., N. W. cor. Centre, through to Reade St.; $10,000,000 steel and granite structure for the preservation of the real-estate records of New York County; interior finish marble, bronze and mahogany; offices of the Register, County Clerk, Surrogate, and Tax and Law Departments;. The 32 granite monoliths cost $30,000 each. The sculpture includes emblematic figures by Bush-Brown and Martiny and statues of 8 men prominent in the city's history. John R. Thomas and Horgan & Slattery, Architects; John Peirce, Builder.

Chesebrough B!dg.   Aquarium   Fire-Boat Station   Naval Landing   Fire-Boat in Action   City Prison (Tombs)   Bridge of Sighs over Franklin St.   Criminal Court Bldg., Centre St.   White St.

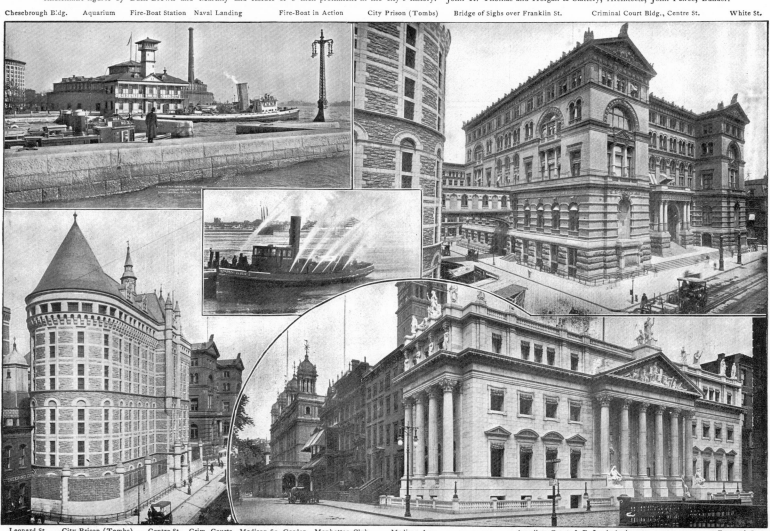

Leonard St.   City Prison (Tombs)   Centre St.   Crim. Courts   Madison Sq. Garden   Manhattan Club   Madison Ave.   Appellate Court, J. B. Lord, Arch.   East 25th St.

MUNICIPAL BUILDINGS. Fire-boat station at the Battery, the "New Yorker" at pier, Harbor Police launches in Naval Landing basin, Fire-Boat "Boody" in action. Criminal Courts Bldg., connected by "Bridge of Sighs" with City Prison; offices of District Attorney, trial rooms of Special and General Sessions and Criminal Branch of Supreme Court. City Prison, on site of Tombs, dismal structure of Egyptian architecture; prisoners held here pending trial. Appellate Division of Supreme Court, $750,000 marble building of great beauty, adorned by symbolic statues and mural paintings.

Broome Street Tabernacle   Broome Street   Centre Street, Subway Bridge Loop Under Street   Police Headquarters, Hoppin & Koen, Arch.   Grand Street

POLICE HEADQUARTERS, Centre St. to Centre Market Pl., Broome to Grand Sts.; 310 ft. long; 46 ft. at Broome St. end; 88 ft. at Grand St. end; imposing Indiana-limestone building, granite base; cost $1,500,000; most complete and perfectly appointed police-headquarters in world; office of Commissioner and Chief Inspector; Detective Bureau and Rogues Gallery; School of Instruction, large drill-room and gymnasium; play-room for lost children; 75 cells in basement. Gillespie, Walsh & Gillespie, Builders. Uniformed force of 9,500 men. Gen. Theo. A. Bingham, Com'r.

Cliff Street   Chapel Court extension Schieren Building   Schieren Building   Ferry Street

CHARLES A. SCHIEREN COMPANY, 30-38 Ferry St., S. W. cor. Cliff; foremost leather-belting manufacturers in America; founded 1868 by Charles A. Schieren (Mayor of Brooklyn, '94-95), with small capital, the business now extends throughout the United States and to foreign countries; situated in "The Swamp," the leather district for over two centuries; plot, 32,000 sq. ft., one of largest individual holdings south of the Brooklyn Bridge; modern development of this big section begun by Mr. Schieren erecting two 10-story fireproof loft-buildings, '05 and '07.

Broadway   R. G. Dun & Co.'s Mercantile Agency   Reade St.

DUN BUILDING, N. E. cor. Broadway and Reade St.; 15 stories; 223 ft. high; headquarters of famous Mercantile Agency, which furnishes accurate records and ratings of
merchants throughout the world; publishes Dun's Review, Domestic and International.

Pearl Street   Scott & Bowne Building; 12 stories; Marc Eidlitz & Son, Bldrs.   New Chambers Street

SCOTT & BOWNE, S. W. cor. Pearl and New Chambers Sts.; manufacturing chemists;
famous the world over for their preparation of cod-liver oil known as Scott's Emulsion;
pioneers in the development of lower East Side as a great manufacturing-district.

Washington St.   Fairchild Building   Laight St.

FAIRCHILD BROS. & FOSTER, 74-76 Laight St.; manufacturing chemists; f'd '79;
famous for preparations of digestive ferments and other pharmaceutical products; Fairchild's
Essence of Pepsine, Panopepton, Peptogenic Milk Powder, Peptonising Tubes, etc.

North River   121-127 Charlton Street   E. R. Durkee & Co.   Washington St.

E. R. DURKEE & CO., 534-540 Washington St., cor. Charlton St., typical ten-story
factory and warehouse building of America's foremost spice and condiment importers and
manufacturers, famous for Durkee's and Gauntlet brands, synonyms of quality.

New York Life Annex   Lafayette St.   New York Life, Home Office, McKim, Mead & White, Arch.   Leonard St.   Bradstreet Mercantile Agency   Broadway   Catharine Lane

NEW YORK LIFE INSURANCE COMPANY, Home Office, 346 Broadway, white marble office-building occupying entire block, annex across Lafayette St.; organized 1845; largest international life insurance corporation; insurance in force $2,125,000,000; assets, $500,000,000, including $14,000,000 in real estate, yielding $1,200,000 in rents; annual income $100,000,000; disbursements, $60,000,000. Darwin P. Kingsley, Pres.; Thomas A. Buckner, Vice-Pres.; John Claflin, Thomas P. Fowler, Woodbury Langdon, J. G. Milburn, Anton A. Rayen among directors.

Church Street   Worth Street   Sixth Avenue "L"   The H. B. Claflin Co.   West Broadway   Thomas Street

THE H. B. CLAFLIN COMPANY, West Broadway to Church St., Worth to Thomas Sts.; largest wholesale dry-goods house in America, handling the entire products of many domestic and foreign mills; one of the largest importing firms in the country; manufacturers and converters of many lines of cotton goods. Founded 1843 by Horace Brigham Claflin; now stock company with $9,000,000 capital. John Claflin, President; J. C. Eames, Vice-President; G. E. Armstrong, Secretary; D. N. Force, Treasurer; S. W. Eames, Ass't Treasurer.

West 20th Street   O'Neill's, founded 1867   West 21st Street   Sixth Avenue "L"   Adams', founded 1886   West 22d Street

O'NEILL-ADAMS CO., DEPARTMENT STORES, Sixth Avenue, 20th to 22d Street, greatest retail-establishment on this shopping-thoroughfare; two enormous dry-goods stores united under one management. The O'Neill and Adams buildings will soon be connected by tunnel under 21st Street. This great store has three quarters of a million square feet of floor space, 5,000 employees, 100,000 customers a day, and does a business of many millions a year. More than a hundred departments carried in each building. This store does the largest business in New York, in millinery, cloaks, suits and furs. Its furniture department occupies three floors of the Adams building. Combined to form one of America's greatest establishments. Adams building erected 1901. O'Neill-Adams Co., chartered '07. Capital $6,100,000.

City Hall Park   City Court   Hall of Records   Centre St   Park Row   Tryon Row   Brooklyn Bridge Terminal   "The Sun"

PARK ROW, from Printing House Square; Tryon Row, long occupied by "Staats-Zeitung," coming down to make way for bridge-terminal and municipal office-building; station of Subway under plaza, expresses continuing under Park Row, through Broadway to South Ferry and Brooklyn, locals taking loop under City Hall Park; 50,000 people an hour pass here in rush hours.

COPYRIGHT 1907 BY IRVING UNDERHILL

Mulberry St.   Jersey St.   Hawley & Hoops   Lafayette St.

HAWLEY & HOOPS, Lafayette, Jersey and Mulberry Streets, on line of the Subway, below the Bleecker Street Station; manufacturers of chocolates and confectionery; occupying one of the largest and best-equipped plants of its kind, and supplying an extensive trade throughout this country and abroad.

Astor Place   Mercantile Library, est. 1820   Eighth St.   Wanamaker's New Store, 217 ft. 6 in. high, D. H. Burnham & Co., Arch.   Subway Entrance   Ninth St.   Wanamaker's (formerly Stewart's)

WANAMAKER'S, Fourth Avenue to Broadway, Eighth to Tenth Sts., connected under Ninth St.; in traffic-centre of city, entrance direct from subway; Hudson Companies' trains through tunnels from New Jersey to pass under Ninth St. to Fourth Ave.; iron store on north, largest in world when built by the famous merchant-prince, Alexander T. Stewart, in 1867; acquired in 1896 by John Wanamaker, the greatest retail-merchant; in partnership with Robert C. Ogden, now retired; new $4,000,000 16-story department-store, completed in 1907, tallest store in world.

Bank of the Metropolis   Hartford Building   Union Square   "Flat-Iron"   H. K. Browne's Statue of Washington   Everett House   Fourth Avenue   Mercantile Building   Union Square Hotel

UNION SQUARE, between Broadway and Fourth Ave., and 14th and 17th Sts.; scene of reception of Gen. Washington by citizens on Evacuation Day, Nov. 25, 1783; of Croton Water Celebration, Oct. 14, 1842; and of great Union Defence Mass Meeting in 1861; 3.48 acres; set apart as a public park in 1809; for a generation the centre of hotel district; now in retail shopping-section. The Park contains the Browne statue of Lincoln, Bartholdi's Lafayette, and fountain by Donndorf presented by D. Willis James.   Tammany Hall, founded 1789, is East of Square on 14th St.

Lackawanna Terminal, Hoboken Hamburg-American and N. German Lloyd Piers Gansevoort Market   Nat. Biscuit Co.   Castle Point   Cunard Piers   Ch. Holy Apostles   Union Ferry Terminal

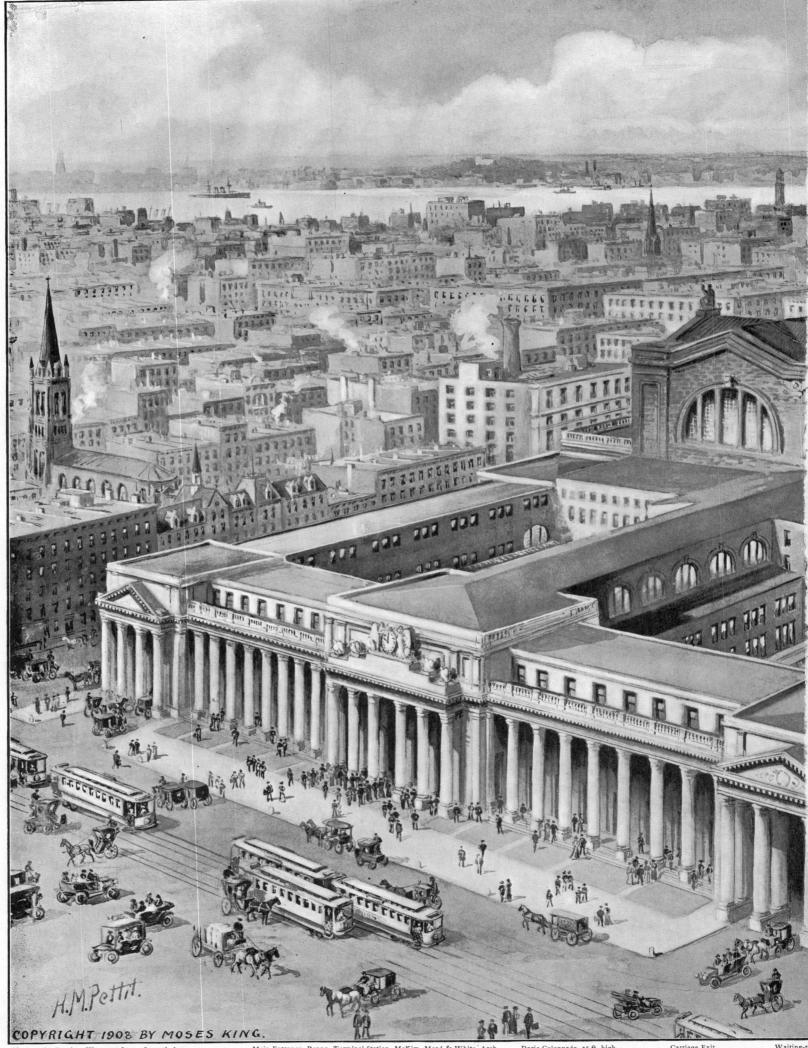

Ch. St. John Baptist West 31st St.   Seventh Ave.   Main Entrance, Penna. Terminal Station, McKim, Mead & White, Arch.   Doric Colonnade, 35 ft. high   Carriage Exit   Waiting-ro

PENNSYLVANIA RAILROAD TERMINAL, 7th to 8th Aves., 31st to 33d Sts., $12,000,000 station, central feature of $90,000,000 improvement by which the Pennsylvania trains are brought through tw
to connection with Long Island Railroad, and by Hell Gate Bridge to N. Y., New Haven & Hartford tracks.   The station will be 780 by 430 ft., rising 60 ft. above the street level and going 40 ft. below
main concourse, 100 by 590 ft., under both 31st and 33d Sts., gives access to trains by two stairways to each platform; sub-concourse, 60 by 340 ft., for passengers leaving trains; train shed, 340 by 210 f

under the Hudson River into great train-yard from 10th to 8th Aves., 60 ft. below surface, through station accommodating 21 tracks, at depth of 40 ft., thence under 32d and 33d Sts. and under East River ; arcade from main entrance on Seventh Ave., 45 ft. wide, 225 ft. long, to main waiting-room, 320 by 110 ft., and 150 ft. high, largest in the world; two smaller waiting-rooms, 58 by 100 ft. each; ge entrance on Seventh Ave. at 31st St., to plaza and cab-stand 20 ft. below surface; exit at 33d St. Baggage-room east of main waiting-room, under arcade, with 430 ft. frontage for transfer wagons.

58

LUNCH & ICE CREAM

SHOELACES

PRETZELS

VEGETABLES

NEWSBOYS

RECREATION PIER

CHINATOWN

IMMIGRANTS

CENTRAL PARK ENTRANCE

GREELEY SQUARE

STATEN ISLAND FERRY

SNOW TIMES

23ᵈ ST. AND FIFTH AVE.

MULBERRY BEND

GERMAN IMMIGRANTS

STREET CLEANERS

LEMONADE

FRUIT

BROOMS AND BASKETS

STREET SCENES. "White Wings" at work. Carting snow to dump. The Plaza, 5th Ave. and Central Park South, in winter. Newsboys under "L" Station at Greeley Square. Lunch carts back of "Herald" Bldg. Lemonade cart in 42d St. "Flat-Iron" corner, Fifth Ave. Hotel, in background. Crosstown cars in 34th St. Family parties on Recreation Pier. Shoestring man near Grand Central Station, "L" station across 42d St. Greeley Square and Statue, looking down Broadway. Fruit vender in shopping district, 6th Ave. and 20th St. Shopping in Mulberry Bend. Free-Ice Depot. Doyers St., centre of Chinese quarter. Selling pretzels in Sixth Ave. A curb merchant. Boarding-house runners at Barge Office. Staten Islanders coming from ferry boat. Immigrants, just landed, going through Battery Park. Sidewalk merchant. Photo. by Byron.

Nineteenth St.   Main Entrance   Broadway   Lord & Taylor's Marc Eidlitz & Son, Builders   Twentieth St.   Lord & Taylor's Fifth Ave. Extension

LORD & TAYLOR, dry goods, Broadway, 20th St. and Fifth Ave., in the heart of the shopping district. One of the largest, oldest and most trustworthy establishments in America, with an international reputation for quality. Established 1826, by Samuel Lord and George W. Taylor; incorporated, 1903. Wholesale and retail business, with extensive mail-order trade. Especially noted for silks, linens, dress-fabrics, hosiery and underwear, and fashionable garments for women and children. Occupies the greater part of a city block. Edward P. Hatch, President.

Subway Express Station, 4th Ave. and 14th St.   Steinway Hall, erected 1866   Irving Place

STEINWAY & SONS, Steinway Hall, 107-109 E. 14th St.; headquarters of famous pianos that have taken highest awards for half a century at international expositions; factories at Steinway, Astoria; Park Ave., 52d to 53d St.; and Hamburg, Germany.

Fifth Ave. Hotel   Broadway   Lincoln Trust Co.   Fifth Ave.   Madison Sq.

LINCOLN TRUST CO., 208 Fifth Avenue and 1128 Broadway; two branches; capital, $1,000,000; President, Frank Tilford. 2d Vice-Pres., Owen Ward; Executive Com., Louis Stern, Chairman. Transacting a general banking and fiduciary business.

COPYRIGHT 1907 BY GEO. P. HALL & SON

Fifth Ave.   Brunswick Bldg,   Apartment Hotel   Madison Square   S. P. C. A.   Mad. Sq. Garden   Mad. Sq. Apts.   Dr. Parkhurst's Ch.   Met. Annex   Metropolitan Life   Bartholdi   Fuller ("Flat Iron") Bldg., 300 ft. high, erected by the Geo. A. Fuller Co.

MADISON SQUARE, intersection of Fifth Ave., Broadway and 23d St., one of the busiest centres of the city, magnificent setting for the 658-ft. tower being added to the Metropolitan Life block, on site of old Madison Square Presbyterian Church (Dr. Parkhurst's), which now occupies ornate building with dome. Here, between the Bloomingdale Road (Broadway) and the Boston Post Road (Third Ave.), in 1811, a vast tract was set apart as a parade ground, of which 6.84 acres are preserved for public uses in Madison Square, where are some of the oldest trees in the city. Hidden by the trees, at Madison Ave. and 25th St., is the Appellate Division of the Supreme Court, the handsomest courthouse in the world, designed by J. B. Lord, and ornamented with symbolic statues.   The Brunswick Building, 225 Fifth Ave., on Hotel Brunswick site.

Madison Square   Broadway   The "Flat-Iron"   Fifth Ave., looking South   Fifth Ave.   W. 24th St.   Albemarle   Stern Bros., 23d St.

FULLER BUILDING, called the "FLAT-IRON," at junction of Fifth Ave., Broadway and 23d St.; 300 ft. high; 120,000 sq. ft. floor-space on plot of 7,690 sq. ft., with 13,340 sq. ft. additional under sidewalks; D. H. Burnham & Co., Architects; Island Realty Co., owners.   Fifth Ave., with Sohmer Building, Presbyterian Building and Methodist Book Concern on west side.

Fifth Ave.   Sommers'   West 23d St.   Stern Bros.   McCreery's   6th Ave. "L"   Fifth Ave.   Fifth Ave., Hotel

SHOPPING CENTRE, Twenty-third St., westward from Fifth Ave. and Broadway; famous stores for three-quarters of a mile south and two-thirds of a mile north on Broadway; mile and a half on Fifth Ave., Sixth Ave. devoted to retail dry-goods business.   Fifth Avenue Hotel, erected 1858, famous political headquarters; Hitchcock, Darling & Co. (Elmer A. Darling and Chas. N. Vilas), Prop'rs.

West 47th St. West 48th St. Broadway, looking north Brewster & Co.
BREWSTER & CO., Broadway, 47th to 48th Sts.; one of the oldest and foremost firms of carriage-makers and superb automobile builders in America; established 1856; incorporated 1903; famous in this country and Europe as builders of the finest vehicles, from sulkies to road coaches, and complete line of automobiles. Capital, $1,500,000; William Brewster, Pres.; H. D. Brewster, Treas.

W. 34th St. Macy Bldg., DeLemos & Cordes, Archs.; Geo. A. Fuller Co., Bldrs. Broadway W. 35th St. Herald Sq. Theatre Metro. Opera
R. H. MACY & CO., Herald Square, B'way and Sixth Ave., 34th to 35th St.; largest department-store under one roof in America; 26 acres floor space; 6,000 employees; 500 delivery wagons marked with Red Star of firm; 150,000 to 250,000 customers a day; $35,000,000 business a year; $500,000 spent in advertising; restaurant seating 1,500. Owned by Isidor and Nathan Straus.

Broadway W. 22d St. "Flat-Iron," D. H. Burnham & Co., Arch. Scribner's Fifth Ave.
FULLER BUILDING, called "Flat-Iron," Broadway, Fifth Ave. and 23d St., first great triumph of steel-frame construction; built by the George A. Fuller Co.; owned by Island Realty Co., subsidiary companies of U. S. Realty & Imp. Co., H. S. Black, Pres.

W. 28th St.   Second National Bank, McKim, Mead & White, Arch.   Fifth Ave.
SECOND NATIONAL BANK OF THE CITY OF NEW YORK, N. W. cor. Fifth Ave. and 28th St.; F'd 1863; pioneer, in 1869,
providing especial accommodations for women customers; capital and surplus, $2,500,000; deposits, $10,000,000; assets,
$15,000,000; 5-story brick and stone bank erected by Geo. A. Fuller Co. James Stillman, Pres.; Jos. S. Case, Cashier.

Soc. Prev. Cruelty to Animals   Madison Avenue   Madison Square Garden, McKim, Mead & White, Arch.   East 26th St.   Manhattan Club
MADISON SQUARE GARDEN, Madison to 4th Ave., 26th to 27th St.; occupying entire city block, 425 by 200 ft.; tower
341 ft. high; statue of Diana, 13 ft. high, by Augustus St. Gaudens; erected 1890; cost $3,000,000; largest amphitheatre
in America, 300 by 200 ft., 80 ft. high, arena 268 by 122 ft.; seats 12,000.   Garden Theatre and Concert Hall.

Mad. Sq. Garden Appellate Court   Dr. Parkhurst's Church   Met. Annex.   Met. Life Bldg., N. LeBrun & Sons, Architects   Madison Ave.   East 23d St.   Metropolitan Bank

METROPOLITAN LIFE INSURANCE COMPANY, 1 Madison Ave., magnificent carved marble office-building, most elegantly finished and most valuable in the world; facing Madison Square, occupying entire block, with Post Office and Bank in Fourth Ave. end, and Annex across 24th St.; tower, 48 stories, 658 ft. high, tallest structure in the world, 103 ft. higher than Washington Monument; headquarters of greatest industrial-insurance corporation, organized 1868; nearly 10,000,000 policies in force; assets, $200,000,000. John R. Hegeman, Pres.

West 32d St.   Broadway   Imperial Hotel   West 31st St.
IMPERIAL HOTEL, Broadway, 31st to 32d St.; exquisite mural decoration; most comfortable and popular house in heart of theatre, shopping and hotel district, close to new Penna. R. R. and Hudson Co's. terminals.   Robert Stafford, Proprietor; Copeland Townsend, Manager.

COPYRIGHT 1905 BY IRVING UNDERHILL.
W. 43d St.   "Times" Bldg., C. L. W. Eidlitz, Arch.   Seventh Ave.   Broadway   Hotel Astor
NEW YORK TIMES, Times Square; founded 1851; half a century at Park Row and Spruce St.; new building, 362.7 ft. high, erected 1904-5; subway passes under building, station in basement; presses 57 ft. below surface; central location.   Adolph S. Ochs, Pres.

Hotel Martinique, H. J. Hardenbergh, Arch.   W. 33d St.
HOTEL MARTINIQUE, Broadway, 32d to 33d Sts., facing Greeley Sq.; in heart of theatre and shopping district; $2,000,000 fireproof hostelry close to Penna. R. R. and McAdoo Terminals; 16-story addition erected 1908-9; proprietors also of Hotel St. Denis.

West 33d Street   Sixth Avenue "L" Station   Saks & Co.   West 34th Street   R. H. Macy & Co.   Metropolitan Opera House   "Times" Bldg.   "Herald"

BROADWAY, from terminal of the Hudson Companies subway to Times Square, with two of the big department-stores on the left, facing Herald Square; upper end of the great retail shopping-district which begins at Eighth St., and beginning of New York's Rialto, the new theatre-district centring at 42d St.; heart of the hotel section; Broadway, here known as "The Great White Way," is thronged day and night, half a million shoppers and playgoers visiting this part of the city every twenty-four hours; two $2,000,000 20-story hotels are to flank Broadway at 33d St.

R. H. Macy & Co.   Met. Opera   "Times"   Astor   Broadway   "Herald"   W. E. Dodge Statue   Sixth Ave.   "L" Road   Hippodrome

HERALD SQUARE AND BROADWAY, north from "L" Station at 33d St., showing the Rialto, or "Great White Way," extending from 34th St. to Times Square, centre of largest theatre district in world; filled with shoppers and theatrical folk by day and playgoers by night. The "Herald"; founded 1835 by James Gordon Bennett, Sr., now conducted by his son, and evening edition, "The Telegram," occupy building of early Florentine design. SIXTH AVENUE is filled with retail shops; cupolas of the Hippodrome indicate where the club district touches theatre section.

Fifth Ave.   Bristol Bldg.   Huyler's   Fifth Ave. Tr. Co.   W. 43d St.   Sherry's   Fifth Ave. Bank   St. Nicholas Church   E. 42d St.

FIFTH AVENUE, north from 42d St. to Hotel Gotham at 55th St.; fashionable thoroughfare daily filled with equipages of wealthy; a congested business-centre; city's foremost clubs on avenue and on 43d, 44th and 45th Sts.; famous Delmonico's, founded 1828, at 44th St. across from Sherry's; Temple Emanu-El at 43d St.; Grand Central Sta. two blocks east on 42d St.; proposed to widen avenue by using stoop space for sidewalks.

W. 34th St.   Knickerbocker Trust Co.   Aeolian Hall   W. 35th St.   Gorham's   Brick Pres. Ch.   Fifth Ave.   Altman's

FIFTH AVENUE, north from 34th St. to St. Nicholas Collegiate Church at 48th St.; Murray Hill section, for half a century centre of fashion, now given to business and occupied by some of foremost retail-houses. Robert Murray homestead was just east of site occupied by Tiffany's; on Sept. 15, 1776, Mrs. Murray delayed Howe as he led his army past her house, enabling Washington to retreat to Harlem Heights.

Cambridge Bldg.   W. 33d St.   Waldorf-Astoria   Knickerbocker Tr.   Brick Pres. Ch.

WALDORF-ASTORIA, Fifth Ave.; most famous hotel in America; Waldorf, 33d St. cor., built by Wm. Waldorf Astor; Astoria, 34th St., by Col. J. J. Astor; 214 ft. high; Henry J. Hardenbergh, Arch.; 1,400 rooms in combined hotels. George C. Boldt, Prop.

W. 32d Street   Reed & Barton Bldg.   Fifth Avenue   Waldorf

REED & BARTON, N. W. cor. Fifth Ave. and 32d Street; silversmiths; new 11-story building. An elegant establishment of the famous workers in silver and gold, in the heart of the new jewelry-district; downtown salesroom, 6 Maiden Lane.

East 37th St.   Tiffany Building, McKim, Mead & White, Arch.   Fifth Ave.

TIFFANY & CO., S. E. cor. Fifth Ave. and 37th St.; exquisite $1,000,000 marble store of famous jewelry-firm; founded by the late Charles L. Tiffany in 1837; on Union Square, 1870-1905; international reputation for fine settings for precious stones; John C. Moore, Pres.

Fifth Ave.   Gorham Building, McKim, Mead & White, Arch.   W. 36th St.

THE GORHAM COMPANY, S. W. cor. 36th St.; foremost silversmiths in the world, famous for original, artistic designs and finest workmanship; building, erected 1905, regarded as one of the most effective on Fifth Ave.; salesroom, 23 Maiden Lane; Edward Holbrook, Pres.

Fifth Ave.   Knox Bldg.   West 40th St.   New York Club

KNOX BUILDING, S. W. cor. Fifth Ave. and 40th Street, headquarters of most famous hat firm in world; founded 1838 by Charles Knox at 110 Fulton St. $1,000,000 structure; down-town store in new Singer Building; factories, Brooklyn.

Seventh Avenue   W. 41st St.   Commercial Trust Co.   Broadway

COMMERCIAL TRUST CO., Broadway, N. W. cor. 41st St.; banking house and office building erected 1908; transacts a general banking and trust-company business. R. R. Moore, President, G. J. Baumann, Vice-President; Ames Higgins, Secretary.

Broadway looking South   Greeley Statue, erected by the printers of the U. S.   Martinique   W. 32d St.   Imperial   Grand   Greeley Square   Union Dime Savings Institution   Sixth Ave.

GREELEY SQUARE, formed by intersection of Broadway, 6th Ave. and W. 32d St.; named in honor of Horace Greeley, founder of the "Tribune." The Pennsylvania Railroad tunnels pass under 32d and 33d Sts., from the great terminal one block west to Long Island City. The Hudson Companies' tunnels from New Jersey run under 6th Ave. to terminal facing the square.

THE UNION DIME SAVINGS INSTITUTION, f.d. 1859; over 90,000 depositors; $26,000,000 deposits; $28,000,000 assets; to erect banking house on 6th Ave. at 40th St.; Charles E. Sprague, Pres.

Hotel Belmont   Lincoln Nat. Bank   Knickerbocker Hotel   "Times"   Hotel Manhattan

FORTY-SECOND ST., Park Ave. west to Broadway; Grand Central Station, at right, one of great gateways of the city, where trains from north, east and west land thousands of passengers every hour; Subway under 42d St.; terminus of Belmont tunnel from Queens.

Fifth Ave.   Sherry's   W. 44th St.   Soc. Mechanics & Tradesmen

SHERRY'S, Fifth Ave., S. W. cor. 44th St.; fashionable restaurant, with great banquet hall, conducted by Louis Sherry, the noted caterer; bachelor apartments on upper floors. In the centre of the club and hotel district and close to the leading theatres.

St. Bartholomew's Church   P. O., Sta. H   Tiffany Studios   St. Nicholas Church   Buckingham   St. Patrick's   Gotham   St. Regis   Savoy   Hall of Education

Vanderbilt Ave.   N. Y. Central Terminal, 42d St. façade   Depew Place   Train Shed   N. Y. Central R. R. Offices, 200 x 400 ft.   Lexington Ave.

NEW YORK CENTRAL & HUDSON RIVER R.R. TERMINAL (Grand Central Station), E. 42d St., Madison to Lexington Aves.; main station 300 x 680 ft.; P.O.; offices Vanderbilt lines and yards, occupy 19 city blocks; 34 express tracks 15 ft. below surface; 15 local tracks 40 ft. below St.; larger train capacity than any station; lobby, 90x300 ft.; concourse, 160 x 470 ft., 150 ft. high; entrance arches 33 ft. wide, 60 ft. high. W. H. Newman, Pres. Terminal also N. Y., N. H. & H.R.R. Both operated by electricity within 32 mile radius. Cost of improvement, $50,000,000.

Fifth Ave.   Delmonico's   East 44th St.

DELMONICO'S, Fifth Ave., N. E. cor. 44th St.; most famous restaurant in America; scenes of many notable banquets; fd. by John Delmonico in 1828 at 23 William St., now on sixth site, having kept pace with uptown movement; branch, Beaver St., since 1835.

W. 44th St.   Fifth Ave. Bank, opp. Sherry's and Delmonico's   Fifth Avenue

FIFTH AVENUE BANK, N. W. corner 44th Street; fd. 1875; shares, par value $100, now worth $3,700 bid; capital and surplus, $2,024,400; deposits, $13,755,175; assets, $15,779,575; dividends 100% per annum.   A. S. Frissell, President.

Central Park, East Drive St. Gaudens' Statue of Sherman   Van Norden Tr. Co.   Netherland   East 59th St.   Savoy Hotel   Bolkenhayn

THE PLAZA, looking up Fifth Ave. from Cornelius Vanderbilt Mansion at 58th St.; showing carriage entrance to Central Park; Savoy Hotel and Hotel Netherland, two of the most sumptuously appointed hostelries in the world, opp. new Plaza Hotel.   The Metropolitan Club, most exclusive and most wealthy in the world, is at 60th St., and residence of Commodore Elbridge T. Gerry at 61st St. Here are miles of homes of men of affairs—Col. John Jacob Astor at 65th St.; Havemeyer, 66th St.; George J. Gould, 67th St.; Sen. W. A. Clark, 77th St.; Andrew Carnegie, 91st St.

Park & Tilford   Netherland   Savoy   Plaza Bank St. Regis Fifth Ave. Gotham   Cornelius Vanderbilt Residence Sherman Statue   The Plaza Hotel   Central Park South

THE PLAZA, looking down Fifth Ave. to St. Patrick's Cathedral, from S. E. cor. of Central Park, showing five of the city's greatest hotels, representing the highest development of modern times in the art of caring elegantly for the comfort of wealthy patrons; finest location in the city, on high ground, at the social centre of New York, on the avenue of fashion, close to Central Park, convenient to the theatres and shopping district on the south, and connected by the Park drives and West 72d Street with the new residential section developed along Riverside Drive and West End Avenue.

W. 58th St.   The Plaza Hotel, 252 ft. high; Henry J. Hardenbergh, Arch.; the Geo. A. Fuller Co., Builders   Central Park South   Central Park

THE PLAZA HOTEL, Fifth Avenue, 58th St. to Central Park West; world's largest and most costly hotel; model of elegance and delicate beauty; 19 stories; cost $12,500,000; five marble staircases; two great dining-rooms; ball-room accommodating 500; $500,000 worth of rooms rented before hotel opened; 10,000-ton steel frame erected in 7 months; 578,000 sq. ft. of tiles used in fireproofing; 100 cooks in main kitchen.   Unsurpassable site for a hotel, facing Park and Plaza.   Owned by U. S. Realty & Imp. Co., Harry S. Black, Pres.   Fred. Sterry, Managing Director.

COPYRIGHT 1908 BY MOSES KING

East River   Penna. R. R. Power House   Long Island City   Astoria in foreground   Edison Power House, 39th St.   Blackwell's Is. Bridge, Connecting Ry.   Metropolitan Power House   Hallett's Point

EAST RIVER BRIDGES, with view of Manhattan from Harlem to Battery, New Jersey west of the Hudson River, Blackwell's Island in East River, Long Island City and Astoria Section to east.   HEL
HELL GATE BRIDGE, longest steel arch in world, 1,000 ft. long; 220 ft. high; heaviest, 80,000 tons; granite abutments; concrete towers 200 ft. high; carrying four tracks of Connecting Railway, which
Bronx Kills to N Y., New Haven & Hartford R.R; connection with Penna. main line through tunnels under East River, Manhattan and the Hudson.   Cost, $14,000,000.   Blackwell's Island Br

Hell Gate Bridge, Gustav Lindenthal, Arch. and Eng'r   Ward's Island   Edison Power House   Harlem River   Manhattan State Hospital for Insane   East River

TE, turbulent and difficult passage, where East River makes a sharp turn, meeting point of the tides of Long Island Sound and New York Bay, 26-foot channel formed by blowing up reefs after 25 years' work. es Penna. R. R. freight cars from floats at Bay Ridge, runs through Brooklyn and Queens, and by bridge and 17,000 ft. of steel viaduct crosses Hell Gate, Ward's Island, Little Hell Gate, Randall's Island and . 7). Williamsburg, Manhattan and Brooklyn Bridges (pp. 6 and 7.) **City owns 41 bridges, total length 13½ miles, cost, $100,000,000; is building six more; land occupied worth $1,000,000,000.**

South Wing, completed 1889   East 81st St.   East Wing, 344 x 200 ft., completed 1901, Thomas Dwyer, Builder   Main Entrance   Northeast Wing, 1907

METROPOLITAN MUSEUM OF ART, Central Park, facing Fifth Ave. at 82d St.; inc. 1871; first permanent building, 233 x 104 ft., centre of present group, occupied 1880; additions, '89 and '94, made area 233 x 344 ft.; $2,000,000 East Wing, '01, contains Hall of Sculpture, 166 x 48 ft.; as designed by Richard M. Hunt to cover 18½ acres and cost $20,000,000. Developed largely by the late Henry G. Marquand and the late Gen. Louis P. di Cesnola; becoming one of world's richest museums under presidency of J. Pierpont Morgan. Sir C. Purdon Clarke, Director

AMERICAN MUSEUM OF NATURAL HISTORY, Manhattan Square, W. 77th to 81st St., Columbus Ave. to Central Park West; founded '69; opened '77; 77th St. façade cost $4,438,000, completed '99; Cady, Berg & See, Architects; total cost (est.) $20,000,000; one of the largest natural-history museums in world; collections worth $10,000,000; more than half a million visitors annually; buildings erected and running expenses paid by city; scientific expeditions conducted from the fees of 2150 members and an income of $1,047,750 endowment, to which Morris K. Jesup, for years president of the Museum, added $1,000,000 by will at his death in 1908; Prof. Henry Fairfield Osborn, President; Hermon C. Bumpus, Director.

R. H. Macy & Co.   W. 40th St.   New York Public Library, Carrère & Hastings, Architects   Fifth Avenue   W. 42d St.   Bryant Park

NEW YORK PUBLIC LIBRARY, Astor, Lenox and Tilden Foundations, Fifth Ave., 40th to 42d St.; $6,000,000 white-marble structure on old reservoir site on Murray Hill; 366 by 246 ft.; main stack-room 274 ft. long, with seven tiers. Astor library, founded 1849; Lenox, 1870; Tilden Trust, 1887; consolidated, 1895; 37 branches in operation, circulating 5,000,000 volumes a year, including 21 Carnegie libraries; 29 more to be built; 5,000 readers a day in reference branches; 1,600,000 volumes. John Bigelow, President of Trustees; Dr. John S. Billings, Director.

1. DE WITT CLINTON HIGH SCHOOL, 10th Ave., 58th to 59th St.; 77 teachers; 1,458 pupils.   2. MORRIS HIGH SCHOOL, 166th St. and Boston Road, The Bronx; 92 teachers; 2,208 pupils.   3. WADLEIGH HIGH SCHOOL, 114th St., near 7th Ave., Harlem; 118 teachers; 2,270 pupils.   4. HIGH SCHOOL OF COMMERCE, 65th St., near Broadway; 65 teachers; 1591 pupils.   The city has 19 High Schools, with 1,093 instructors and 24,620 pupils, and maintains night classes in 11 of these.   Cost of schools, 1908, $31,641,323.

Murray Hill Hotel Park Ave. Hotel Belmont, Warren & Wetmore, Arch. E. 42d St. Lincoln N. B.

HOTEL BELMONT, Park Avenue, 41st to 42d St.; tallest hotel in world, 292 ft. high; 258,400 sq. ft. floor area; subway curves under bldg. from Park Ave. into 42d St.; built by Subway Realty Co., 1905; leased by Aug. Belmont Hotel Co., B. L. M. Bates, Mgr.

W. 42d St.   Hotel Knickerbo .er, Marvin & Davis, and Bruce Price, Arch.   Broadway

HOTEL KNICKERBOCKER Pr-adway, S. E. cor. 42d St.; beautifully decorated, mural paintings by Maxfield Parris   ~eric Remington; bas reliefs, John Flanagan; Trowbridge & I   ..cts of interior. James B. Regan, Prop.

Broadway, looking north   Rutgers Presb. Church   W. 73d St.   The Ansonia, 200 ft. high

THE ANSONIA, Broadway, 73d to 74th Street; largest, highest and most elaborate apartment-hotel in world; unusually large and fine suites; erected 1902 by W. E. D. Stokes. Close to "L" and Subway express stations and Riverside and Central Parks.

West 55th St   Hotel Woodward   Broadway

HOTEL WOODWARD, S. W. cor. Broadway and 55th Street, elegant 12-story hostelry, in centre of new hotel and automobile district, close to theatres; central location for sight-seeing; modern conveniences; built and owned by N. E. Clark; T. D. Green, Mgr.

RESIDENCES. 1. Ex-U. S. Senator Wm. A. Clark, 5th Ave. and 77th. 2. Bishop H. C. Potter, Riverside Drive and 89th. 3. Louis C. Tiffany, 27 E. 72d. 4. Harry Payne Whitney, 2 W. 57th. 5. Vanderbilt twin-houses, 5th Ave.; Henry C. Frick, 51st St. cor.; Wm. D. Sloane, 52d St. 6. Isaac V. Brokaw, 5th Ave. and 79th. 7. Geo. J. Gould, 5th Ave. and 67th. 8. Andrew Carnegie, 5th Ave. and 91st to 92d. 9. E. T. Gerry, 5th Ave. and 61st. 10. Mrs. C. Vanderbilt, 5th Ave., 57th to 58th. 11. James Stillman, 9 E. 72d. 12. J. P. Morgan, Madison Ave. and 36th, with private art-gallery; M. Eidlitz & Son, Builders. 13. J. D. Rockefeller, 4 W. 54th. 14. Joseph Pulitzer, 11 E. 73d. 15. Chas. M. Schwab, West End Avenue to Riverside Drive, 73d to 74th. 16. E. J. Berwind, 2 E. 64th. 17. Col. John Jacob Astor, 5th Ave. and 65th. 18. H. O. Havemeyer, 5th Ave. and 66th. 19. Stuyvesant Fish, 25 E. 78th. 20. William K. Vanderbilt, 5th Ave. and 52d.

THEATRES. 1. Casino, Broadway and 39th St., and Lyric, 42d St., S. S. and Lee Shubert, Managers. 2. New Amsterdam and Aerial Gardens, 42d. 3. Savoy, 34th, Charles Frohman. 4. Majestic, Columbus Circle, Shuberts. 5. Grand Opera House, 23d and 8th Ave., J. H. Springer. 6. New York Theatre, 45th St. end, Klaw & Erlanger, and Criterion, 44th St. end, Charles Frohman. 7. Broadway, 41st, Klaw & Erlanger. 8. Belasco, 42d, David Belasco. 9. Hudson, 44th, H. B. Harris. 10. Victoria and Paradise Roof, 42d, Oscar Hammerstein. 11. Hippodrome, 6th Ave., 43d to 44th, Shuberts. 12. Lyceum, 45th, Daniel Frohman. 13. Madison Square Garden. 14. Garrick, 35th, Charles Frohman. 15. Carnegie Hall, 57th and 7th Ave., H. M. Barry, Pres. 16. Metropolitan Opera, Broadway, 39th to 40th, Heinrich Conried, Director. 17. Cooper Union, forum and free school, founded by Peter Cooper.

St. Nicholas Park and Terrace City College, Main Bldg. Geo. B. Post & Sons, Arch. Thomas Dwyer, Builder W. 140th St. Gymnasium Townsend Harris Hall Chemistry Bldg. Convent Ave. Mech. Arts Bldg.

COLLEGE OF THE CITY OF NEW YORK, St. Nicholas Terrace to Amsterdam Ave., W. 140th to W. 138th St.; imposing $4,000,000 group of fieldstone and terra cotta buildings, occupied 1905; founded 1847 as free Academy; City College, 1866; four-year collegiate course, 1,045 students; three-year preparatory department, in Townsend Harris Hall and in old college building at 23d St. and Lexington Ave., 2,896 pupils; 207 instructors. Free tuition; supported by City at annual cost of $500,000. Edward M. Shepard, Chairman. Dr. John H. Finley, Pres

Harlem River   Webb Academy   Chancellor's Residence   Professors' Residences   The Bronx   Ohio Field   Gymnasium   Gould Hall

Hall of Sciences Philosophy Hall of Fame Library Campus Hall of Languages McKim, Mead & White, Arch. Physics Chemistry Biology

NEW YORK UNIVERSITY, Sedgwick to Aqueduct Aves., W. 179th to W. 181st St., University Heights, the Bronx; founded 1829; building erected, '32-5 on Washington Sq.; splendid group on Heights occupied '94; new 10-story building on old site for Schools of Pedagogy, Law and Commerce; 12 departments, 310 instructors, 3,800 students; medical school, First Ave. and E. 26th St.; veterinary school, 141 W. 54th St. Hall of Fame for Great Americans, colonnade 506 ft. long, $250,000 gift of Miss Helen Miller Gould. Rev. Dr. Henry M. MacCracken, Chancellor.

PHILANTHROPIC INSTITUTIONS. 1. Lying-In Hospital, 2d Ave., 17th to 18th Sts., gift of J. P. Morgan. 2. Methodist Episcopal Hospital, 7th Ave. and 6th St., Brooklyn, Geo. I. Seney, Founder. 3. New Mills Hotel, 7th Ave. and 36th. 4. N.Y. Eye and Ear Infirmary, 2d Ave. and 13th, founded 1820. 5. St. Luke's Hospital, W. 113th, Morningside Hts. 6. Society for Relief of Ruptured and Crippled, Lexington Ave. and 42d. 7. Church Missions House, 4th Ave. and 22d. 8. Webb's Academy and Home for Ship-Builders, Fordham Hts. 9. Hebrew Orphan Asylum, Amsterdam Ave., 136th to 138th. 10. Sloane Maternity Hospital, Amsterdam Ave. and 59th, Wm. D. Sloane, Founder. 11. Roosevelt Hosp., 9th Ave., 58th to 59th. 12. Presbyterian Hosp., Madison Ave. and 70th; Eidlitz & Son, Bldrs. 13. French Ben. Soc. Hosp., 450 W. 34th. 14. Mt. Sinai Hosp., 5th to Madison Ave., 100th to 101st. 15. Soc. Prev. Cruelty to Animals, Madison Ave., 26th.

CHURCHES. 1. St. Paul the Apostle, Columbus Ave. 60th St., Paulist Fathers. 2. Madison Ave. M. E., cor. 60th, Wallace MacMullen. 3. St. Nicholas Collegiate, 5th Ave. and 48th, D. S. Mackay. 4. Divine Paternity, Central Park West 76th, Uni., Frank O. Hall. 5. Temple Beth-El, 5th Ave. 76th, Samuel Schulman. 6. Holy Trinity Chapel (Rhinelander Memorial), E 88th, Frederic Courtney. 7. Broadway Tabernacle, cor. 56th, Cong., C E Jefferson. 8. First Christian Science, Central Park West 96th, E. F. Hatfield. 9. St. Francis Xavier, 42-48 W. 16th, Jesuit Fathers. 10. St. Patrick's Cathedral, 5th Ave. and 50th, John M. Farley, Abp.; M. J Lavelle. 11. Grace, Broadway and 10th, Wm. R. Huntington. 12. St. Bartholomew's, Madison Ave. and 44th, Leigh in Parks. 13. Holy Trinity, Clinton and Montague Sts, Brooklyn, J. H. Melish. 14 First Baptist, I. M. Haldeman. 15. St. Mary the Virgin, 139 West 46th Street, George M. Christian. 16. St. Agnes' Chapel, West 92d Street, William T. Manning. 17. First Presbyterian, Fifth Avenue and 11th Street, Howard Duffield.

KING'S BIRDS-EYE VIEW OF BROOKLYN
Sketched by TOR ALBROT BUNNELL
COPYRIGHT 1908 BY MOSES KING

Williamsburg Bridge   Broadway Ferries   Wallabout Bay   Navy Yard   Manhattan Bridge   Brooklyn Bridge   Fulton Ferry   Columbia Heights   Pierrepont Stores   Prentice Stores   N. Ger. Lloyd West Indies Line   Union Stores   Atlantic Basin   Red Hook   Erie Basin   N. Y. Bay

BROOKLYN BOROUGH, 77.62 square miles, from the East River to Atlantic Ocean, from New York Bay to Queens Borough. Population, 1908, 1,492,970. Settled 1623; incorporated 1834; consolidated with New York 1898. Taxable property, land and improvements, $1,216,026,385; real estate exempt from taxation, $92,866,547; personalty, $109,195,525; franchises, etc., $180,492,870; total, $1,598,581,327. 48 parks of 1663 acres, including Prospect, 516 acres, most beautiful in the world; 44 miles of parkways, 1,459 miles of streets. Brooklyn is a city of homes, with 225,000 school children, yet its 4,000 factories in 1907 produced goods valued at $400,000,000. Busiest shipping-district in the world; N. Y. Dock Co., Atlantic Basin (40 acres), Erie Basin (161 acres), Bush Terminal, South Brooklyn, largest piers in the world.

Fleet Street   The Dime Savings Bank of Brooklyn   De Kalb Avenue   Fulton Street

THE DIME SAVINGS BANK OF BROOKLYN, DeKalb Avenue and Fleet Street, Brooklyn, one of the three largest and strongest savings-institutions in the borough; at the "hub" formed by the radiating avenues and car lines that lead to the homes of 1,500,000 people; founded in 1859; magnificent new banking-house erected in 1907; over 70,000 depositors. Resources, $34,500,000; surplus, $2,130,000. J. Lawrence Marcellus, President; Russell S. Walker, Treasurer; Frederick W. Jackson, Secretary. Mowbray & Uffinger, Architects.

Bond Street   Frederick Loeser & Co's, Francis H. Kimball, Architect   Fulton St. "L," Brooklyn Rapid Transit   Elm Place Addition, Subway Station opposite

FREDERICK LOESER & CO'S DEPARTMENT STORE, Fulton St., at junction with DeKalb Ave., Bond St. to Elm Pl., occupying two city-blocks in heart of Brooklyn shopping-district, where all railway, surface and "L" lines radiate; founded 1869 at Fulton and Tillary Sts., moved to present site 1887; enlarged ten times; immense floor-space, with large warehouses and distributing stations in every section of Brooklyn. Has unique system of actually guaranteeing prices as low or lower than the same article can be bought for elsewhere. Brooklyn's best store.

60 Wall St. Bank Commerce Lawyers Title Woodbridge Bldg. St. Paul Park Row Am. Tract "World" "American" N. Y. Life Woolworth Bldg, 272 ft. high Public School, 62 Wanamaker's Bridge tower, 38,214 cu. yards masonry

Army Pier Mallory Steamship Piers Fulton Ferry Fish Market Fulton Market New Haven Line Norwalk Line Roosevelt St. Ferry Clyde W. Indies Line Catharine Ferry Joy Line Furman St., Brooklyn

EAST RIVER, from Columbia Heights, Brooklyn, showing the Manhattan skyline from Wall St. north, with the busiest water-front in the world; coast and sound liners berth along the Manhattan shore; on the Brooklyn side, just south of the bridge tower, are the ferries to Fulton St. and to Jersey City; from Fulton St. south are the piers and stores of the New York Dock Co, which extend around Red Hook to Conover St., a distance of three miles, and include the Atlantic Basin, which alone has three miles of wharfage and piers at which nine great ocean steamships can be berthed at once. At the piers in the view are accommodated the Booth, Lamport & Holt, and Red "D" lines, and the great warehouses shown are Roberts and Phelps Bros. Stores. N. Y. Dock Co., capital, $17,000,000; David H. King, Jr. Pres.; offices, Maritime Bldg, 8 Bridge St.

Court St.　　Montague St.　　Mechanics' Bank　　Fulton St.　　"L" Station

MECHANICS' BANK, Court and Fulton Sts., Brooklyn, facing Borough Hall; f'd 1852; largest State bank on Long Island; capital and surplus, $1,755,670; deposits, $10,939,300; assets, $13,414,000; five branches; Geo. W. Chauncey, President.

Erected 1905　　The Peoples Trust Co., Mowbray & Uffinger, Arch'ts　　Montague St.

THE PEOPLES TRUST COMPANY, 181-183 Montague St., Brooklyn; founded 1889; branches in Bedford and Wallabout sections; one of the finest banking-houses in borough; deposits, $13,700,000; assets, $15,900,000; Charles A. Boody, President.

Fulton St. "L"   Hall of Records   Kings County Court House   Municipal Bldg., back of Borough Hall, to be replaced by $2,000,000 structure   Polytechnic Institute   Court St.

BROOKLYN BOROUGH HALL, facing Park at Fulton and Court Sts.; City Hall prior to consolidation, 1898; white marble, 102 x 162 ft., 75 ft. high; offices of Borough President. Brooklyn has 18,374 inhabitants to the sq. mile; in 1907 8,311 buildings were erected in the borough at a cost of $63,159,176; its area is 77.62 sq. miles, which is room for 7,800,189 people at the present density of population in Manhattan. During rush hours 70,000 people cross the East River an hour by bridges and ferries; the Subway under East River has a capacity of 24,000 an hour.

Lawrence St.   Telephone Building, 81 Willoughby St.   Willoughby St.

THE N. Y. & N. J. TELEPHONE CO., Gen. Offices, Bkn.; 140 central offices, 21 in Bkn. and Queens, 4 on Staten I.; 150,000 'phones; 415,000 miles of wire. U. N. Bethell, Pres.; W. D. Sargent, 1st and J. C. Reilly, 2d Vice-Pres.; H. F. Thurber, Gen. Mgr.

Financial district, continues Wall Street

LAWYERS' TITLE INSURANCE & TRUST CO., 188-190 Montague Street, Brooklyn; main building running through from Liberty St. to Maiden Lane, Manhattan; new 16-story building going up at 160 Broadway; Edwin W. Coggeshall, Pres. & Gen. Mgr.

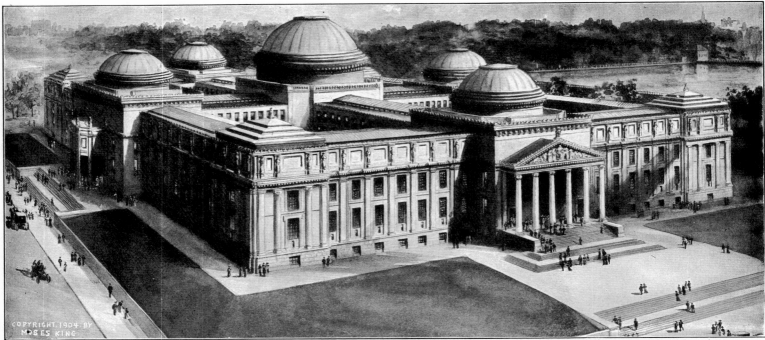

Washington Ave.   Institute Park, 50 acres   Brooklyn Institute as planned by McKim, Mead & White, Arch.   Eastern Parkway   Reservoir

BROOKLYN INSTITUTE OF ARTS AND SCIENCES, near Plaza entrance to Prospect Park, Brooklyn; founded as the Apprentices' Library, 1823; 12-acre site valued at $1,000,000; first section of $5,000,000 group, 560 ft. sq. with four interior courts, completed '97; second section, '04; third section '08; lectures in 29 departments; art classes, school of pedagogy, biological laboratory, library of 35,000 vols.; Franklin W. Hooper, Director; Frederic A. Lucas, Curator-in-chief of Museum; A. Augustus Healy, Pres.; Charles A. Schieren, Vice-Pres. and one of founders.

STATUES AND MONUMENTS. 1. Gen. Henry W. Slocum, by MacMonnies, Eastern Parkway and Bedford Ave. 2. "The Pilgrim," J. Q. A. Ward, Central Park near E. 72d St. 3. J. S. T. Stranahan (MacMonnies), Plaza Entrance Prospect Park. 4. Alexander Hamilton's Tomb, Trinity Churchyard. 5. Martyrs' Monument, Trinity Churchyard, facing Pine Street; commemorating patriots who died in British prisons. 6. Robert Fulton's Tomb, Trinity Churchyard, near Broadway and Rector Street. 7. Gen. William Tecumseh Sherman (Augustus St. Gaudens), Plaza entrance, Central Park. 8. Henry Ward Beecher (Ward), facing Borough Hall, Brooklyn. 9. Gen. Franz Sigel, Riverside Drive.

ARMORIES. 1. Seventh Regiment, Park Ave., 66th to 67th Sts.; org. 1806; Col. Daniel Appleton. 2. Twenty-second Regiment, Broadway, 67th to 68th; Col. W. B. Hotchkin. 3. Squadron A, Madison Ave. & 94th; Maj. O. B. Bridgman. 4. Ninth Regiment, 14th St., org. 1812; Col. W. F. Morris. 5. Eighth Regiment, Park Ave., 94th to 95th; Col. E. F. Austin. 6. Seventy-first Regiment, 4th Ave., 33d to 34th; 236 ft. high; Col. W. G. Bates. 7. Fourteenth Regiment, 8th Ave., 14th to 15th, Brooklyn; org. 1847; Col. John H. Foote. 8. Sixty-ninth Regiment, Lexington Ave., 25th to 26th, org. 1851; Col. Edward Duffy. 9. Squadron C, Bedford Ave., Union to President Sts., Brooklyn; Maj. Charles I. Debevoise. 10. Twenty-third Regiment, Bedford Avenue, corner Pacific Street, Brooklyn; Col. W. A. Stokes. 11. Thirteenth Coast Artillery, Sumner and Putnam Avenues, Brooklyn; Col. David E. Austen.

Long Island City Queens Borough | Blackwell's Island in East River | Blackwell's Is. Bridge to E. 59th St. | Central Park 839.9 acres | St. Luke's Hospital | Cathedral of St. John the Divine | Brooklyn Borough | Williamsburg Bridge | Plaza Hotel | St. Patrick's Cathedral

H.M.Pettit
COPYRI
BY MOSE

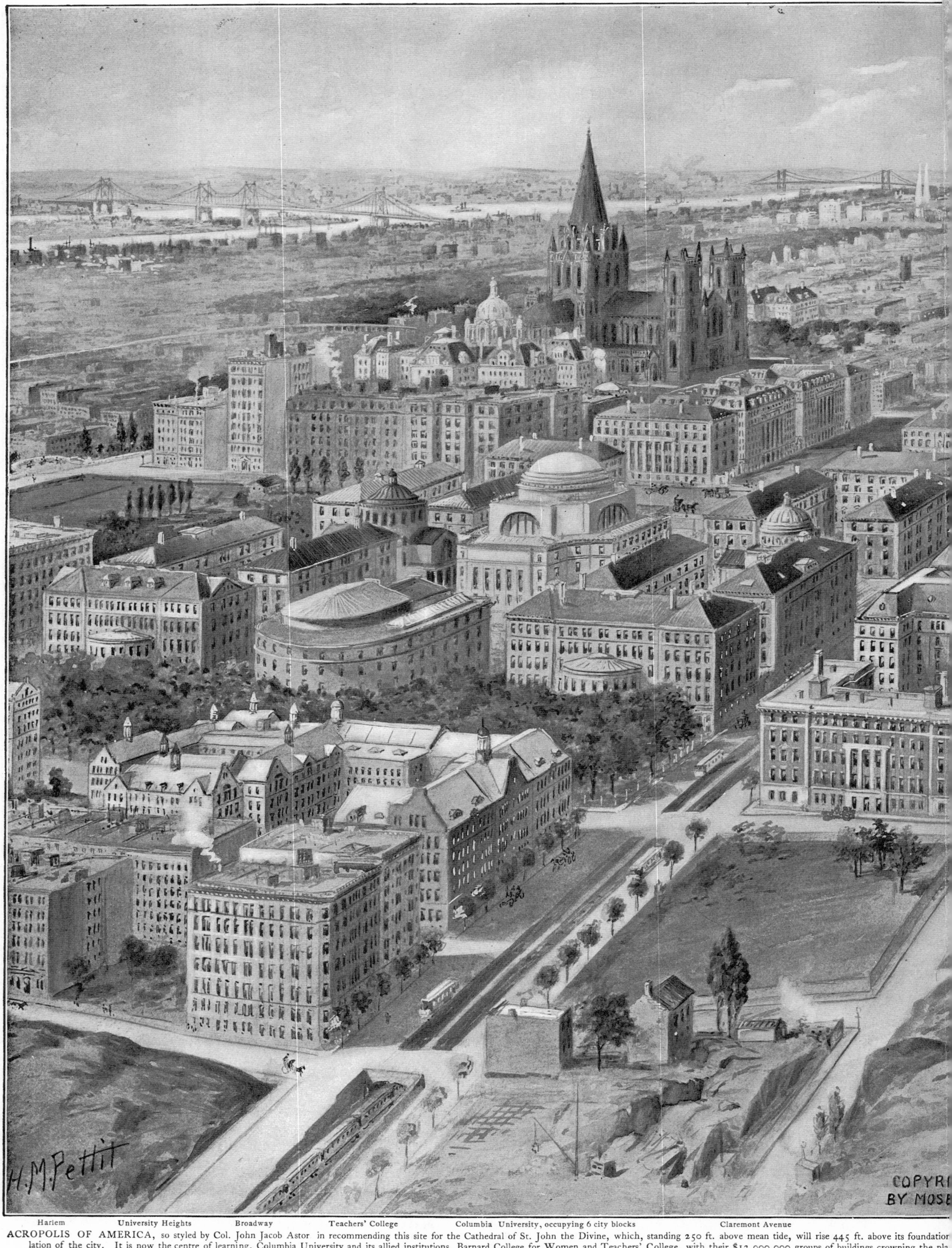

Harlem | University Heights | Broadway | Teachers' College | Columbia University, occupying 6 city blocks | Claremont Avenue

ACROPOLIS OF AMERICA, so styled by Col. John Jacob Astor in recommending this site for the Cathedral of St. John the Divine, which, standing 250 ft. above mean tide, will rise 445 ft. above its foundatior lation of the city. It is now the centre of learning, Columbia University and its allied institutions, Barnard College for Women and Teachers' College, with their $12,000,000 groups of buildings crowning the pla a great Water Gate is to honor Robert Fulton, whose invention of the steamboat made the commercial greatness of the city and nation possible. Columbia, founded as King's College in 1754, has 11 faculties,

e visible 25 miles away.   By the time this $10,000,000 work is completed, giving America the finest and most splendidly located cathedral in the world, Col. Astor predicts that this will be the centre of popu-
t is, with the exception of a small plot on Washington Heights, the highest ground on Manhattan Island.   Here stands the tomb of Gen. Grant, commemorating his services in preserving the Union; and
structors, 5,000 students and an endowment of $18,700,000.   Dr. N. M. Butler, President.   Barnard, founded 1889, Laura D. Gill, Dean.   Teachers' College, founded 1886, J. E. Russell, Dean.

Cathedral St. John the Divine Belmont Chapel St. Luke's Hospital Apartment Houses Morningside Park, 31¼ acres St. Nicholas Ave. Manhattan Ave. MORNINGSIDE PARK, a natural bluff extending from Cathedral Parkway (110th St.) to W. 123d St., crowned by Cathedral Heights, upon which is being erected a $10,000,000 cathedral of the Episcopal Church, with massive spire 445 ft. high, designed by Heins & La Farg, begun 1892; adjoining is the $3,000,000 St. Luke's Hospital, founded 1846 by Rev. Dr. Muhlenberg. 3,500 patients a year.

Wadleigh High School Harlem River, in distance W. 111th Street Cathedral Parkway 110th St. Sta., 6th & 9th Ave. "L" North end Central Park HARLEM, residence-place of 500,000 people, viewed from Cathedral Heights; Morningside Park in foreground; 150 trains an hour pass over the high "L" structure, which has three tracks 73 ft. above the street, and makes a double curve from 8th into Columbus Ave.; enormous modern apartment-houses, replacing the old-fashioned flats, are tripling the residential capacity of Harlem, which was founded in 1658.

OTIS ELEVATOR WORKS, Yonkers, N. Y., that has supplied the product so well known in New York and has made possible the modern skyscraper. Founded 1853 by E. G. Otis, inventor of the first practical belt-geared elevator, from which he developed the steam elevator in 1866. Plant employing 1,600 people turns out ten complete elevators a day. Otis Elevator Company incorporated Nov. 1898. Otis elevators successfully used in every important city and in the tallest structures in the world—the Eiffel Tower, 1,000 feet high, and the Singer Building, Metropolitan Life Tower, etc., reaching the upper floors in one continuous run. Otis offices in all principal cities. Otis Bros & Company formed 1867; hydraulic elevators introduced 1871; electric elevators 1888. Plant employing 1,600 people turns out ten complete elevators a day.

BROADWAY & 41ST ST.

PARK & TILFORD
LENOX AVENUE AND 136TH STREET

BROADWAY & 101ST ST.

WAREHOUSE
152-156 W. 36TH ST.

BROADWAY & 21ST ST.

COLUMBUS AVE. & 72ND ST.

SIXTH AVE. NEAR 9TH ST.

PARK & TILFORD

ORIGINAL STORE

5TH AVE. & 59TH ST.

Sixth Ave. Store, second site occupied by firm   First Store, 35 Carmine St., 20 by 30 ft.   Fifth Ave. Branch, between Van Norden Trust Co. and Hotel Netherland

PARK & TILFORD, largest retail grocery-house in the world, seven stores in Manhattan; founded in 1840 at 35 Carmine Street with $300 capital, by Joseph Park and John M. Tilford; incorporated 1890; capital, $3,000,000. Frank Tilford, son of one of the founders, entered employ of firm in 1870, became Vice-President 1891, President since 1906 and practically sole owner of the business. Extensive importers of wines and cigars, the name of the house being a recognized guarantee of quality. General Offices, 917 Broadway.

PARKS.   1. Van Cortlandt Mansion, Van Cortlandt Park, The Bronx.   2. Poe Park and Cottage, The Bronx.   3. Pell Oak, Pelham Bay Park.   4. Claremont Park and Zbrowski Mansion, The Bronx.
5. Antelopes, Zoological Park, The Bronx.   6. Washington Square and Arch, lower end 5th Ave.   7. Jeannette Park, Coenties Slip.   8. Buffaloes, Zoological Park.   9. Bronx River, Bronx Park.
10. Japanese Tea House.   11. Soldiers' and Sailors' Arch, Plaza entrance Prospect Park, Brooklyn.   12. Lullwood Bridge, Prospect Park.   13. Restaurant and Shelter, Prospect Park.   15, 19. Ocean
Parkway Entrance Prospect Park, groups of wild horses, winter and summer views.   17, 18. Boundary Walk and Bicyclists' Rest, Prospect Park.   20, 21. Sheep on Common and Boat
Landing, Prospect Park.   22. Fort Greene Park, Brooklyn.   23. Fort Hamilton.   24. Automobile Parade, Ocean Parkway.   25. Parade Ground Pavilion, Van Cortlandt Park.

PARKS. 1. Bridge over Bronx River, Bronx Park. 2. Road in Bronx Park west of Falls. 3. Botanical Museum, Bronx Park; Darius O. Mills, Pres. 4. Falls, Bronx River. 5. Bird House, Zoological Park. 6. Conservatories, Bronx Park. 7. Flying Cage, Bronx Park. 8. Skating on Lake in Central Park. 9. The Dell, Central Park. 10 Bridge near the Ramble. 11. Swan Boats. 12. Terrace and Bethesda Fountain. 13. Bridle Path. 14. Sacred Ox. 15. The Mall, main promenade of Central Park, which covers 839 9 acres, valued at $200,000,000. 16 Camel family, Betsy, Prince and Frank. 17. Reservoir. 18 Common. 19. View in heart of Central Park. 20 Leo. 21. Menagerie, Central Park, and Arsenal, offices of Park Board. 22. Polar Bear. 23. Cooper Square, where 3d and 4th Aves. meet in the Bowery. 24. Hudson Park, Hudson and Leroy Sts. 25. Harlem River Speedway at Washington Bridge; 100 ft. wide, extends from 155th to 208th Sts.; cost $3,025,000.

STATUES AND MONUMENTS. "Commerce," ideal figure in bronze, Central Park, Circle entrance. Prof. S. F. B. Morse, by Byron M. Pickett, Central Park, near 5th Ave. and 72d St. Alexander Hamilton (W. O. Partridge), Hamilton Club, Brooklyn. Gen. Lafayette (Bartholdi), Union Square. Obelisk, 200-ton monolith, 3400 years old, brought from Egypt 1880. Daniel Webster (Thomas Ball), Central Park, 72d St. and West Drive. W. H. Seward (Randolph Rogers), Madison Square. Gen. Worth monument, 5th Ave. and 25th St. Soldiers' and Sailors' Monument, white marble, columns 35 ft. high, Riverside Drive near 89th St. Admiral Farragut (Augustus St. Gaudens), N. W. cor. Madison Square. Dr. J. Marion Sims, Bryant Park. Nathan Hale (MacMonnies), City Hall Park. Washington Irving (Beer), Bryant Park. Richard M. Hunt Memorial, 5th Ave. above 7oth St., bust by D. C. French. DeWitt Clinton, City Hall. Abraham de Peyster, Bowling Green. John Ericsson (J. Scott Hartley) Battery Park.

CLUBS. 1. Bar Association, 42 W. 44th St. 2. N. Y. Historical Society, Central Park West, 76th to 77th, founded 1804. 3. Century Association, 7 W. 43d, '47; Academy of Medicine, 17 W. 43d; and Racquet and Tennis Club, 27 W. 43d. 4. Union League Club, 5th Ave. and 39th. 5. American Fine Arts Society, 215 W. 57th, and Geo. J. Gould's Gymnasium. 6. Engineers' Club, 32 W. 40th. 7. N. Y. Athletic Club, Central Park South and 6th Ave. 8. University Club, 5th Ave. and 54th. 9. New York Club, 20 W. 40th. 10. Lambs' Club, 128 W. 44th. 11. Union Club, 5th Ave. and 51st, '36. 12. Metropolitan Club, 5th Ave. and 60th. 13. City Club, 57 W. 44th. 14. Columbia Yacht Club, Hudson River, off W. 86th. 15. N. Y. Yacht Club, 37-41 W. 44th, fd. '44. 16. Progress Club, Central Park West and 88th. 17. Harvard Club, 27 W. 44th. 18. American Geographical Society, 15 W. 81st.

HALL OF RECORDS, Centre St. entrance; statues by Philip Martiny.   CHURCH MISSIONS HOUSE, Fourth Ave., cor. 22d St.   COLLEGE OF CITY OF NEW YORK, Convent Ave., entrance.
MADISON SQUARE PRESBYTERIAN CHURCH.   CUSTOM HOUSE GROUPS, America and Europe, by Daniel C. French.   GRACE EPISCOPAL CHURCH, Broadway above 10th St.
APPELLATE COURT; Wisdom, by F. W. Ruckstuhl.   CUSTOM HOUSE GROUPS, Asia and Africa, by French.   CHAMBER OF COMMERCE, main entrance, figures symbolical of Commerce
CHAMBER OF COMMERCE, statues adorning façade; Alexander Hamilton, Financier, by Philip Martiny; Gov. DeWitt Clinton, father of the Erie Canal, by Carl Bitter; John Jay, Jurist, by Bitter

Gimbel's   W. 33d St.   "L" Station   Saks & Co.   Metropol tan Opera   "Times"   Herald Square   "Herald"   Sixth Ave.   Site of Hotel McAlpin

BROADWAY, from Greeley Square to Times Square, showing city's greatest thoroughfare intersected by Sixth Ave. and 34th St. with three great department stores at the left; upper end of most **im-portant** retail shopping district in the world, which extends from Eighth St.; centre of largest hotel district; beginning of New York's Rialto, the theatre district centering at 42d St.; Broadway, here known as "The Great White Way," from the brilliance of the electric signs, is visited each day by half a million shoppers and playgoers. "HERALD," founded 1835.

Original paper cover

KING'S VIEWS OF NEW YORK

FUTURE NEW YORK is preeminently the city of skyscrapers. Its first steel-frame structure, the Tower Building, at 50 Broadway, reaching a height of 129 ft., was regarded as a skyscraper, with its 10 stories; now there are in Manhattan 1,048 buildings of 11 stories or more. The skyline reached 612 ft. in the Singer Tower, 700 ft. in Metropolitan, 792 ft. in Woolworth, and the new Pan-American Building is to be 801 ft. high. Of the 92,749 buildings in Manhattan, 2,956 are fire-proof, 286 semi-fire-proof, and 6,963 frame, 82,544 brick and wood.

New York Skyline. D-183
From N.Y.
Copyright 1916 By Irving Underhill, N.Y.

Municipal Bldg., 580 ft.   Woolworth, 792 ft.   Park Row Bldg.   W. U. Telegraph   City Investing   Singer   Trinity Bldg.   Am. Surety   Bankers' Trust   Manhattan Life   Adams Bldg.   42 B'way   Standard Oil   Bowling Green Offices   Whitehall Bldg.

Home Life   Fall River Line   Underwood Bldg.   Hudson Terminals   Penna. & West Shore Ferries   Central Bldg.   West St. Bldg.   U.S. Express   Empire Bldg.   Hamburg-Am. Bldg.   Columbia Bldg.   Hudson River

SKYLINE OF LOWER MANHATTAN from Jersey City, showing world's highest building, Woolworth, 792 ft. and greatest Municipal Building; the Park Row Bldg., 382 ft., first structural wonder of the 20th century; three marvels of 1908: 200,000 ton twin Hudson Companies' Buildings, 34-story City Investing Bldg., and 612-ft. Singer Tower, the three accommodating 41,000 tenants. Manhattan Island, 19.65 sq. mi., purchased in 1626 from Indians for about $24, land value now $4,100,000,000 exclusive of area occupied by streets; total realty value with improvements, is $6,250,000,000, average $450,000 per acre. The island has 2,538,606 inhabitants, lower end has office population of 400,000; land here is worth from $100 to $600 a sq. ft. and office-space rents at from $1 to $40 a sq. ft., making profitable the erection of costly sky-scrapers.

Whitehall Building, 416 ft. high   Bowling Green Offices   Columbia Bldg.   Standard Oil   Manhattan Life, 350 ft.   City Investing   Singer   Equitable Trust   Liberty Tower   Park Row Bldg.   Sixty Wall St., 362 ft.   Am. Tract "World"   Erie R. R. Pier   East River

Public Baths   Battery Park   Old Barge Office   Custom House   Staten Island Ferry   South Brooklyn Ferry   Brooklyn Ferries   Broad Exchange Building   Cotton and Coffee Exchanges   Beaver Building   Coenties Slip   Canal Boat Terminal   Compania Transatlantica

MANHATTAN, as seen from Governor's Island, showing the remarkable skyline formed by the gigantic sky-scrapers, with the 34-story annex to the Whitehall Building, 416 ft. high, the City Investing Building, 486 ft., the Singer Tower, 612 ft., the buildings rising one above another like castellated cliffs, affording a remarkable spectacle when illuminated at night; here the Hudson and East Rivers form New York Bay, whose broad channels stretch seven miles to the Narrows, while there are 14 square miles of anchorages; this is the commercial and geographical center of New York, with the berths of the transatlantic steamships on the Hudson and the centre of the coast-trade on the East River; over 6,000 craft daily traversing these waters; about 3,000 immigrants a day are landed at the Barge Office, $3,500,000 is the daily average of imports of foreign merchandise.

New York, Skyscrapers, D-557
From Governor's Island
Copyright 1911 By
Irving Underhill, New York.

© UNDERHILL

East River   Wall St. Ferry   Army Pier   N. Y. & Cuba Mail S. S. Co.   United Fruit Co.   Fulton Ferry   Burling Slip   Fulton Market   Bay State Line   Hartford Line   Peck Slip   Tidewater Trasp. Co.   Chelsea Line   James Slip

MANHATTAN FROM BROOKLYN, view of the skyscrapers of the financial district and lower business section of the city from Columbia Heights, showing the busy East River, center of the enormous coastwise and Long Island Sound commerce; the oldest part of the harbor, where ships were built in the early days of the city; modern piers now being erected, the shipping capacity of this part of the waterfront trebled within five years.   Fulton Market a landmark since 1821; Fish Market, in the newer building, overhanging the water, the most important institution of the sort in America.   From the Army Pier supplies are shipped to the American possessions in the Orient.   The low ground between the Park Row Building and the waterfront, known as "The Swamp," is the Leather District.   The chemical industries centre about the Woodbridge Building.

Manhattan Approach to Brooklyn Bridge   Williamsburg Bridge   Williamsburg section of Brooklyn   Manhattan Bridge   East River   Navy Yard   Brooklyn Bridge   Empire Stores   Fulton Ferry   Booth Steamship Piers   New York Dock Co., Piers and Stores

BROOKLYN, view from Manhattan, showing the great manufacturing districts on either side of Wallabout Bay, where the United States Government maintains its greatest navy yard, and the upper part of the extensive system of piers and stores that make Brooklyn the greatest point in the world for the trans-shipment of merchandise, goods being received by trucks from factories and by cars carried on floats, lighters and steamers, and forwarded to every land.   From Fulton Ferry south for three miles are the piers and stores of the New York Dock Co., which extend to the mouth of the East River, along Buttermilk Channel and around Red Hook, and include Atlantic Basin, which alone has three miles of wharfage and can berth nine ocean steamships.   The East River at this, its narrowest point, is the busiest stream in the world, with 6,000 craft passing daily.

Isolation Hospital Transfer Boats   Physicians' Residence   Hospital   Slip for Ferry to Barge Office   Immigration Depot, largest in the world

ELLIS ISLAND, the Gateway of the New World, in New York Bay off the Battery. All immigrants are taken from steamers on barges and examined here by the Department of Commerce before being permitted to enter America. The criminals, paupers, diseased and contract-laborers are deported at the expense of the steamship companies, the rest are landed at the Barge Office. Of 1,481,639 aliens arriving by ships in New York in 1913, 1,015,184 were immigrants, and 12,000 were deported; 365,855 were travelers from foreign countries. Total immigration into U. S. in 1913, 1,355,000.

SWINBURNE ISLAND, in Lower Bay, two miles from the Narrows; Hospital ship "Illinois," at anchor; physician's residence; pest houses; crematory; place of detention for persons suffering from the
more serious infectious diseases who arrive in the port on ships, chiefly used in cases of cholera, small-pox, typhus, bubonic plague and yellow fever; burying ground at Seguin's, S. I.; Dr. Joseph
J. O'Connell, Health Officer of the Port, Rosebank, S. I.; no large number of patients here since Asiatic-cholera epidemic of 1892; passengers and crews of 12,000 vessels examined in 1913.

HOFFMAN ISLAND, in Lower Bay, one mile from Narrows, place of detention of well persons arriving on infected vessels and for those suffering from minor infectious diseases; all ships report to Health
Officer of the Port at Quarantine, the boarding-station at Rosebank, S. I., just within the Narrows, in New York Bay; if cases of infectious diseases are discovered, patients are removed to Swinburne
Island, those exposed to infection are held for observation on Hoffman Island, and the ship is disinfected; vessels from infected ports thoroughly disinfected; quarantine remarkably thorough.

Tompkinsville   Fire Boat Station   Borough Hall   Brighton Heights Reformed Church   Ferry Slips   St. George   Baltimore & Ohio Freight Terminal   New Brighton   Kill van Kull

STATEN ISLAND, RICHMOND BOROUGH, 57.19 sq. mi., bet. N. Y. Bay and Lower Bay, separated from N. J. by Kill van Kull, S. I. Sound and Arthur Kill; population, 99,186, least
densely populated of the five boroughs; value taxable realty $81,558,246, an increase of 20 per cent. in four years; total realty value, $100,000,000; desirable residence-section, brought within 20
minutes of Whitehall St., Manhattan, by swift municipal ferryboats; 341 miles of streets and roads; 51 miles of water front; Todt Hill, 413 ft. above sea level, is highest point in city.

East River   Atlantic Basin   Buttermilk Channel   Red Hook   Erie Basin   Gowanus Bay   Bush Terminal   Bay Ridge   Upper Bay   Narrows

Governor's Island Landing   Staten Island Ferryboat   Quartermaster's Dock   Fort Columbus   Officers' Residences   Castle William   Addition to Island   New York Bay

GOVERNOR'S ISLAND, view from the Battery; U. S. Army headquarters, Atlantic Division, Department of the East; originally an island of 65 acres, bought from Indians by Gov. Van Twiller, 1634; Army Post since 1803; enlarged 1905-11 to 120 acres by building sea wall and filling in; piers to be erected for transports and ordnance ships; most important military depot in America with complete equipment, arms and ammunition for an army of 100,000 men; separated from Manhattan by East River, with ferry to Whitehall St.   Castle William, built 1812, now military prison.

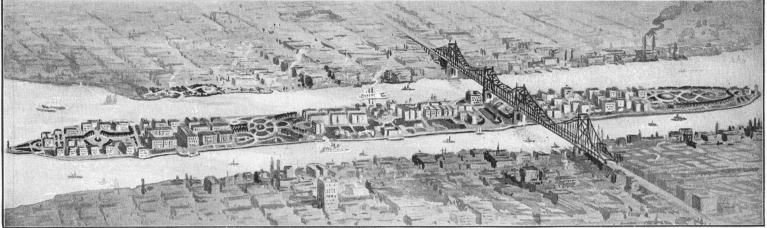

Hallett's Cove   Metropolitan Hospital   Workhouse   New York City Home for the Aged and Infirm   Queensboro Bridge   Penitentiary   City Hospital   Ferries to E. 26th and E. 52d Sts.

BLACKWELL'S ISLAND, 120 acres in East River from 50th to 86th Sts.; $25,000,000 property devoted to charitable and correctional purposes at expense of $2,000,000 annually to city; Metropolitan Hospital, Homœopathic, founded 1875, 9,000 patients a year; Workhouse, for those convicted of minor offences, average number of prisoners, 1,200; City Home for Aged and Infirm, founded 1846, average number of inmates, 3,500; Penitentiary, for those sentenced to less than a year, average number 1,825; City Hospital, founded 1849, 800 beds, 7,000 patients a year.

Harlem River   Children's Home   "Maryland" ferrying Colonial Express train from New Haven tracks at Mott Haven to Penna. R. R., Jersey City   Little Hell Gate

RANDALL'S ISLAND, 100 acres, at mouth of Harlem River, separated from the Bronx on the north by the Bronx Kills and from Ward's Island on the south by Little Hell Gate, with the Sunken Meadow and the East River on the east.   N. Y. City Children's Hospital, 500 patients; School for Feeble Minded, 800; Custodial Asylum for idiots, 700; famous for Nathan Straus' demonstration of the life-saving effects of pasteurized milk.   Thirty acres at south end occupied by House of Refuge, where manual training is provided for 900 juvenile delinquents.

Long Island Sound   Belden Point   Marine Observatory   Pelham Bay   Church of St. Mary, Star of The Sea   Hofbauer's Boat House   Dixon's Boat House

CITY ISLAND, famous yacht rendezvous, in Long Island Sound, off Pelham Bay Park, connected by bridge with Rodman's Neck section of Park; with mono-rail line, 1½ miles long, to Bartow Station, N. Y., New Haven & Hartford R.R. and surface line from Marshall's Corner to Belden Point.   Pelham Bay, to the north, shut in by Hart's Island, and Eastchester Bay, to the east, form admirable anchorages for pleasure craft, and City Island is a centre of boat building, repairing and sail making.   Within city limits, 19 miles from City Hall.

Barge Office   Produce Exchange   Governors Island Ferry   Staten Island Ferry   Hamilton Ave. Ferry   Atlantic Ave. Ferry   South Brooklyn (39th St.) Ferry   Brooklyn Bridge   East River

MUNICIPAL FERRY TERMINAL, East River from Whitehall to near Broad St.; 700 ft. long; main cornice 64 ft. above mean tide; turrets, 100 ft. high; $3,000,000 steel, copper and glass structure, with seven slips for the boats plying to Staten Island and on three Brooklyn lines; waiting rooms, each 150 by 65 ft.; concourse, 30 ft. wide, and exterior loggia, 15 ft. along South St.; offices of Dock Department, 700 by 70 ft., above waiting-rooms; glass-covered playground on roof; Walker & Morris, Architects. Hamilton and Atlantic Avenue Slips yet to be rebuilt.

Lower end of Manhattan   Fulton Ferry   Brooklyn Bridge   Empire Stores   Brooklyn Factories   Tower, Manhattan Bridge   East River   Battleship "Connecticut"   Pike Street, Manhattan

MANHATTAN BRIDGE, wire cable, double-deck suspension bridge, greatest traffic capacity of any in world, part of thoroughfare constructed 1901–'9 from the Bowery at Canal Street to extension of Flatbush Avenue, Brooklyn; swung from two steel towers, 336 feet high, resting on masonry pedestals which are 32 feet above and 92 feet below water line; the four cables weigh 6,300 tons and are made of 37,888 wires; length of bridge, 6,855 ft.; width, 120 ft.; 4 trolley tracks; 4 "L" tracks; 35-ft. roadway; two 11-ft. promenades; cost, $13,400,000; land, $6,300,000.

Williamsburg   Manhattan Tower   Navy Yard   East River   Arbuckle Coffee Mills   Fort Greene Park   Brooklyn Tower   Fulton Ferry

BROOKLYN BRIDGE, over East River from City Hall, Manhattan, to Sands St., Brooklyn; epoch-making achievement in bridge construction, begun Jan. 3, 1870, opened May 24, 1883; original cost $10,000,000; operating expenses and repairs to 1914, $23,649,256; receipts, $23,623,466; suspended on four cables, each of 5,296 wires, each 3,578 ft. long; permanent load, 14,680 tons; length of river span, 1,595 ft.; total length 6,537 ft.; width, 85 ft.; crossed in 1913 by 1,399,785 trolley cars and 1,383,842 "L" cars; daily by 275,000 people and 3,000 vehicles.

Manhattan   Astoria in the distance   Avenue A   Almshouse, Blackwell's Island   Sound Liner   Ravenswood Park   Penitentiary   City Hospital   Long Island City

QUEENSBORO BRIDGE, over East River and Blackwell's Island, East 59th St. and 2d Ave., Manhattan, to Jane and Academy Sts., Long Island City; great cantilever structure costing with approaches $25,000,000; rests on six masonry piers; 7,636 ft. long; west span, 1,182 ft.; clear height over channels, 135 ft.; height of island towers, 324 ft.; width 86 ft.; two decks with 53 ft. roadway, four trolley and two railroad tracks and two promenades; begun 1901, opened March 30, 1909, affording direct route to Queens Borough, which has 130.8 sq. mi. and 387,444 population.

Grand St. Ferry Manhattan Tower   East River   Greenpoint   Havemeyer Sugar Refineries   Approach to Broadway, Brooklyn

WILLIAMSBURG BRIDGE, crossing East River from Delancey and Clinton Sts., Manhattan, to Broadway, Brooklyn; combined cantilever and suspension bridge, opened Dec. 19, 1903; approach extended 1904 to the Bowery by demolishing ten half-blocks of tenements.   Length, 7,200 ft.; river span, 1,600 ft.; width, 118 ft.; two roadways, two "L" tracks, four trolley tracks; two promenades; cost, $10,000,000; 41,634 tons of steel; crossed daily by 475,000 people; through trolley-cars between Manhattan shopping district and Brooklyn; Brooklyn "L" thro' Center St. subway loop.

Washington Bridge Park   The Bronx   N. Y. Central R. R.   Harlem River   High Bridge Station   McComb's Dam Park   Speedway   Water Tower High Bdge. Pk.   Wash'ton Heights

HARLEM RIVER from Fort George, with the Bronx on the left, Washington Heights on right.   Washington Bridge, in foreground, at 181st St., beautiful steel and granite structure, 2384 ft. long, 80 ft. wide.   High Bridge, at 175th St., 1460 ft. long, carries old Croton Aqueduct over river at height of 116 ft. to pumping station and high-service reservoir; aqueduct completed 1842; capacity 90,000,000 gallons a day.   Second aqueduct, completed 1890, carries 290,000,000 gallons a day under Harlem at 135th St.   At 158th St. is Putnam R.R. drawbridge.

Northern New Jersey　　Watchung, or Orange Mountains　　Lake Country　　Hackensack Meadows　　Weehawken　　Palisades　　Central Park

PATERSON

PASSAIC

RUTHERFORD

MONTCLAIR

EAST ORANGE

HOBOKEN

PASSAIC RIVER

HACKENSACK RIVER

NEWARK

JERSEY CITY

HUDSON RIVER

BOROUGH OF MANHATTAN

EAST RIVER

ELIZABETH

NEWARK BAY

BAYONNE

NEW YORK BAY

ELIZABETHPORT

KILL VON KULL

RAHWAY RIVER

STATEN ISLAND SOUND

BOROUGH OF RICHMOND
STATEN ISLAND

THE NARROWS

GRAVESEND BAY

ARTHUR KILL

LOWER BAY

ATLANTIC

Tottenville　　Prince Bay　　Midland Beach　　Great Kills　　New Dorp　　South Beach　　Fort Wadsworth　　Fort Hamilton　　Sea Gate　　Coney Island　　Prospect Park

THE CITY OF NEW YORK, within dotted lines, 326.9 square miles, including Boroughs of Manhattan, Brooklyn, The Bronx, Queens and Richmond, consolidated 1898.　Population, 1914, 5,583,871; suburba[n] including $1,100,000,000 owned by city; grand total, $10,505,000,000; increase in real-estate assessments in 1913, $127,203,871.　Cost of city government, 1914, $192,995,551; largest items, schools, $38,20[ ] worth of piers built by the city.　Shipped by water in 1913, $1,800,000,000 worth of goods, one-half going to foreign ports.　Street railways, including Subway and "L" lines, have 1,564 miles of track and carried 1,772,[ ]

KING'S BIRD'S EYE VIEW
OF
GREATER NEW YORK
COPYRIGHTED 1911 BY
MOSES KING.

...ghton Beach   Manhattan Beach   Oriental Hotel   Bergen Beach   Rockaway Inlet   Barren Island   Rockaway Park   Duck Marshes   Alverne   Edgemere   Rockaway
...ulation, 2,180,000. Taxable property, land and improvements, $8,049,859,912; franchises, etc., $630,000,000; personalty, $325,422,140; total, $9,005,282,052; real estate exempt from taxation $1,500,000,000;
...; interest on debt, $37,745,836. Parks, 7,946 acres; cemeteries, 2,155 acres; miles of streets, 4,720. Water-front, 555 miles; piers and bulkheads have a total wharfage space of 227 miles, including $100,000,000
...568 passengers in 1913. City owns $70,000,000 Subway with 81 miles of tracks and is building 322 miles more for operation with existing privately owned systems, at a cost of $366,000,000, making 618.7 miles in all.

U. S. BATTLESHIP NEW YORK, super-dreadnaught, largest battleship completed, built in New York Navy Yard, begun Sept. 11, 1911, launched Oct. 30, 1912, commissioned April 1, 1914; cost $6,400,000; displacement, 28,367 tons; 565 ft. long, 95 ft. beam, draught, 28.5 ft.; speed, 21 knots; 28,100 horsepower; 10 14-in. breech-loading rifles, largest and heaviest installed on any war vessel, capable of hurling every minute seven tons of steel-encased explosives 14 miles; 21 5-in. rapid-fire guns; 10 smaller guns; 4 21-in. torpedo tubes; 63 officers and 1,000 men.

HAMBURG-AMERICAN STEAMER "VATERLAND," largest steamship in the world; built by Blohm & Voss at Hamburg, launched April 3, 1913; arrived in New York on maiden voyage May 21, 1914, averaging 23.2 knots an hour from Cherbourg to Sandy Hook, crossing in 5 days, 7 hours; highest speed 26.3 knots an hour; 950 ft. long, 100 ft. beam, nine decks above the water line; draught, 36.5 ft.; height above water, 100 ft.; double skin; 54,500 tons; 93,000 horsepower; uses 1,100 tons of coal a day; accommodations for 4,000 passengers and crew of 1,134.

CUNARD LINE'S STEAMER "AQUITANIA," launched April 21, 1913, at Clydebank, Scotland, arrived in New York June 5, 1914, on maiden trip, having averaged 23.65 knots an hour. Largest British steamship afloat, 901 ft. long, 97 ft. beam, 92.5 ft. deep from boat deck to keel, 47,000 tons, room for 3,250 passengers and crew of 1,000, built with double skin, average space of 15 ft. between inner and outer shells; outer hull 41 water-tight compartments, inner ship 84, with 16 bulkheads; turbine engines of 77,000 horsepower. Eleven ft. longer than twin-ships "Lusitania" and "Mauretania." Speed record of Atlantic held by "Mauretania," which in Sept., 1910, crossed from Daunt's Rock to Sandy Hook, 2,781 knots, in 4 days, 10 hours, 41 minutes, averaging 26.06 knots or 29.97 land miles an hour. Jan. 26, 1911, made 676 knots.

THE HUDSON RIVER DAY LINE STEAMER "WASHINGTON IRVING," licensed to carry 6,000 passengers, largest license ever issued; deck area for passengers, 66,564 sq. ft. Most commodious and sumptuous craft ever operated in inland waters; all boilers and machinery below decks; length 416.5 feet, beam 86.5 feet; 6,000 horse power, compound engines; speed 25 miles per hour; all windows plate glass; interior finished in rich hard woods; dining room on main deck; large luncheon rooms forward below; grand promenade one-seventh of a mile in circuit; orchestra arranged so as to be heard on four decks. Cost nearly $1,000,000; every available safety appliance. Day line established 1863. Fleet includes "Washington Irving," "Hendrick Hudson," "Robert Fulton," "Albany." Operated by daylight on Hudson between New York and Albany.

QUEBEC STEAMSHIP COMPANY'S STEAMER "BERMUDIAN", Steel Steamer, with all modern luxuries. 10,518 tons displacement; 425 feet long, 50 feet beam. Newest, fastest and only steamer landing passengers at dock in Bermuda without transfer by tender. Sails weekly. The company have maintained steam communication with Bermuda and West Indies over 30 years. Also operate a line to St. Thomas, St. Croix, St. Kitts, Antigua, Guadeloupe, Dominica, Martinique, St. Lucia, Barbados and Demerara. A. E. Outerbridge & Co., Agents, 29 Broadway.

OLD DOMINION LINE STEAMER "MADISON," flag-ship of fleet of six 4,000-ton coastwise liners, operating daily service between New York, Old Point Comfort and Norfolk, Va., approximate time 19 hours to Norfolk, connecting with the Old Dominion steamers for Richmond, via the James River, 12 hours, and Newport News, Smithfield, Petersburg, Portsmouth, Hampton, and Virginia Beach; connection is also made with steamers for Baltimore and Washington. Piers and general offices at Pier 25, N. R., foot of North Moore St.

HOLLAND-AMERICA LINE STEAMER "STATENDAM", being built for service between New York and Rotterdam via Boulogne-sur-Mer; 45,000 tons displacement; length, 740 ft; beam, 86 ft; depth of hull, 48 ft; accommodations for 3,600 passengers; companion ships, "Rotterdam", "New Amsterdam", "Noordam", "Ryndam", and "Potsdam", noted for steadiness, safety and comfort, with perfection in service and cuisine; equipped with wireless and submarine signal devices; hulls of steel with colossal bilge keels; pier at Fifth St., Hoboken, N. J.; offices at 24 State St., New York.

STEAMER "BERKSHIRE", Hudson Navigation Co., New York, Albany and Troy, the largest river steamer in the world; length 440 feet; 500 staterooms; private suites with baths and private balconies; searchlight 175,000 candle power having a carrying capacity of 100 miles; with Steamers "C. W. Morse", "Trojan" and "Rensselaer" maintains nightly service between Pier 32, Hudson River (North River) and Albany and Troy, where connections are made with trains for the North, East and West. The Comfortable and Popular way for travelers on the Hudson River.

Hudson River   N. Y. Central R.R.   W. 44th St. Pier   Esplanade over railroad and covered street for trucks   W. 45th St. Pier   Warehouses
NEW STEAMSHIP PIERS, largest in the world, under construction on the Hudson River from 44th to 48th st., for berthing of huge modern express steamships; piers each 1,050 ft. long, 150 ft. wide, with berths 360 ft. wide and 44 ft. deep, cut into the solid rock. This work has necessitated construction of largest coffer dam in the world, 800 ft. long, costing $497,500 to hold back a head of water 68 ft. high, 55,000,000 gallons of water being pumped out to permit dry blasting. Piers to cost $1,500,000 each. R. A. C. Smith, Commissioner of Docks and Ferries.

Marginal Street, 250 ft. wide   International Mercantile Marine Piers (Atlantic Transport, Red Star, White Star and American Lines)   Jersey Central Ferry to Communipaw   Lackawanna Ferry to Hoboken   Erie Ferry to Jersey City   Crosstown Lines on West 23d St.
CHELSEA PIERS, Hudson River, from ferry terminals at West 23d St. to New West Washington Market at Little West 12th St.; nine granite steamship piers, erected by the city, 1902-7 at a cost of $15,000,000; each 125 ft. wide and from 800 to 853 ft. long; two of them with fender extensions of 100 ft., making them 900 and 925 ft. long; berths for 16 of the largest ocean liners, with 250 ft. width of water between piers; steel superstructures, double-decked, 78 ft. high; first steamship to land at the new piers the "Lusitania," on her maiden trip in 1907; Cunard Line occupies the three southern piers, Nos. 53, 54 and 56; French Line, 57; Atlantic Transport, 58; Red Star, 59; White Star, 60 and 61; American Line, 62.   1,381,639 passengers arrived in ocean steamships in 1913 and 462,131 sailed; total, 1,843,770.

Hoboken   Hudson River   West Shore and Penna. R.R. Ferries   Starin and D. L. & W. Pier, Fall River Line   West St.   Jersey Central
WEST STREET, looking north from Cortlandt St., with 200 ft. wide marginal street, giving access to piers and ferries; thoroughfare constantly congested with trucks hauling merchandise, view shows West Shore and Pennsylvania R. R. ferry house, Lackawanna and Starin Terminal, N. Y. Central, Providence and Fall River Lines, crossed by foot bridges for passengers to ferries.

Brooklyn Bridge   "L" Terminal   39th St. Terminal   South Ferry   South Ferry (Atlantic Ave. Ferry)   Staten Island Ferry   Governor's Island Ferry
MUNICIPAL FERRY TERMINALS, at South Ferry (Atlantic Ave. Ferry), which, with Hamilton Ave. line, has slips between the big modern $3,000,000 steel, copper and glass ferry-houses from which the city operates huge screw-propeller double-decked ferryboats to 39th St., South Brooklyn, and to Staten Island; each ferry-house has main waiting room 150 x 65 ft.

STATUE OF LIBERTY, Bedloe's Island, New York Bay, 1¼ miles from the Battery; colossal figure of Liberty Enlightening the World, largest made in modern times, constructed by Eiffel, presented to America by the French, electric torch 306 ft. above water, highest beacon in the world. Pedestal rests on largest concrete monolith. War Department Signal Corps School on island.

Liberty Statue, 151 ft., by Auguste Bartholdi; Pedestal 155 ft., by R. M. Hunt, Arch.

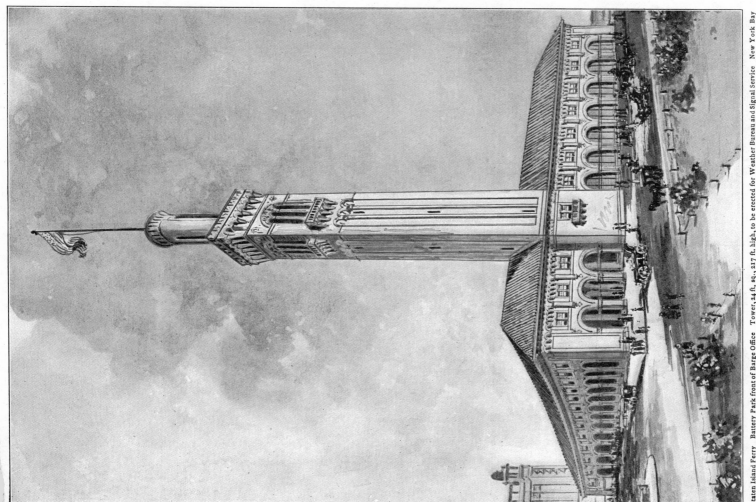

BARGE OFFICE, at the Battery, modern steel and brick building replacing granite pile erected in 1880, 210 by 217 ft.; pier 185 ft. long for revenue cutters; slip for Ellis Island ferry boats; offices of customs boarding officers and immigration service; headquarters of the U. S. Revenue Cutter Service, office of Shipping Commissioner; loggia 15 ft. deep along curved north front and west side.

Staten Island Ferry Battery Park front of Barge Office Tower, 24 ft. 49, 217 ft. high, to be erected for Weather Bureau and Signal Service New York Bay

Produce Exchange Roof   Whitehall Street   Produce Exch. Branch P. O. in basement, at Bridge St. end   Custom House, Cass Gilbert, Arch., John Pierce, Builder, Dudley Field Malone, Collector of the Port   Bowling Green   Battery Place

U. S. CUSTOM HOUSE, facing Bowling Green at foot of Broadway, occupying entire block between Whitehall and State Sts., to Bridge St.   Emblematic Groups—Asia, America, Europe, Africa—by Daniel C. French
(1626) and Government House (1787) and later headquarters of steamship lines.   Embelished with stately Doric colonnades; cartouche emblematic of America, by Carl Bitter, crowning attic; great commercial nations represented on the cornice, in this order—Greece and Rome,
by F. E. Elwell; Phœnicia, by F. W. Ruckstuhl; Genoa, by Augustus Lukeman; Venice and Spain, by F. M. L. Tonetti; Holland and Portugal, by Louis St. Gaudens; Scandinavia, by Albert Jaegers; Germany, by Johannes Gelert; France and England, by Charles Grafly.

Washington Bldg.   Adams Bldg.   Broadway Bankers' Trust Custom House   Battery Park Bldg.   Chesebrough Bldg.   U. S. Army Bldg.   Immigrant Missions

BATTERY PARK, showing Washington Building, first skyscraper, on site of Kennedy Mansion, once Washington's headquarters; Broadway vista, Bowling Green, in front of Custom House; imposing façade of $7,200,000 Custom House on State St., the early thoroughfare of fashion; Battery Park, 21.2 acres, has a sea-wall commanding unobstructed view of harbor; the "L" skirts inner side of park, hidden by the trees, and Municipal Subway passes underneath to South Ferry, with twin tunnels under East River to Brooklyn; new subway loop being built under park.

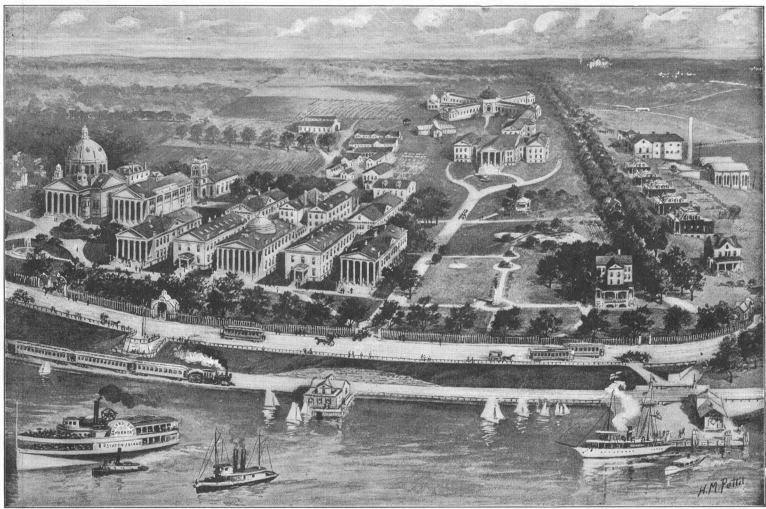

Chapel   Music Hall   Main Buildings   Storehouses   Sanitarium and Hospital   Governor's Residence   Employees' Homes

SAILORS' SNUG HARBOR, Richmond Terrace, New Brighton, Staten Island, facing Kill van Kull; largest and wealthiest charitable institution in the world; founded 1801 by Capt. Robt. Richard Randall, who bequeathed a farm worth $4,600 for the care of aged and infirm American merchant-marine sailors; which property, along Broadway, below 14th St., has became so valuable that it yields an income of over $700,000 a year.   Institution opened 1831; grounds cover 196 acres; 890 inmates; 300 employees.   Captain A. J. Newbury, Governor; James Henry, Comptroller.

Public Baths   Battery Park   Entrance to the Aquarium   Fire Boat Station   New Jersey Shore

THE AQUARIUM, on the Battery sea wall, containing in 122 glass tanks the finest collection of living fishes ever displayed.   The building was erected in 1807 on a small island and was called Fort Clinton; in 1822, joined to the mainland by filling in, it became a place of amusement known as Castle Garden and Jenny Lind sang there in 1850; from 1855 to 1892 it was the immigration depot, which was moved to Ellis Island, and in 1896 the old Fort was converted into an aquarium; visited annually by 2,400,000 people; 6,000,000 food fish hatched and distributed each year.

Schermerhorn Bldg.   First National Bank   No. 1 Wall St.   Trinity Church   Manhattan Life

ONE WALL STREET, S. E. cor. Broadway, until 1910 the most expensive plot in New York, costing $598.21 a square foot, ground floor and basement rents for $37,500 a year; 18 stories; 217 ft. high; profitable utilization of costly plot, only 29 ft. 10 in. front on Broadway, and 39 ft. 10 in. on Wall Street, made possible by steel-frame construction and especially compact elevators.

N. German Lloyd   Bowling Green Offices   Int. Mer. Marine   Stevens House   Hamb.-Am.   Empire Bldg.   Standard Oil   Seaboard Bk.   Produce Ex. Bk.

BROADWAY, from beginning of 15-mile thoroughfare to Trinity Building, viewed from new Custom House; 10 trans-Atlantic steamship lines on left, Hamburg-American on site of first dwelling of white men on island. Petroleum industry of world centres in 17-story Standard Oil Building. Bowling Green Offices, 229 ft. high, largest in city when built by Spencer Trask.

Sea Wall   Aquarium   Fire Boat Station   Naval Landing   Dock Dept. Pier   Iron Steamboat Pier   Lehigh Valley R. R. Pier   Penna. R. R. Piers   Whitehall Bldg., 1903   Whitehall Annex, 1911

BATTERY PARK and **WHITEHALL BUILDING**, Battery Pl., West to Washington Sts.; one of the largest office buildings in world; 550,000 sq. ft. rentable area; 11,000,000 cu. ft.; original $1,000,000 building, 20 stories, 254 ft. high, opened 1903; $4,600,000 addition, 34 stories, 416 ft. high, completed 1911; frontage, 180 ft. on Battery Pl., 264 ft. on Washington St., 307 ft. on West St., garden on Washington St. to secure light and air to all suites; area of combined plots, 51,515 sq. ft., or 21 city lots; 30 high-speed electric traction elevators.

Beaver Street   Produce Exchange, George B. Post, Architect   Whitehall St.   Bowling Green   Stone St.   Kemble Bldg.

NEW YORK PRODUCE EXCHANGE, fronting on Bowling Green; organized 1861; $3,000,000 building, 307 by 150 ft., occupied 1884; clock tower, 40 by 70 and 240 ft. high; trading room, second floor, 220 by 144 ft. and 60 ft. high, daily scene of the largest volume of trading in grain and provisions of any exchange in the world; 2,140 members, representing every important shipping centre in America.   Important factor in improvement of the waterfront and the building of the $101,000,000 barge-canal across New York State.   John Aspegren, President.

South Brooklyn   Gowanus Bay   Bay Ridge   Narrows   Governor's Island   Staten Island   Kill van Kull   Liberty   Constable Hook, N. J.

East River   Mutual Life   Liberty Tower   Bankers' Trust   Broadway   Singer   City Investing   Whitehall   Railroad Freight Piers   Hudson River   West St. Bldg.

BROADWAY, from the Woolworth Building, showing the deep ravine formed by the huge skyscrapers, with the financial centre of the world at the left, and the Hudson and East Rivers uniting to form in New York Bay the world's greatest harbor, with Governor's Island separated from Brooklyn by Buttermilk Channel. Wall Street is marked by the Bankers' Trust, with its pyramidal cap, the Hanover National Bank adjoining on this side, and in the group on this side of Broadway are banks that hold in their vaults an aggregate of half a billion dollars in cash.

Hamburg-American Building, Formerly Aldrich Court

HAMBURG-AMERICAN LINE, 45 Broadway, site of first building erected (1613) by white men on Manhattan Island; purchased 1907, finest steamship-offices in America; 431 steamships touching 370 ports.

Pearl St.   Fraunce's Tavern, preserved under care of Sons of the Revolution   Broad St.

FRAUNCE'S TAVERN, S. E. cor. Broad and Pearl Sts.; residence built 1725 by Etienne De Lancey; two stories added and opened as a tavern in 1762 by Samuel Fraunce; Washington's headquarters 1776; farewell address to his officers delivered in "long room" 1783; bought by the city in 1903 for $340,000 and restored.

Rector St.   Sixth Ave. "L"   U. S. Express Bldg., 320 ft. high   Hudson West St. Bldg., 324 ft.   Trinity Parochial School   Trinity Church Spire, 284 ft. high   Trinity Bldg., 308 ft.

TRINITY CHURCH, Broadway at the head of Wall St.; founded 1696; third church on present site, completed 1846; 192 ft. long, 80 ft. wide; $40,000 bronze doors and $100,000 marble altar and reredos, gift of the Astor family; the parish owns $10,000,000 worth of productive real estate in lower part of city, yielding an income of over $750,000 a year, used to maintain nine chapels, 12 schools and 20 parishes that do missionary work in poorer sections of city; Alex. Hamilton's grave marked by pyramid near Rector St.; Robert Fulton's body nearby.   Rev. Dr. Wm. T. Manning, Rector.

Trinity | Trinity Building | Thames St. | U. S. Realty Building | Cedar St. | 308 ft. high

TRINITY BUILDING, 111 Broadway, and U. S. REALTY BUILDING, 115 Broadway; twin offices in English Gothic; assessed at $11,900,000; frontage, 129.5 ft.; 260 to 275 ft. deep; 552,873 sq. ft. floor area; each building rests on 70 pneumatic caissons, sunk 75 ft.; steel frame of Realty Building erected by Geo. A. Fuller Co. in 63 days, stone work in 146 days, trim, 45 days.

Trinity Bldg. | Dix Chapel | Equitable | Am. Surety Co. | Trinity, 284 ft. high | First Nat. Bank | Bankers' Trust | Union Trust

TRINITY CHURCH, head of Wall St.; wealthiest parish in America; finest, pure Gothic architecture; erected 1846 on site of original church (1697); churchyard, 391.5 ft. front on B'way, average depth to Trinity Pl., 243 ft.; land worth $40,000,000; tombs of Alexander Hamilton, Robert Fulton, Martyrs' Monument, tombstone of 1681. Morgan Dix Memorial Chapel erected 1913.

Adams Building   Tin Pot Alley   Broadway, looking North

ADAMS BUILDING, 57–61 Broadway, 32 stories, 486 ft. high, 105 ft. frontage on Broadway, 209 ft. on Tin Pot Alley; Francis H. Kimball, architect; cost $2,000,000. Chase National Bank, founded '77, on ground floor; deposits, $115,623,000; A. H. Wiggin, President.

Johnston Bldg.   Blair Bldg.   Stock Exchange   Hanover Bank   Bank of Commerce   Broad Exchange

CURB MARKET, Broad St. looking toward Sub-Treasury on Wall St. and the Nassau St. end of the Equitable Bldg.; unique open-air market for the sale of stocks that are not listed on the exchanges; scene of great animation daily from 10 a. m. to 3 p. m.

MOSES KING Inc
PUBLISHER   NEW YORK

Jersey Central Ferry   Metropolitan Line West St. Bldg. Hudson Terminal Penna. R.R. Piers U.S.Express   Whitehall Bldg.   Dock Dept.   Adams Bldg. Naval Landing   Bowling Green Offices Washington Bldg.   Aquarium

SKYSCRAPERS OF LOWER MANHATTAN, where the business interests of 100,000,000 people centre in enormous steel, fireproof buildings that have risen, most of them within fifteen years, to meet the rapidly inc Banking power of New York $3,961,000,000, or 17% of bank'ng resources of entire nation.   Here are the headquarters or agencies of $16,000,000,000 worth of railroads, of manufacturing concerns with a capita tions with $4,600,000,000 resources.   The post offices handle 12,500 pieces of mail a minute and the city spends $90,000 a day on postage. $7,500,000 worth of goods are manufactured in the city every w

Richard Rummell del.
N.Y.
COPYRIGHT 1911

g demands for office room in the new world·centre.   Here is the largest of the 12 Federal Reserve Banks, N. Y. State forming District No. 2, with 478 banks whose combined capital and surplus amount to $744,000,000.
30,000,000,000, of business enterprises that represent investments aggregating $240,000,000,000, here centres the business of 150 fire-insurance companies with $500,000,000 assets, and 200 life-insurance corpora-
g day in 34,000 factories employing 685,000 wage earners.   There are about 17,000 telephone conversations every minute and 18,000 fares a minute are paid to the traction companies during the rush hours.

Beaver St.   Cotton Exch.   William St.   Hanover Sq.   Seligman Bldg.

COTTON EXCHANGE, Beaver and William Sts.; organized 1870; $1,000,000 building occupied 1885; 450 members; E. K. Cone, President. America produced in 1913 14,128,902 bales of world's supply of 16,500,000; exported 8,235,687.

Wall St.   Bankers' Trust   Head of Broad St.   Nassau St.   Hanover Bank

BANKERS' TRUST BUILDING, Wall St., N.W. cor. Nassau; 39 stories, 540 ft. high; on site of Gillender Building, 19 stories, 1897-1910; site cost $825 sq. ft.; highest price ever paid anywhere in world; $93,000,000 in deposits; E. C. Converse, Pres.

Hanover St.   Wall St.   McKim, Mead & White, Architects   William St.

NATIONAL CITY BANK, built 1841 for Merchants' Exchange; Custom House, '62-07; bought for $3,265,000; four stories added for $3,000,000; bank founded 1812; capital and surplus, $62,000,000; deposits, $190,000,000.   F. A. Vanderlip, Pres.

Central Tr. Co.   Centre of Wall St.   No. 60 Wall St., Clinton & Russell, Arch.   Equitable Trust Co., Francis H. Kimball, Arch.   Mills Building   Mutual Alliance Trust Co.

SIXTY WALL ST., through to Pine St.; 362 ft. high; conspicuous landmark; visible from the ocean; contains Wall St. Branch P.O., second only to General P.O. in receipts. International Banking Corp., branches in 17 foreign cities; capital, $9,500,000. Gen. Thos. H. Hubbard, Pres.

EQUITABLE TRUST CO., 37-43 Wall St.; 327 ft. high; erected 1907. Branches at 222 Broadway and 618 Fifth Ave. Trust Co. occupies main floor; capital and surplus, $13,200,000; deposits, $82,000,000; assets, $89,000,000. Alvin W. Krech, President.

Atlantic Bldg.   1 Wall St.   Trinity   Bank of America   Hanover Bank

WALL STREET CANYON, financial heart of America, occupied entirely by banks, financial institutions and allied interests; Stock Exchange at left; the U. S. Sub-Treasury at the right, and 39-story Bankers' Trust replacing Gillender Building.

J. P. Morgan & Co.   Mills Bldg.   50 Broad Street   Blair Com. Cable   Stock Exchange

BROAD STREET, south from Wall, line of canal in New Amsterdam days, with bridge near present Exchange Place, where merchants met daily to trade; now centre of world's largest market in securities. Produce Exchange shows beyond Mills Building.

National City Bank Atlantic Mutual Equitable Trust   Wall St.   Banking House of J. P. Morgan & Co.   Broad St. opposite Stock Exchange   Mills Building

J. P. MORGAN & CO., S. E. cor. Wall and Broad Sts., opposite Sub-Treasury; most famous international banking house; founded as Drexel, Morgan & Co., in 1871 by the union of Drexel & Co. and Junius S. Morgan and his son, J. Pierpont Morgan, who became the most powerful banker in the world and on his death in April, 1913, was succeeded by his son of the same name.   Magnificent and unique new banking house, built of huge blocks of flawless white marble in 1913-14 at a cost of $2,000,000 on plot worth $4,000,000; Trowbridge & Livingston, Architects.

Nat. City Bank Atlantic Mutual Morgan & Co. Trinity Banking Row

WALL STREET, from Hanover St. to Trinity at Broadway, new banking house of J. P. Morgan & Co. at Broad Street, No. 1 Wall Street dominating the vista. A little more than a century ago first bank in State founded here; now banking centre of world.

Wall Street Bank of America William St.

BANK OF AMERICA, in block occupied by Sub-Treasury and Assay Office; founded 1812 on present site; Oliver Wolcott, first president; capital and surplus, $7,500,000 deposits, $27,800,000; assets, $44,000,000. William H. Perkins, President.

Sub-Treasury Assay Office Row of Banks National City Bank Drexel Bldg. J. P. Morgan & Co.

WALL STREET, Nassau to East River; banking centre of New York; on north side of street; Bank of Manhattan Co., founded 1799; Merchants' National, 1803; Bank of America, 1812; Bank of New York, N. E. cor. William St., 1797; Mechanics' & Metals Nat'l Bank, 1810; Central Trust Co., 1875; International Bank; Seamen's Bank for Savings, 1829, at Pearl St. South side, J. P. Morgan & Co.; Mutual Alliance Trust Co.; Equitable Trust Co., 1899; U. S. Trust Co., 1853; Metropolitan Trust Co., 1881; Atlantic Mutual Ins. Co., 1842; National City Bank, 1812.

American Exchange National Bank, 16 stories, 235 ft. high   N. Y. Clearing House, built 1896; R. W. Gibson, Arch., Marc Eidlitz & Son, Bldrs.   National Bank of Commerce, 20 stories, 274 ft.

NEW YORK CLEARING HOUSE, 77-83 Cedar St., conservator of sound banking; association of 29 national banks, 17 state banks and 15 trust companies, with $179,900,000 capital, $297,000,000 surplus and $2,000,000,000 net deposits; formed 1853; average daily clearings, 1913, $323,833,400; total, 60 years, $2,419,273,696,081; record day, Nov. 3, 1909, $736,461,548; trust companies admitted May, 1911; Francis L. Hine, President Clearing House Association; William Sherer, Manager; W. J. Gilpin, Assistant Manager; A. W. Higgin, Chairman.

Commercial Cable Bldg., 275 ft. high   Stock Exchange, George B. Post, Architect; cost $3,000,000   Wilkes Bldg.   Stock Exchange Extrance   Wall St.   Trinity

NEW YORK STOCK EXCHANGE, Bread St., through to New, with entrance on Wall St., founded May 17, 1792; carved white-marble building, occupied May, 1903; board room, 138 by 112 ft. and 80 ft. high, with ceiling in gold relief; façade of Corinthian columns each 52 ft. high; sales in 1913, 83,470,693 shares of stock worth $7,170,862,086 and $476,914,499 of bonds; record day in stocks, April 30, 1901, 3,190,857 shares; in bonds, Nov. 11, 1904, $15,085,500; 1,100 members; trading, 10 a. m. to 3 p. m.; H. G. S. Noble, President.

National Park Bank, Donn Barber, Arch.

Statues symbolical of Commerce over Entrance   Alexander Hamilton, Financier   DeWitt Clinton, Governor   John Jay, Jurist   Liberty Place

NATIONAL PARK BANK, 214 B'way; Ann & Fulton Sts.; fd. 1856; capital and surplus, $19,400,000; deposits, $96,000,000; assets, $122,500,000; R. Delafield, Pres.

CHAMBER OF COMMERCE, 65 Liberty St., cor. Liberty Pl.; organized in Fraunces Tavern April 5, 1768; $1,500,000 carved marble building dedicated Nov. 11, 1902, by Pres. Roosevelt; foremost commercial body in America, potent influence in the nation and in development of city by waterway and harbor improvements; 1,600 members.   Seth Low, President.

Seligman Bldg.   Beaver St.   Consolidated Exchange, Clinton & Russell, Architects   Broad St.

CONSOLIDATED STOCK EXCHANGE, S. E. cor. Broad and Beaver Sts.; the centre of seven exchanges; formed '85 by union of the Mining Stock Exchange (founded '75) and five other boards; from April, '88, to Aug.,'07, occupied building at Broadway and Exchange Pl.; Aug. 26, '07, moved into new $300,000 home erected on $870,000 site; trading room, 95 by 82 ft., contains 12 trading posts for railroad and industrial stocks and mining shares; 12,087,301 shares stock and 1,577,239 mining shares dealt in 1913; 850 members; M. E. de Aguero, Pres.

Jersey Central Bldg.　Fulton Street　Cedar Street　The West Street Bldg., Cass Gilbert, Arch ; John Peirce Co., Bldrs.　Albany Street　Singer Bldg.　Washington Life

THE WEST STREET BUILDING, West St., Albany to Cedar; 24 stories; 324 ft. high; erected by West St. Improvement Co., Gen. Howard Carroll, Pres.; built of steel, granite and terra cotta; cost $4,000,000; facing 250 ft. marginal street and Jersey Central and Penna. R. R. ferries.　Restaurant top floor.　Offices of Lackawanna R. R., Du Pont De Nemours Powder Co., etc.

Park Row Bldg.　Fulton Bldg., 50 Church St.　Dey St.　Hudson Terminals, River View　Cortlandt Bldg.; 30 Church St.　Cortlandt St.　P. R. R. Ferries

HUDSON TERMINALS, Church St. Cortlandt to Fulton; twin structures, together the largest offices in the world, 18,150,000 cu. ft.; weighing 200,000 tons, resting on biggest coffer-dam, 400x178 ft., 75 to 98 ft. deep; 22 stories, 275 ft. high; 39 elevators; office room for 20,000 people.　Trains from Hudson & Manhattan Co. twin tunnels under Hudson enter station in basement.

Woolworth   Roof St. Paul's Chapel   Federal Bldg.   Park Row   Municipal Bldg.   St. Paul Bldg.   Nat'l Park Bank

BROADWAY AND PARK ROW, view from the "Evening Mail" Building, looking north east; busiest section of the city, with half a million people daily passing through these thoroughfares and adjacent streets. Park Row leads past the Brooklyn Bridge Terminal to the Bowery at Chatham Square and was known as Chatham Street until 1886, when the Aldermen changed the name.

St. Paul   Liberty Tower, Maiden Lane Bldg.   Equitable   Singer   "Mail"   City Investing   W. U. Teleg.

BROADWAY CANYON, from the Woolworth Building south; showing the deep ravine formed by the huge skyscrapers that have been erected in response to the enormous demand for office room in the world's business centre; an amazing development when it is considered that Broadway two centuries ago was a cow path to a clearing called The Common, afterwards City Hall Park.

Broadway Entrance, City Investing Bldg.   Wessels Bldg.   Cortlandt St.   Façade City Investing Bldg.   Church St.

CITY INVESTING BUILDING, Broadway, Cortlandt and Church Sts.; 34 stories; 486 ft. high; plot of 27,000 sq. ft., 1⅓ acres floorspace, room for 6,000 tenants; corridor 38 ft. wide from Broadway to Church Street, 315 ft.; entrance direct to Sixth Ave. "L" road; 21 elevators; light and air protected by control of adjoining properties; City Investing Co., Owners; Robert E. Dowling, Pres.

Washington Life Bldg.   Bourne Annex   Liberty St.   Singer Bldg., Ernest Flagg, Arch.   City Investing Bldg.   Telephone Bldg.   Cortlandt St.   Waterman Bldg.

SINGER BUILDING, N. W. cor. Broadway and Liberty St.; 47 stories; 612 ft. high; towers, resting on 36 caissons sunk to bed rock 92 ft. below curb, rising 421 ft. above main building, 65 ft. sq., weighing 18,365 tons, braced to withstand wind pressure of 330 tons against any face; 16 Otis traction elevators; entire building, 9½ acres floor space; 5,000 tenants. Built by The Singer Mfg. Co.

Am. Exch. Nat. Bank   Cedar St.   Equitable Building, Thompson-Starrett Company, Contractor   Pine St.   Am. Surety Co.

EQUITABLE BUILDING, Broadway, Cedar to Pine St., through to Nassau St., 38 stories; 537.5 ft. high; 45 acres floor space; rooms for 15,000 workers; 48 elevators, whose combined lift would be four miles; erected by the Equitable Office Building Corporation at a cost of $29,000,000; Gen. T. Coleman Du Pont, President; E. R. Graham, Architect; on site of famous Equitable Building destroyed by fire, Jan. 9, 1912.   Equitable Life Assurance Society, founded 1859, assets $528,442,491; insurance in force $1,500,000,000; W. A. Day, President.

68 William St.   Casualty Company of America   Cedar St.

CASUALTY COMPANY OF AMERICA, 15-story building on the northeast corner of William and Cedar Streets; founded in 1903; strong company writing personal accident, health and disability insurance, automobile and team risks, burglary, employers' liability, workmen's compensation, plate glass and elevator insurance, fidelity, surety and contract bonds,

City Investing, 486 ft.   Singer, 612 ft.   Woolworth, 792 ft.   Park Row Bldg., 382 ft.   Municipal Bldg., 580 ft.

U. S. Realty, 306 ft.   Washington Life, 273 ft.   American Exchange Natl. Bank, 235 ft.   Evening Mail   Silversmiths' Bldg 264 ft.

BROADWAY, from Cedar St. north, deep canyon through which flows the greatest human tide in the world, 220,000 people passing in a business day; additional subways being built under parallel streets on either side; headquarters of big manufacturing and commercial concerns; Jewelry District to right; Guaranty Trust Co. at Liberty St.; Lawyers Title Ins. & Trust Co.

Chamber of-Commerce   Liberty St.   Liberty Tower   Nassau St.

LIBERTY TOWER, N. W. cor. Liberty and Nassau Sts.; 31 story building on plot 57.9 by 82.1 ft., on site of old Bryant Building; 401 ft. high; typical of the development of large office area on small plots in response to the demands of business downtown.

Liberty St.   German-American Bldg., Hill & Stout, Arch.   Maiden Lane   Royal Bldg.

GERMAN-AMERICAN INSURANCE CO., Liberty St. and Maiden Lane; 21 stories, 281 ft. high, rests on largest caissons, 42 feet below cellar. Org. 1872; cap., $2,000,000; risks, $240,000,000; surplus, $9,250,000; assets, $22,000,000; W. N. Kremer, Pres.

Emigrant Industrial Savings Bank   County Court House   City Hall   "World"   "Tribune"   41 Park Row   Potter Building   Mail St. end of Federal Building

CITY HALL PARK from Broadway, with Hall of Records, Municipal Building and Newspaper Row in the background; here, a mile from the Battery, were the northern limits of the city when the City Hall was begun in 1803; now Manhattan Borough extends 12 miles to the north, to the Ship Canal at Spuyten Duyvil; the Bronx carries the city line to Yonkers, and Mount Vernon, 16 miles away; the limits of Queens are 16 miles away; Brooklyn extends to the Atlantic Ocean, 11 miles, and Richmond Borough stretches away to the lower bay, Tottenville being 20 miles away. The old County Court House, famous as Tweed's $10,000,000 job, is to be removed when new building is completed in Civic Centre to the north, and the City Court Building and Federal Building are also to go, leaving the classic City Hall as the only structure in the Park.

Royal Bldg.   Fulton St.   Downing Bldg.   Bennett Bldg.   Market and Fulton Bank

FULTON STREET, from Gold St. westward; the main thoroughfare between the Hudson River ferries from New Jersey and the Fulton St. ferry to Brooklyn; congested from early morning to night with trucks carrying merchandise, lined with retail shops of all kinds.

Stock Exchange Roof   Hanover Bk.   Bank of Com.   Mutual Life   Am. Tract   Sub-Treasury

NASSAU STREET CANYON, from U. S. Sub-Treasury, on Wall St., in heart of financial district, through banking-section and jewelry district, to Printing House Square; most congested thoroughfare in the world, 10,000 people passing in an hour.

Mail St.   Federal Building   Astor House   St. Paul's   Barclay St.   Woolworth Building, designed by Cass Gilbert   Park Place   Broadway

WOOLWORTH BUILDING, Broadway, Barclay St. to Park Pl.; tallest building in the world, 55 stories, 792 ft. high; begun 1910, completed April, 1913; plot, 152 x 197 ft., cost $4,500,000; foundations, with caissons 19 ft. in diameter sunk to bed rock 110 to 130 ft. below sidewalk, cost $1,000,000; building, about $8,000,000; main building 29 stories; tower, 86 x 84 ft., 36 stories above main building; light on top visible 96 miles at sea; stores and arcade on ground floor; Irving National Exchange Bank on first floor; built by F. W. Woolworth.

South Brooklyn   Governor's Island   Produce Exchange   Narrows   Staten Island   Banker's Trust   Equitable Building   U. S. Express   Trinity and   Liberty
Buttermilk Channel   East River   240 ft. high   Harbor   Battery   540 ft.   537 ft.   320 ft.   U. S. Realty   306 ft.

Equitable Trust, 327 ft.   Morgan & Co.   Mutual Life   Stock Exchange   Hanover Bk.   Nat'l Bank of Com.   Postal Life   Nassau St.   Liberty Tower, 401 ft.   Chamber Commerce   Am. Ex. Bank   Trin. & U. S. Realty, 308 f   Lawye

FINANCIAL DISTRICT, where $2,500,000,000 worth of skyscrapers and other business buildings cluster on the lower end of Manhattan Island, with an office-population of 350,000 with over a mi.on peop
38 stories; 175, 14 to 20 stories; 822, 11 to 13 stories; the highest are 750, 700, 612, 580, 540 and 486 ft., one is to be 801 ft. high; the block bounded by Broadway and Church St. and Cortlalt and
world; these structures, built of steel, protected and enclosed with imperishable brick, with partitions and floors fireproofed with hollow tiles, with window frames, fittings and doors of metal, with ve glass

Maiden Lane Bldg.　　Singer Building・　　Broadway　|　Cortlandt Street　　Waterman Pen Building　　　　　　　　　　　　　　N. Y. Telephone Co.　　Hudson Terminal

to and fro each day, 24,000 an hour through Broadway alone; of 1,161 buildings in Manhattan of ten stories or more, the tallest have 58, 55, 47, 45 and 41 stories respectively; 8, from 31 to 38 stories; 42, 21 to ovides office room for 20,000 people, and if the hundred small blocks below Fulton St. are similarly built up there will be room for 2,000,000 to work daily in this financial and commercial clearing-house of the are the safest in the world, as proved by the Baltimore fire and the San Francisco earthquake; they rest on bed-rock, pneumatic caissons being sunk to the required depth, 92 ft. in case of the Singer Building.

Roof of County Court House "World" "Sun" "Tribune" Am. Tract City Hall 41 Park Row Potter Bldg. Park Row Bldg. St. Paul Bldg. Broadway Singer City Investing Home Life Hudson Terminal Nat. Shoe & Leather Bank

BROADWAY AND PARK ROW, view from Dun Building; showing the remarkable development of the century since the City Hall was built on "The Commons"; in 1811 the first Tammany Hall had just been completed, its walls surviving in the "Sun" Building; Martling's Tavern was on the site of the American Tract Building; the Park Theatre faced the lower end of the park, now the Federal Building; the Brick Presbyterian Church stood on the site of the old "Times" Building, now 41 Park Row; the Debtors' Prison was east of the City Hall, near Chatham St. (now Park Row), which led to the bouweries, or farms, along what is now the Bowery; the Bridewell, or City Prison, was west of the City Hall, near Broadway; Columbia College was west of Broadway between Barclay and Murray Sts.; Potter's Field was where Court House now stands.

Fourth Ave. Bible House Cooper Union St. Gaudens' Statue of Cooper Third Ave. "L" 7th St. Old Tompkins Market

COOPER SQUARE, where Fourth and Third Aves. merge into the Bowery. COOPER UNION, founded 1859 by Peter Cooper; is a free school of sciences and art, with $4,000,000 endowment. There are 72 instructors and over 4,000 pupils. John E. Parsons, President. BIBLE HOUSE, 8th to 9th Sts., built 1852 by American Bible Society, organized 1816; 100,000,000 Bibles issued in 98 years.

EAST SIDE, typical view in the melting pot of the races, where men and women of all nationalities are developed into American citizens; the great congested district of lower Manhattan, north of the Brooklyn Bridge and east of the Bowery, is the most densely populated in the World, with 300,000 people living in 370 acres; 40 per cent of the city's inhabitants are foreign born whites.

City Hall   Hall of Records   Centre Street Façade   Chambers Street through Arcade   McKim, Mead & White, Architects   Park Row   Brooklyn Bridge Entrance   "World"

MUNICIPAL BUILDING, Park Row and Centre Street, facing City Hall Park ; $20,400,000 offices for city departments, largest structure of sort in world, housing 6,000 city employees; resting on 116 pneumatic caissons, sunk to bed rock, in some places 260 ft. below the street and 239 ft. below water level ; the most difficult foundations ever constructed, costing $2,000,000 ; building 381x168x158 ft. with 600,000 sq. ft. floor space ; 34 stories (15 in tower) ; 580 ft. high, including 24-ft. figure of Civic Fame ; begun 1908, occupied 1914 ; six-track subway station in basement.

Williamsburg Bridge   Site for New County Courts   Municipal Building, 580 ft.   Navy Yard   Manhattan Bridge   East River   Brooklyn Bridge   Brooklyn

Stewart Building   Chambers St.   Emigrant Industrial Savings Bank   Hall of Records   Broadway   City Hall   New Brooklyn Bridge Terminal   "World"   "Sun"   "Tribune"   No. 41 Park Row   Potter Building   Beekman Street

CIVIC CENTRE, City Hall Park, as it will be when its restoration is made possible by removal of Federal Building, County Court House and City Court, preserving the classic City Hall, erected over a hundred years ago, in the setting intended for the seat of the municipal government, with the new Court House to the north along Centre Street, which leads to the City Prison (Tombs), Criminal Courts, Public Health Building and Police Headquarters. Close to the new Court House it is proposed to erect city departments in the Municipal Building and Hall of Records, the new County Court House to provide quarters for the United States Courts. The unsightly sheet iron shed at the Manhattan end of the Brooklyn Bridge is to be replaced by an ornamental terminal so arranged as to practically abolish the "bridge crush" of the rush hours.

No. 206 Broadway   St. Paul's Chapel   "Evening Mail"   Equitable   Singer City Investing   N.Y.Law School   6th Ave. "L" on Church St.   Hudson Terminals

ST. PAUL'S CHAPEL, Trinity Parish, Broadway, Vesey to Fulton St., oldest church building on Manhattan Island, erected 1764 then facing riverfront; Washington's pew marked by shield of U. S.; Gov. Clinton's by that of state.   Graves of famous persons in churchyard.   Brick building in churchyard houses offices of Trinity Parish.   Erected in wheatfield now surrounded by world's greatest buildings.   "Evening Mail" across Fulton St.; Hudson Terminals across Church St.; Western Union at Dey St., City Investing at Cortlandt St. and Singer Tower at Liberty St.

Dun and Stewart Bldgs.   Broadway, looking north   Old General Post Office and U. S. Courts   Park Row   "World"   Potter Bldg.   Park Row Bldg.

FEDERAL BUILDING, one of the finest granite buildings in the world, 144-ft. façade at intersection of Broadway and Park Row, with 262½ ft. on each thoroughfare and 279 ft. on Mail St. U. S. District and Circuit Courts and old General Post Office, which has 47 branches, 251 sub-stations; 38 post offices, 78 branches, 435 sub-stations in entire city.   1,600 mails dispatched daily, 1,700 received; receipts, year ended June 30,'14, $31,000,000; entire city, $38,000,000; Postal savings deposits, $4,500,000; 8,200 clerks and carriers.   Edward M. Morgan, Postmaster.

Frankfort St.   Crowd watching baseball scoreboard   "Tribune," fu. 41   Spruce St.   Am. Tract, 300 ft. high   41 Park Row, Geo. A. Fuller Co., Bldrs.
PRINTING HOUSE SQUARE, Park Row, Nassau and Spruce Sts; newspaper centre 60 years.   "TRIBUNE" Bldg, erected 73;
enlarged '06.   "Sun," founded '33, adjoining, to move to Am. Tract Bldg;   "World" in next block;   "Press," "Commercial" and
"Staats Zeitung," on Spruce St.;   "American," "Evening Mail," "Evening Post" near by.   41 Park Row, old "Times" Bldg.

Manhattan Terminal, Brooklyn Bridge   Pulitzer Bldg.   Frankfort St.   "The Sun"   "The Tribune"
"THE WORLD," PULITZER BUILDING, Park Row, opposite City Hall Park, 309 ft. high, 375 ft. basement to dome;
founded 1860; purchased by Joseph Pulitzer; largest newspaper office building, tallest in city when erected in 1889; enlarged 1907.   Site of historic French's Hotel, purchased 1888 for $630,000.   Morning and evening editions,

NEW YORK COUNTY COURT HOUSE, to be erected in new Civic Centre, along Centre St. north of the Municipal Building, from plans by Guy Lowell, on site having area of 115 city lots, costing $7,568,500; to be surrounded by a circular street 140 ft. wide, with boulevard 125 ft. wide leading to Manhattan Bridge. The building, to cost from $17,000,000 to $25,000,000, will be 700 ft. in diameter and 200 ft. high; four main entrances, each 43 ft. wide and four 13 ft. wide, leading to central hall 150 ft. in diameter; from which elevators reach the upper floors; between the elevators and the court rooms will be an annular air-shaft 32 ft. wide; 16 court rooms on each floor, each two stories high, opening on the outside of the building, and a gallery opening on the air-shaft, with counsel and witness rooms under the gallery; plan inspired by the Coliseum.

Lower West Side   Varick St.   St. John's   Butterick Bldg.   Telephone Bldg.   Metropolitan   Broadway   New York Life   Lower East Side   Tombs

Church St.   Varick St. extended to West Broadway   Wholesale Dry Goods District   Barclay Bldg.   Broadway   Dun Bldg.   Stewart Bldg., Chambers St. façade   Emigrant Industrial Savings Bank

WHOLESALE DISTRICT, viewed from Woolworth Building, greatest jobbing centre in world, wholesale dry goods houses lining Broadway for two miles from City Hall to 23d St. and occupying side streets to West Broadway and Varick St., where the grocery business centres; in the foreground Chambers St. is given over to electrical supplies, and to the south is the crockery district; in lofts throughout this district and east to the Bowery, 200,000 people are employed in manufacturing; to the right is the lower East Side, most populous spot on earth, 600,000 people living in one square mile.

Smith-Gray & Co. Building   Broadway Chambers   Barclay Building   City Hall   Emigrant Industrial Savings Bank   City Court   Park Row

CITY HALL, from Park Row, showing the seat of the City Government in a setting of business buildings. The portico is the scene of official ceremonies. In the central part of the building, second floor front, is the Governor's Room, scene of official receptions; this has been restored to its colonial beauty at a cost of $50,000, half contributed by Mrs. Russell Sage; it contains the chair in which Gen. Washington was inaugurated the first president, the desk on which he wrote his first message and portraits of Revolutionary Chieftains, Governors and Mayors.

Postal Telegraph Bldg.   Home Life   Smith Gray Broadway Chambers   Dun   Stewart

BROADWAY, north from Murray St., the upper end of the office building district and the beginning of the wholesale district; centre for typewriters, office furniture and supplies, library equipment, fire-arms, safes; formerly centre of the wholesale dry goods business.

Howard St.   Printing & Book Binding Department   Lafayette St.

BRADSTREET'S BUILDING, Lafayette St., N. W. cor. Howard. Widely known Mercantile Agency, established over 60 years, connections over civilized world, issues quarterly volume of commercial ratings of bankers, merchants, etc. Executive offices 346 B'way.

Dun Building   Chambers St.   Main Entrance, Hall of Records, flanked by Philip Martiny's groups of Indians and early settlers   Centre St.   Shot Tower

HALL OF RECORDS, Chambers St., N.W. cor. Centre, through to Reade St.; $10,000,000 steel and granite structure for the preservation of the real-estate records of New York County; interior finish marble, bronze and mahogany; offices of the Register, County Clerk, Surrogate, and Tax and Law Departments. The 32 granite monoliths cost $30,000 each. The sculptures include emblematic figures by Bush-Brown and Martiny and statues of 8 men prominent in the city's history. John R. Thomas and Horgan & Slattery, Architects; John Peirce, Builder.

Broadway   R. G. Dun & Co.'s Mercantile Agency   Reade St.

DUN BUILDING, N. E. cor. Broadway and Reade St.; 15 stories, 223 ft. high; headquarters of famous Mercantile Agency, which furnishes accurate records and ratings of
merchants throughout the world; publishes Dun's Review, Domestic and International.

North River   121-127 Charlton Street   E. R. Durkee & Co.   Washington St.

E. R. DURKEE & CO , 534-540 Washington St., cor. Charlton St., typical ten-story
factory and warehouse building of America's foremost spice and condiment importers and
manufacturers, famous for Durkee's and Gauntlet brands, synonyms of quality.

Washington St.   Fairchild Building   Laight St.

FAIRCHILD BROS. & FOSTER, 70-76 Laight Street. Founded 1879. Manufacturers of
Preparations of Digestive Ferments and other Pharmaceutical Products: Pepsencia,
Panopepton, Peptogenic Powder, Peptonising Tubes, Laibose, etc.

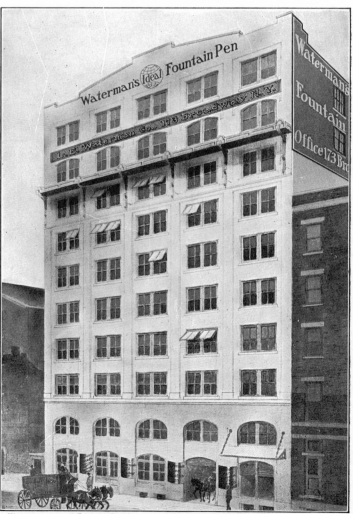

Water St.   Offices 173 Broadway   34-40 Fletcher St.   Front St.

WATERMAN'S IDEAL FOUNTAIN PEN FACTORY, 10-story concrete bldg. devoted
exclusively to making Waterman's Ideal Fountain Pen and Ink; 35,000 sq. ft. floor space;
capacity 1,500,000 a year; other factories, Seymour, Conn., and St. Lambert, Canada.

Broome Street Tabernacle   Broome Street   Centre Street, Subway Bridge Loop under Street   Police Headquarters, Hoppin & Koen, Arch.   Grand Street

POLICE HEADQUARTERS, Centre St. to Centre Market Pl., Broome to Grand Sts.; 310 ft. long; 46 ft. at Broome St. end; 88 ft. at Grand St. end; imposing Indiana-limestone building, granite base; cost $1,500,000; most complete and perfectly appointed police-headquarters in world; offices of Commissioner, Deputy Commissioners and Chief Inspector; Detective Bureau and Rogues Gallery; School of Instruction; large drill-room and gymnasium; Uniformed force of 10,835, including 500 mounted men and 100 bicycle police. Arthur Woods, Commissioner.

Fourth Ave.   Broadway   Union Square   University Pl.   Fifth Ave.   Sixth Ave.   Retail Shopping District

NIGHT SCENE, remarkable photograph taken from the Metropolitan Life Tower at 23d St. and Madison Ave., showing the Singer Tower, at Broadway and Liberty St., 2½ miles to the south, near the centre of the view, and the lights of the Brooklyn Bridge, to the left; the pillars topped by electric lights, just to the right of the centre of the picture, mark Fifth Ave. illuminated for the Hudson-Fulton celebration, September, 1909, and in the right foreground are some of the great stores of the retail shopping district, while the loft buildings of Fourth Ave. fill the left foreground.

Lofts on 4th Ave.   Metropolitan Life   Hotel McAlpin   Broadway   R. H. Macy   Municipal Bldg.   Herald Sq. Bldg.   Skyscrapers

RETAIL SHOPPING DISTRICT, view southward from the Times Building at 42d St., where the human tide surges to and fro through the whole twenty-four hours; at the right on Seventh Ave. is the Pennsylvania Station; here the part of Broadway in the foreground is the centre of the hotel district and the heart of the theatre district, while the retail shops and great department stores line the thoroughfare for two miles. Sixth Ave., crossing Broadway at 34th St., is a shopping thoroughfare nearly its entire length of three miles; at the left the great new stores that have made Fifth Ave. the greatest retail dry goods centre; farther to the left rise the new lofts on Fourth Ave., where the wholesale dry goods trade is developing a new centre; the Metropolitan tower looms up at Madison Square; the skyscrapers of lower Broadway appear in the distance.

Jersey City   Hudson River   Penn R. R. Station   Seventh Ave.   Mills Hotel

THE BOWERY, north from Grand St.; the Bouwerie Lane of the Dutch period, along which were located the "bouweries" or country-seats of the wealthy; afterwards famous for many years for its dance halls, theatres and night resorts; now a busy shopping thoroughfare and the centre of a district given over to small manufacturing and to jobbing houses.

APPELLATE COURT, Madison Ave. and 25th St.; magnificent marble court house erected in 1900 at a cost of $750,000, richly embellished with statuary, paintings and tapestry; occupied by the Appellate Division of the Supreme Court, the court of last resort on appeals from the Supreme Court, except on questions of law, composed of seven justices designated by the Governor.

N. Y. Central and New Haven R. Rs. under Park Ave.

PARK AVENUE, north from 59th St., where the apartment house has reached its highest development in luxurious housekeeping suites some containing 19 rooms and 8 baths and renting for $11,000 a year; branch of municipal subway is being built under 59th St.

Sixth Ave.   South Side of West 29th St.   Seventh Ave.

E. G. SOLTMANN, 134-140 W. 29th St. 12-story modern loft building, example of new type of fireproof construction being widely used for office and light manufacturing purposes. Most extensive plant for production of blue prints and drawing materials.

FIRE AND POLICE DEPARTMENTS. 1. Testing the high pressure service in West St.; water pumped through a system of 108 miles of mains and delivered at a pressure of 300 pounds. 2. Fire Boats in action; equipped with powerful pumps these boats afford efficient protection against water front fires. 3. Motor-driven Fire Apparatus, rapidly supplanting the horse-drawn equipment. 4. City Prison, on site of "The Tombs," Centre St., Leonard to Franklin, erected 1897 to hold prisoners awaiting trial, connected by "The Bridge of Sighs," with (5) Criminal Courts Building.

Third Ave. "L"　　Consolidated Gas Co.'s Building　　E. 15th St.　　Irving Place　　Academy of Music, erected 1866　　Third Ave.　　E. 15th St.　　Consolidated Gas Building as illuminated at night　　N. Y. Edison Co.　　Irving Place
CONSOLIDATED GAS COMPANY'S BUILDING, S. E. cor. Irving Pl. & E. 15th St.; Headquarters of Consolidated Gas Co., largest in world.　George Bruce Cortelyou, Pres.　Building, completed 1914, noted for magnificent exterior illumination and wonderful construction; 257 ft., 19 stories high; 85 ft. on Irving Pl., 297 ft. on E. 15th St. where 5 stories are suspended from huge girders between two 19 story structures over one of 12, built 1912.　Only building with hanging floors.　Two kitchens, one for gas, other for electricity.　Company furnishes nearly 2,000 employees' with noon meal at cost.　Headquarters also of N. Y. Edison Co., New Amsterdam Gas Co., Standard Gas Light Co., United Electric Light & Power Co.　These companies furnish gas and electricity for light, heat and power in Manhattan and Bronx.

Bank of the Metropolis   Decker Bldg.   Hartford Bldg.   "Flat-Iron"   Broadway   "Century"   Metropolitan Tower   Everett Bldg.   Fourth Ave.   Germania Life   Union Square Savings Bank

UNION SQUARE, Broadway to Fourth Ave., 14th to 17th St.; 3.48 acres set apart as a park in 1809; scene of reception to Gen. Washington, Evacuation Day, Nov. 25, 1783; Croton Water celebration, Oct. 14, 1842; Union Defence mass meeting, 1861; for a generation the heart of the hotel district; recently developed as a mercantile centre by the erection of huge loft buildings along Fourth Ave. on sites of the Everett House, at 17th St.; Hotels Clarendon, Florence and Belvedere at 18th St., Ashland at 24th St. and Putnam at 28th St. Subway under Fourth Ave.

Subway Express Station, 4th Ave. and 14th St.   Steinway Hall

STEINWAY & SONS, Steinway Hall, 107-109 E. 14th St., erected 1866; for a quarter of century the most famous concert hall in America; headquarters of best known piano manufacturers.   Factories at Steinway, Long Island and Hamburg, Germany.

Everett Bldg.   Fourth Ave.   Germania Life Bldg.   East 17th Street

GERMANIA LIFE INSURANCE CO. BLDG., N. E. cor. 4th Ave. & E. 17th St.; built 1910; cost $2,200,000; 281 ft. high.   Company fd. 1860; insurance in force over $150,000,000; assets over $50,000,000; income 1914, $9,000,000.

Hudson River   St. Bartholomew's Church   The Palisades   St. Nicholas Collegiate Church   Ritz-Carlton Hotel   St. Patrick's   Gotham   Pla

MOSES KING, INC.
PUBLISHERS.

Vanderbilt Ave.   E. 42d St.   Ligget's Drug Store   Elevated Driveway encircling station, connected with Park Ave. on the north at 45th St. and by bridge over 42d St. with Park Ave. on the south at

GRAND CENTRAL TERMINAL, East 42d St., Vanderbilt to Lexington Ave.; world's largest and most costly railroad station, terminal of the vast system of railroads known as the New York Central lines an 33½ miles of tracks, room for 1,149 cars; four levels—gallery, 90 x 300 ft., at driveway level; main concourse, 120 x 300 ft., room for 10,000 passengers, and waiting room for 5,000 people, at 42d St. lev incoming trains after discharging passengers pass around loops to the train yard under offices east of station; 85,000 tons of steel used in construction of terminal, 3,000,000 cubic yards of earth and rock excava

St. Regis   Netherland   Central Park   Harlem   Park Ave.   Grand Central Palace   Ward's Island   Hell Gate   Queensboro B'idge   East River

Twelve entrances at street level   Depew Place   New York Central General Offices and Branch Post Office   Lexington Ave.

e New York, New Haven and Hartford Railroad; covers 69.8 acres; station proper, 310 x 672 ft., 150 ft. high; below street level, 455 x 745 ft., 45 ft. deep; capacity for 200 trains and 70,000 passengers an hour; 42 tracks for express long distance trains; suburban concourse 25 ft. below street, 25 tracks for suburban trains; under these tracks, baggage and express subways run east and west, connecting with each track; rain yards and approaches, extending to 57th St., will be covered with business blocks, hotels and a great amphitheatre. Old Grand Central Station, erected in the seventies, enlarged 1900, covered 23 acres.

E. 26th St.   Madison Sq. Garden   Manhattan Club   Appellate Court   Metropolitan Annex   Metropolitan Bldg.   E. 23d St.   Broadway   "Flat-Iron" Fifth Ave. Fifth Ave. Bldg.

MADISON SQUARE, showing Fifth Ave. at the right, crossed by Broadway at 23d St.; here, between Bloomingdale Road (Broadway) and the Boston Post Road (Third Ave.) a great tract was set apart in 1811 for a parade ground; 6.84 acres remain, bounded by Broadway and Madison Ave. and 23d and 26th St.; this was for a generation the centre of the hotel and theatre district; the Fifth Avenue Hotel, erected in 1858, for half a century was the most famous hostelry in America; it was torn down in 1908 and the 14-story Fifth Avenue Building was erected on its site.

W. 23d Street   Site of Fifth Avenue Hotel, 1858-1908   Fifth Avenue and Broadway   Opposite Madison Square   Broadway   Albemarle

FIFTH AVENUE BUILDING, office structure, facing Madison Sq. where Broadway crosses Fifth Ave. diagonally, with 197.5 ft. frontage, extending 259.8 ft. along 23d St., 264.7 ft. along 24th St., 18 full city lots, over 13 acres of floor space.   Built of steel, granite, limestone and brick; 14 stories high, Maynicke & Franke, Architects, Fifth Avenue Building Co., owners.   Henry C. Eno, Pres.; Walter E. Maynard, Vice-Pres. and Gen'l Manager; Henry Lane Eno, Treas.   In heart of shopping district, on historic site of Corporal Thompson's Inn, 1830; Franconi's Hippodrome, 1853.

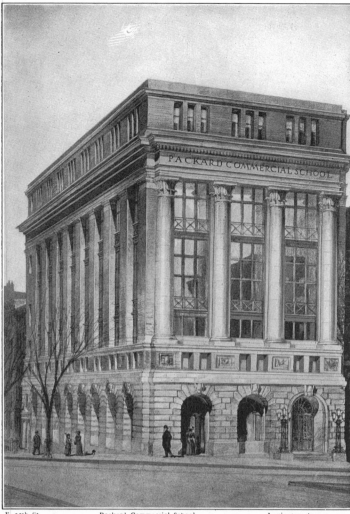

E. 35th St.   Packard Commercial School   Lexington Ave.

PACKARD COMMERCIAL SCHOOL, S. E. cor. Lexington Ave. and East 35th St.; founded in 1858 by S. S. Packard; commercial, stenographic and secretarial courses, also higher accounting and auditing; new fireproof building, occupied August, 1911.

Broadway   Mutual Bank, 49-51 West 33d St.   Fifth Ave.

MUTUAL BANK, new banking house erected 1911; capital and surplus, $700,000; deposits, $7,200,000; assets, $8,000,000; one of the substantial financial institutions of the great retail shopping district. C. A. Sackett, Pres., Hugh N. Kirkland, V. Pres. and Cashier.

Broadway   W. 22d St.   "Flat-Iron," D. H. Burnham & Co., Arch.   Fifth Ave.

FULLER BUILDING, called "Flat Iron," Broadway, Fifth Ave., and 23d St., first great triumph of steel frame construction; built by the George A. Fuller Co.; 300 ft. high; 120,000 sq. ft. floor space on plot of 7,690 sq. ft.; 13,340 sq. ft. under sidewalks.

W. 34th St.   Broadway and Sixth Ave., 206.5 ft. frontage   Liggett's Drug Store   E. 33d St., 150 ft. frontage
HOTEL McALPIN, Broadway, 33d to 34th Sts.; 25 stories, with 3 sub-basements; largest capacity in the world, 1,620 rooms, all light, with 1,100 baths; 1,800 telephones, largest private exchange, 30x120 ft.; 7 miles steam pipes; 115 miles wiring; ball room, 46x84 ft., 25 ft. high; banquet room, 32x80 ft.; club room for men guests, 65x96 ft.; cost, $13,500,000.   Greeley Square Hotel Co.

Soc. Prev. Cruelty to Animals   Madison Avenue   Madison Square Garden, McKim, Mead & White, Arch.   E. 26th St.   Manhattan Club
MADISON SQUARE GARDEN, Madison to 4th Ave., 26th to 27th St.; occupying entire city block, 425 by 200 ft.; tower 341 ft. high; statue of Diana, 13 ft. high, by Augustus St. Gaudens; erected 1890; cost $3,000,000; largest amphitheatre in America, 300 by 200 ft., 80 ft. high, arena 268 by 122 ft.; seats 12,000.   Scene of great political meetings.

Annex   Madison Sq. Presbyterian Church   E. 24th St.   Metropolitan Building, N. LeBrun & Sons, Architects   E. 23d St.

METROPOLITAN LIFE INSURANCE COMPANY, 1 Madison Avenue; magnificent carved marble office building, facing Madison Square; occupying entire block, with arcade to Fourth Avenue and annex across 24th Street; tower, 52 stories, 700 feet high, 75 x 90 feet at base; view of New York and surroundings for 20 miles from top; Home office of the greatest insurance corporation, organized 1868; 13,957,000 policies in force, representing insurance aggregating more than $2,816,000,000   John R. Hegeman, President.

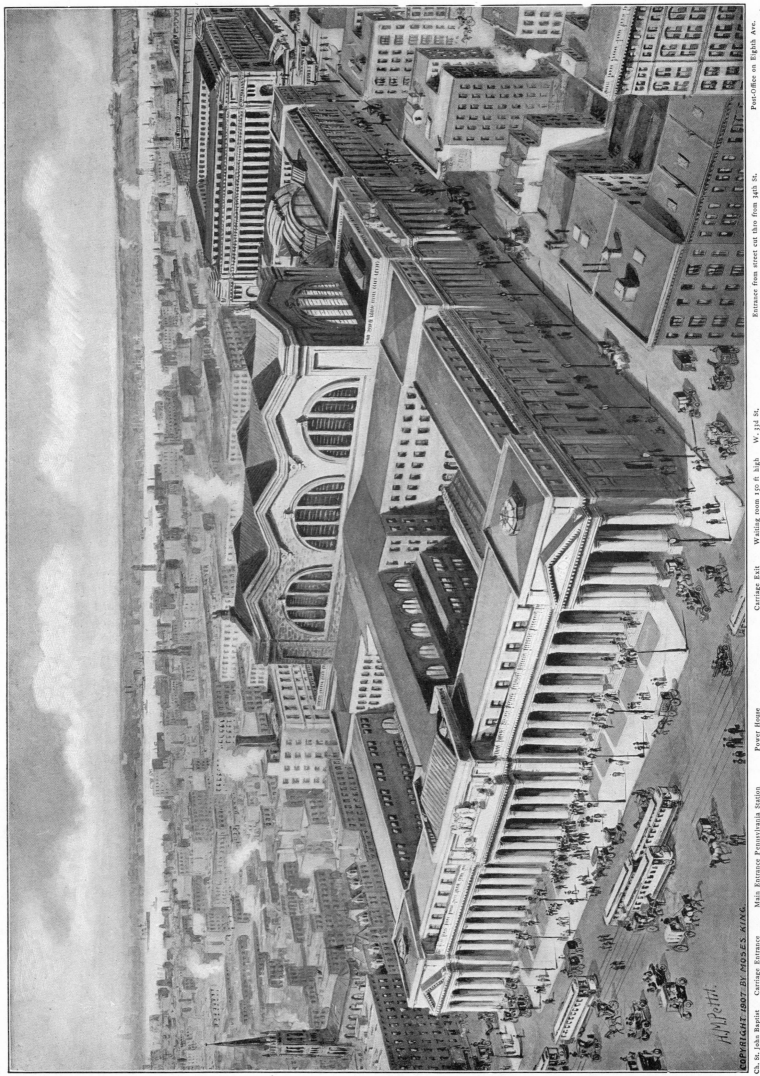

Ch. St. John Baptist   Carriage Entrance   Main Entrance Pennsylvania Station   Power House   Carriage Exit   Waiting room 150 ft high   W. 33d St.   Entrance from street cut thro from 34th St.   Post-Office on Eighth Ave.

PENNSYLVANIA STATION, 7th to 8th Aves., 31st to 33d Sts.; assessed at $19,500,000; 784x430 ft.; arcade, 46 x 216 ft.; two small waiting rooms, each 56 x 100 ft.; two waiting rooms, 277 x 108 ft.; main concourse, 124 x 500 ft. extending under streets, with two stairways to each train platform; exit concourse, 60 x 1088 ft. with elevators to each platform; train shed 340 x 210 ft.; cabstand 20 ft. below street; baggage room under arcade, with 430-ft. platform for transfer wagons; 21,500 ft. train platforms; 39,000 tons structural steel, 27,000 tons structural steel, 650 supporting columns.   Twin tunnels under the Hudson river; train yard at Tenth Ave., 60 ft. below surface; 25 tracks in station; tunnels under 32d and 33d Sts. and East River to Long Island R. R.   Cost of entire work over $100,000,000.   Station opened Sept. 8, 1910.

W. 31st St.   Eighth Ave., opposite Pennsylvania Railroad Station   McKim, Meade & White, Architects   Geo. A. Fuller Co., Builders   W. 33d St.   Ninth Ave.

NEW GENERAL POST OFFICE, Eighth Ave., 31st to 33d Sts., $6,200,000 structure over the station tracks and car yards of the Pennsylvania Railroad, 375 x 335 ft.; offices of the Postmaster and his chief assistants on the second floor front; executive offices of the Railway Mail Service, third floor front; headquarters Sea Post; supply department; letter mail handled on first floor, second class in basement; direct connection by chutes and elevators from each floor with railway mail cars on tracks under the post office; basement occupied in the fall of 1910; entire building in 1914.

RAPID TRANSIT. (1) Hudson Tubes, two to Jersey City at Cortlandt St., two to Hoboken at Christopher St., extension to Newark, lateral tunnel under Jersey City and Hoboken, subway under Sixth Ave. to 33d St., to be extended to Grand Central Station. (2) Eighteenth St. Station and (4) Spring St. municipal subway, leased to Interboro Rapid Transit Co.; Atlantic Ave., Brooklyn, under East River, length of Manhattan, to Van Cortlandt Park, 242d St., Bronx; branch from 96th St. and Broadway, under Central Park and Harlem to Bronx Park; 81.9 miles of tracks; cost, with equipment, $75,000,000. (3) Penn. R.R. tunnels, two under Hudson, four under East River. (5) Viaduct, carrying subway across Manhattan Valley.

Gimbel's   Sixth Ave. "L" Road and Station   Saks & Co.   Herald Square "Herald"   Hotel McAlpin   Broadway   W. 33d St.   Wilson Building

BROADWAY, from Greeley Square to Times Square, showing city's greatest thoroughfare intersected by Sixth Ave. and 34th St. with three great department stores at the left; upper end of most important retail shopping district in the world, which extends from Eighth St.; centre of largest hotel district; known as "The Great White Way," from the brilliance of the electric signs. Branch of new municipal subway is being constructed under this section of Broadway. Hudson Tubes now terminating under elevated R. R. station to be extended to 42d St. to Grand Central.

Saks   R. H. Macy & Co.   Met. Opera "Times" Astor   Broadway   World's Tower   "Herald"   Sixth Ave.   "L" Road   Marbridge Bldg.

HERALD SQUARE AND BROADWAY, north from "L" Station at 33d St., showing the Rialto, or "Great White Way," extending from 34th St. to Times Square, centre of largest theatre district in world; filled with shoppers and theatrical folk by day and playgoers by night. The "Herald," founded 1835 by James Gordon Bennett, Sr., now conducted by his son, and evening edition, "The Telegram," occupy building of early Florentine design. Large office building to occupy block from 35th to 36th St. opp. Herald. SIXTH AVENUE is filled with retail shops.

71st Regiment Armory   Future Dry Goods Centre   Park Ave. Hotel   Hotel Vanderbilt

FOURTH AVENUE, south from 34th St.; important wholesale centre developed within
half a dozen years by the erection of modern fireproof loft buildings; now occupied by
many of the houses that made Broadway the greatest jobbing district of the world.

Hotel Biltmore   E. 44th St.   James Gambrill Rogers, Architect   Vanderbilt Ave.

YALE CLUB, N. W. cor. Vanderbilt Ave. and 44th St.; founded 1897; new building
erected 1914; 100 x 73 ft.; 20 stories; cost $500,000; 1,750 resident members; 1,600
non-residents. Growth of club made former home at 30 West 44th St. inadequate.

108-110-112 West Fortieth Street

WORLD'S TOWER BUILDING, 30 story structure, tallest office building ever built in
the world on this size plot, also one of the most handsome. Owner and builder, Edward
West Browning, who also holds a number of other world's records in the building line.

AMERICAN REAL ESTATE COMPANY. 1. Hendrik Hudson Annex, N. W. cor. 110th St. & Broadway. 2. Hendrik Hudson Apartment Building, 110th St. & Riverside Drive. 3. Merchants Exchange Building, S. W. cor. Fifth Ave. & 17th St., 18 stories. 4. Apartment Building, 40-46 E. 62d St. 5. General Offices American Real Estate Co., 527 Fifth Ave., S. E. cor. 44th St. 6. Arena Building, 39-41 W. 31st St. through to 38-40 W. 32d St. 7. Alta Ave., Park Hill, Yonkers. 8. Apartment House, 163d St. Fox & Simpson Sts., Bronx. 9. Bronx Theatre Building, 150th St. & Melrose Ave. 10. A-re-co Court Apartment Buildings, Westchester Ave. & Southern Boulevard, Bronx. 11. Watson A-re-co Property, Bronx. Company founded 1888; pioneer corporation in buying and improving New York real estate; capital and surplus, $3,247,789. E. B. Boynton, President.

W. 38th St.　　　　424-434 Fifth Ave.　　　　Vantines　　　W. 45th St.　　　West Side of Fifth Ave.　　W. 46th St.

LORD & TAYLOR, dry goods, Fifth Ave., 38th to 39th Sts.; established in 1826 in Catharine St.; many years at Broad- ANDREW ALEXANDER, 548 Fifth Avenue, one of the most famous boot way and Grand St.; at Broadway and 20th St., 1871 to 1914; new store, 600,000 sq. ft. floor space, occupied Feb. and shoe houses in America, noted for style and quality; luxurious and uniquely 24, 1914, ten stories, every modern convenience for shoppers and workers. Joseph H. Emery, President. ornamental building, fashionable branch of main store, 304-308 Sixth Ave.

Cambridge Bldg.　W. 33d St.　Waldorf-Astoria　Columbia-Knickerbocker Trust　Brick Pres. Ch.　St. Patrick's　Tiffany's　Altman's　McCutcheon's　Old Residences, now Shops

FIFTH AVENUE, looking north from 33d St., the famous Murray Hill section, once the heart of fashion, now occupied by some of the world's largest and foremost retail stores, he centre of the largest retail dry goods trade in the world; Waldorf-Astoria, 214 ft. high, 1,400 rooms. The Robert Murray homestead was just east of the site of Tiffany's; on Sept. 15, 1776, Mrs. Murray delayed Gen. Howe as he led the British Army past her home, enabling Gen. Washington to retreat to Harlem Heights. Columbia-Knickerbocker Trust Co., $58,300,000 deposits.

W. 46th St.　　7th Ave.　　New York Theatre　Hotel Claridge　　　"Times"　　　　Hotel Astor　Astor Theatre　Gaiety Theatre　　　　　Broadway　　　　　Globe Theatre

"TIMES" SQUARE, formerly called Longacre, formed by the intersection of Broadway and Seventh Ave., extending from the "Times" Building, at 42d St., to 47th St., centre of the theatre and hotel district; 37 of the foremost playhouses in America within 250 yards, with seating capacity for audiences aggregating 45,000; Metropolitan Opera House two blocks below 42d St.; Hippodrome, largest playhouse in world, one block east; more people pass 42d St. and Broadway in 24 hours than any other point in world; 40 great restaurants, some of world wide reputation, within 400 yds.

Park Ave.　　Hotel Belmont, 292 ft. high　　　　Lincoln Nat. Bank　　42d St. Building　Candler Bldg.　　Hotel Manhattan　　　Liggett's Drug Store　　　Grand Central Station

FORTY-SECOND STREET, looking west from Park Ave., which is to be carried over 42d St. by viaduct and to run around Grand Central Station on the elevated roadway marked by the lamp posts on the right of the picture. Subway under 42d St., which is the busiest thoroughfare in the world, with thousands of passengers arriving every hour from east, west and north; terminus of Steinway tunnel to Queens; Hudson tubes to be extended to this point. Lincoln National Bank, deposits, $16,500,000; huge safe deposit vaults. Headquarters National Progressive Party in 42d St. building.

Murray Hill Hotel   Park Ave.   Hotel Belmont   E. 42d St.   Lincoln Nat. Bank

HOTEL BELMONT, Park Avenue, 41st to 42d St.; tallest hotel in the world, 292 ft. high; 258,400 Sq. ft. floor area; subway curves under bldg. from Park Ave. into 42d St.; built by Subway Realty Co., 1905; leased by Aug. Belmont Hotel Co., B. L. M. Bates, Mgr.

West 58th St.   5th Ave.   Plaza Hotel   Central Park South   Central Park

THE PLAZA HOTEL, Fifth Ave., 58th St., to Central Park South; cost $12,500,000, 19 stories, 252 ft. high, model of elegance and delicate beauty; five marble staircases; two great dining-rooms; ballroom accommodating 500.   Fred Sterry, Managing Director.

Fifth Ave.   Delmonico's   East 44th St.

DELMONICO'S, Fifth Ave., N. E. cor. 44th St.; most famous restaurant in America; scenes of many notable banquets; fd. by John Delmonico in 1828 at 23 William St., now on sixth site, having kept pace with uptown movement; branch, Beaver St., since 1835.

Vanderbilt Ave. Building   E. 43d St.   Vanderbilt Ave.

HOTEL BILTMORE, Vanderbilt to Madison Ave., 43d to 44th St.; 26 stories; 200 x 215 ft.; erected 1912 by N. Y. Central R. R.; Warren & Wetmore, Architects; 1,000 rooms; one of world's finest hotels; cost $4,500,000; Gustav Baumann, Pres.

Fifth Avenue   N. Y. Athletic Club   Central Park   Maine Monument   Gainsborough Studios   Central Park South   Broadway   Columbus Monument   "American"   Eighth Ave.   Thoroughfare Bldg.   Park Theatre   W. 59th St.   N. Y. Nautical College

COLUMBUS CIRCLE, formed by intersection of Broadway and Eighth Ave. at southwest corner of Central Park, beginning of boulevard section of Broadway; subway under Broadway; another being built under Seventh Avenue, turning eastward under Central Park South (59th St.) and crossing Queensboro Bridge.   COLUMBUS MONUMENT, heroic figure of Christopher Columbus, made in Italy, surmounting a column ornamented with bronze reliefs, erected by Italian residents in America; unveiled October 12, 1892, in commemoration of the 400th anniversary of the discovery of America.   MAINE MONUMENT, erected by the contributions of a million Americans in memory of the victims of the blowing up of the Battleship "Maine" in Havana Harbor, Feb. 15, 1898; unveiled May 30, 1913; Attilio Piccirilli, sculptor; cost $175,000.

New York Public Library   W. 42d St.   Bristol Bldg.   Temple Emanu-El   Fifth Ave.

FIFTH AVENUE, north from 40th St. to St. Patrick's Cathedral, for two generations the thoroughfare of fashion, now a congested business section, filled daily with the equipages of the wealthy; club and theatre district on the left; hotels on both sides; subway under 42d St.; retail shops as far as 57th St. Hudson tubes to be extended at lower level to Grand Central Station, two blocks to the right.

W. 44th St.   Times Square (formerly Longacre), formed by intersection of Broadway and Seventh Ave.   W. 45th St.

HOTEL ASTOR, Broadway, 44th to 45th Sts., facing Times Square; built and furnished by William Waldorf Astor, in 1904, at a cost of $7,000,000; enlarged 1909 at a cost of $3,000,000, 900 suites with baths; banquet hall seating 1,200; exquisite restaurant on main floor; private dining rooms; meeting rooms; headquarters Federation of Women's Clubs; roof garden; Wm. C. Muschenheim, Prop.

Amusement Places

THEATRES. 1. Manhattan Opera House, 34th near 8th Ave., seats 3,450. 2. Polo Grounds, 8th Ave. & 155th, the "Giants" home field, scene of National League base ball games, seat 30,000. 3. The Playhouse, 141 W. 48th, 879. 4. Metropolitan Opera House, Broadway, 39th-40th, 3,366; Gatti Casazza, Director. 5. Century, Central Park West & 62d, home of grand opera in English, 2,050; Milton & Sargent Aborn. 6. The Strand, Broadway & 47th, 1,530. 7. New York, Broadway and 45th, 1,750. 8. Belasco, 115 W. 44th, 1,000. 9. Hippodrome, Sixth Ave., 43d-44th, 5,200; largest playhouse in world; Sam S. & Lee Shubert, Inc. 10. Carnegie Hall, 7th Ave. & 57th, 2,860; Carnegie Lyceum, 697; American Academy of Dramatic Arts. 11. Cort, 48th near Broadway, 1,000. 12. Casino, Broadway & 39th; Knickerbocker, Broadway & 38th, 1,352.

Williamsburgh Bridge   Manhattan Bridge   B'klyn Bridge   Singer Tower   Metropolitan Tower   Jersey City   St. Patrick's Cathedral   "Times"   Plaza Hotel   Hudson River

EAST RIVER BRIDGES, with view of Manhattan from Harlem to Battery, New Jersey west of the Hudson River, Blackwell's Island in East River, Long Island City and Astoria Section to east.

COPYRIGHT 1908 BY MOSES KING

East River   Penna. R. R. Power House   Long Island City   Astoria in foreground   Edison Power House, 39th St.   Queensboro Bridge   Connecting Ry.   "L" Power House, 74th St.   Hallet's Point

EAST RIVER BRIDGES, with view of Manhattan from Harlem to Battery, New Jersey west of the Hudson River, Blackwell's Island in East River, Long Island City and Astoria Section to east.   HELL GATE
   HELL GATE BRIDGE, longest steel arch in the world, 1,000 ft. long; 220 ft. high, heaviest, 80,000 tons; granite abutments; concrete towers 200 ft. high; carrying four tracks of Connecting Railway, which
      Bronx Kills to N. Y., New Haven & Hartford R. R.; connection with Penna. main line through tunnels under East River, Manhattan and the Hudson.   Cost, $14,000,000.   Queensboro Bridge (p. 7).

Hell Gate Bridge, Gustav Lindenthal, Arch. and Eng'r.   Ward's Island   Metropolitan Power House, 104th St.   Harlem River   Manhattan State Hospital for Insane   East River

ent and difficult passage, where East River makes a sharp turn, meeting point of the tides of Long Island Sound and New York Bay, 26-foot channel formed by blowing up reef after 25 years' work. es Penna. R.R. freight cars from floats at Bay Ridge, runs through Brooklyn and Queens, and by bridge and 17,000 ft. of steel viaduct crosses Hell Gate, Ward's Island, Little Hell Gate, Randall's Island and msburg, Manhattan and Brooklyn Bridges (pp. 6 and 7.) City owns 47 bridges, including 4 greatest in world; total length 18½ miles, cost $150,000,000; land occupied worth $1,000,000,000.

Obelisk   South Wing, completed 1889   East 81st St.   East Wing, 344x200 ft. completed 1901, Thomas Dwyer, Builder   Main Entrance   Northeast Wing, 1907   North Wing, 1913

METROPOLITAN MUSEUM OF ART, Central Park, facing Fifth Ave. at 82d St., inc. 1871; centre of present group, occupied 1880; additions, '89, '94, '01, '07, '13; designed by Richard M. Hunt to cover 18½ acres and cost $20,000,000. Developed by late Henry G. Marquand and the late Gen. Louis P. di Cesnola; becoming world's richest museum under presidency of the late J. Pierpont Morgan, '04-'13. 40,000 exhibits added in 8 years; $50,000,000 Morgan collections; 839,419 visitors in 1913; expenses $375,000. Robert W. De Forest, Pres. Edward Robinson, Director.

Columbus Ave.   6th & 9th Aves. "L"   Northern half of group and Central Tower not yet built   77th St. façade cost $4,438,000; Cady, Berg & See, Archs.   Reservoirs in Central Park   Central Park West

AMERICAN MUSEUM OF NATURAL HISTORY, Manhattan Square, W. 77th to 81st St.; founded '69; opened '77; largest natural-history museum in world; collections worth $12,000,000; 600,000 visitors annually; buildings erected and running expenses paid by city; scientific expeditions conducted from the fees of 3,700 members and income from endowment of $7,000,000 to which Morris K. Jesup, for years its president, added $1,000,000 by bequest and his widow $5,000,000; Prof. Henry Fairfield Osborn, President; Dr. Fredk. A. Lucas, Director.

W. 40th St.   American History, 2d floor rear   Periodical Room, Main floor   Art Gallery, 2d floor front   Carrère & Hastings, Architects   Main Entrance, Fifth Avenue Circulating Department, on 42d St.
NEW YORK PUBLIC LIBRARY, Fifth Ave., 40th to 42d St.; $9,000,000 marble building; cornerstone laid Nov. 10, 1902; opened May 23, 1911; 390x270 ft.; two inner courts, each 80 ft. sq.; main stack room, 270 ft. long, 7 tiers; 2,133,608 volumes, room for 3,000,000; 7,300 periodicals on file.   Astor Library, 1849; Lenox, '70; Tilden Trust, '87; consolidated, '95; 43 circulating branches, 8,111,785 books taken out in year by 325,000 people.   442,091 readers in libraries.   Geo. L. Rives, Pres   Edwin H. Anderson, Director.

1. DE WITT CLINTON HIGH SCHOOL, 10th Ave., 58th to 59th St.; 138 teachers; 3,654 pupils.   2. MORRIS HIGH SCHOOL, 166th St. and Boston Road, The Bronx; 125 teachers; 3,218 pupils.   3. WADLEIGH HIGH SCHOOL, 114th St., near 7th Ave., Harlem; 141 teachers; 3,045 pupils.   4. HIGH SCHOOL OF COMMERCE, 65th St., near Broadway; 100 teachers; 2,774 pupils. 23 High Schools; 2,053 instructors and 50,511 pupils; 16 Night High Schools.   Cost of schools 1914, $38,203,406.   T.W. Churchill, Pres. Bd. of Education.

Central Park, East Drive   St. Gaudens' Statue of Sherman   Fifth Ave.   Metropolitan Club   Plaza Br. Union Trust Co.   Hotel Netherland   E. 59th St.   Savoy Hotel

FIFTH AVENUE, looking north from the Plaza, 58th to 59th St.; showing carriage entrance to Central Park; Savoy Hotel and Hotel Netherland, two of the most sumptuously appointed hostelries in the world, opposite Plaza Hotel, and the Plaza Branch of the Union Trust Co.   The Metropolitan Club, most exclusive and most wealthy in the world, is at 60th St., and residence of Commodore Elbridge T. Gerry at 61st St.   Here are homes of men of affairs—George J. Gould, 67th St.; Henry C. Frick, 70th St.; former Senator W. A. Clark, 77th St.; Andrew Carnegie, 91st St.

E. 59th St.   Savoy Hotel   Fifth Ave. Bus   Hotel St. Regis   Fifth Ave.   Hotel Gotham   Vanderbilt Residence   W. 58th St.

THE PLAZA, looking down Fifth Ave. to St. Patrick's Cathedral, from S. E. cor. of Central Park, showing three of the city's greatest hotels, representing the highest development of modern times in the art of caring elegantly for the comfort of wealthy patrons; finest location in the city, on high ground, the social centre of New York, on the avenue of fashion, close to Central Park, convenient to the theatres and shopping district on the south, and connected by the Park drives and West 72d Street with the new residential section developed along Riverside Drive and West End Ave.

The Palisades | Hudson River | Fort Lee Ferry | Fort Washington Point | Washington Heights | Grant's Tomb | Apartment Houses

W. 97th St. Pier   N. Y. Central R. R.   Bloomingdale Boat Club   Columbia University Boat House   Riverside Park   Riverside Drive   The Clifden

RIVERSIDE PARK and DRIVE north from W. 98th St. to Grant's Tomb, Fort Washington Point in the middle distance, Recreation Pier beyond boat house erected for Columbia University crew by Edwin Gould where the Hudson affords ample room for rowing and the speeding of power boats; here the "flat" finds its highest development in magnificent apartment houses. Riverside Drive, varying in width from 90 to 168 ft., extends three miles from 72d St. to 129th where it is carried by viaduct over Manhattan Valley to an extension which reaches to Dyckman St.

Soldiers' Monument | Apartment Houses | Belnord and Bretton Hall | The Apthrop | The Lombard | The Wellsmore

Riverside Park   Riverside Drive   W. 75th St.   Geo. H. Macy Residence   W. 74th St.   W. H. Beardsley Residence   W. 73d St.   Charles M. Schwab Residence

RIVERSIDE PARK, W. 72d St. to W. 129th, along Hudson River; 140 acres, acquired by the city 1872-1901. RIVERSIDE DRIVE, from W. 72d St. to the Soldiers' and Sailors' Monument at 89th St. This is the finest residence district in the city, where lots 100 ft. deep are worth from $1,200 to $1,600 a front foot on the Drive, from $700 to $1,100 on the adjacent side streets; Schwab residence, occupying the block from 73d to 74th St. through to West End Ave. is assessed at $1,700,000; other residences range in value from $200,000 to $350,000.

RESIDENCES. 1. Ex-U.S. Senator W. A. Clark, 5th Ave. & 77th. 2. Wm. H. Barnard, Riverside Drive & 89th. 3. L. C. Tiffany, 27 E. 72d. 4. Old H. P. Whitney Residence, 2 W. 57th. 5. Vanderbilt twin houses, 5th Ave.; H. C. Frick, 51st St. cor.; Wm. D. Sloane, 52d St. 6. Mrs. Isaac V. Brokaw, 5th Ave. and 79th. 7. Geo. J. Gould, 5th Ave. and 67th. 8. Andrew Carnegie, 5th Ave., 91st to 92d. 9. E. T. Gerry, 5th Ave., 61st. 10. Mrs. C. Vanderbilt, 5th Ave., 57th to 58th. 11. James Stillman, 9 E. 72d. 12. J. P. Morgan, Madison Ave., 36th, with private art-gallery. 13. J. D. Rockefeller, 4 W. 54th. 14. Mrs. Joseph Pulitzer, 11 E. 73d. 15. Chas. M. Schwab, Riverside Drive, 73rd to 74th. 16 E. J. Berwind, 2 E. 64th. 17. Mrs. John Jacob Astor, 5th Ave , 65th. 18. Mrs. H. O. Havemeyer, 5th Ave., 66th. 19. Stuyvesant Fish, 25 E. 78th. 20. W. K. Vanderbilt, 5th Ave., 52d.

Sacred Heart Convent   Columbia University   Grant's Tomb   Riverside Drive Viaduct   Hebrew Orphan Asylum   The Palisades   Hudson River

St. Nicholas Park and Terrace   City College, Main Bldg.   Geo B. Post & Sons, Arch.   Thomas Dwyer, Builder   W. 140th St.   Gymnasium   Townsend Harris Hall   Chemistry Bldg.   Convent Ave.   Mech. Arts Bldg.

COLLEGE OF THE CITY OF NEW YORK, St. Nicholas Terrace to Amsterdam Ave., W. 140th to W. 138th St.; imposing $4,000,000 group of fieldstone and terra cotta buildings, occupied 1905; founded 1847 as free Academy; City College, 1866; four-year collegiate course; three-year preparatory department, in Townsend Harris Hall; evening collegiate courses and extension lectures; 5,209 pupils; 260 instructors. Free tuition; supported by City at annual cost of $685,000. F. P. Bellamy, Acting-Chairman. Dr. Adolph Werner, Acting-President.

Harlem River   Webb Academy   Chancellor's Residence   Professors' Residences   The Bronx   Ohio Field   Gymnasium   Gould Hall

Hall of Sciences   Philosophy   Hall of Fame   Library   Campus   Hall of Languages   McKim, Mead & White, Arch.   Physics   Chemistry   Biology

NEW YORK UNIVERSITY; Sedgwick to Aqueduct Ave., W. 179th to W. 181st., University Heights, the Bronx; founded 1829; building erected '32-5 on Washington Sq.; splendid group on Heights occupied '94; new 10-story building on old site for co-educational Schools of Pedagogy, Law and Commerce and Graduate School; 12 departments, 409 instructors, 5,039 students; medical school, First Ave. and E. 26th St. Hall of Fame for Great Americans, colonnade 506 ft. long, $250,000 gift of Miss Helen Miller Gould (Mrs. F. J. Shepard). Dr. E. E. Brown, Chancellor.

Institutions of

Philanthrophy

PHILANTHROPIC INSTITUTIONS.   1. Woman's Hospital, 110th St. near Amsterdam Ave.; 114 beds.   2. Bellevue, E. 26th to 29th, 1st Ave. to E. River, 1235 beds.   3. Rockefeller Institute for Medical Research, E. 66th & Ave. A.   4. Roosevelt Hospital, W. 59th & 9th Ave.; 350 beds.   5. Presbyterian, E. 70th & Madison Ave.; 330 beds.   6. French, 450-458 W. 34th. 7. Montefiore Home for Chronic Invalids, Woodlawn Ave. Gun Hill Road; 450 beds.   8. Babies' Hospital, Lexington Ave. & 55th; 80 beds.   9. Mt. Sinai, 5th Ave. and 100th; 493 beds.   10. St. Luke's, W. 113th and Amsterdam Ave.; 300 beds.   11. Lying-in, 2d Ave., 17th-18th, 167 beds.   12 Municipal Lodging House, 432-438 E. 25th; 400 beds.   13. Mills Hotel No. 3, 7th Ave. & 36th; 1875 rooms.   14. Hospital for Ruptured and Crippled Children, 321 E. 42d; 250 beds.

CHURCHES

CHURCHES. 1. St. Paul the Apostle, Columbus Ave., 60th St., Paulist Fathers. 2. First Baptist, Broadway 79th St., I. M. Haldeman 3. St. Thomas, 5th Ave., 53d St., Ernest M. Stires.
4. Divine Paternity, Central Park West, 76th St., Oliver M. Hall. 5. First Christian Science, Central Park West, 96th St., R. P. Verrall. 6. St. Patrick's Cathedral, Fifth Ave., 50th to
51st St., M. J. Lavelle. 7. Chapel of Intersession (Trinity Parish) Broadway, 155th St., Milo H. Gates. 8. Transfiguration (Little Church Around the Corner), East 29th St.,
G. C. Houghton. 9. Grace, Broadway, 10th St., C. L. Slattery. 10. Our Lady of Esperanza, Riverside Drive, 156th St., A. Buisson. 11. St. Agnes' Chapel (Trinity
Parish), West 92nd St., W. W. Bellinger. 12. Broadway Tabernacle, cor. 56th St., C. E. Jefferson. 13. Temple Beth-El, 5th Ave., 76th St., Samuel Schulman.

KING'S BIRDS EYE VIEW OF BROOKLYN

Drawn by 70 ELROIT RUSSELL
COPYRIGHT 1908 BY MOSES KING

BROOKLYN BOROUGH, 77.62 square miles, from the East River to Atlantic Ocean, from New York Bay to Queens Borough.   Population, 1914, 1,916,655.   Settled 1623; incorporated 1834; consolidated with New York 1898.   Taxable property, land and improvements, $1,680,013,591, franchises, etc., $120,919,054; personalty, $46,296,870; real estate exempt from taxation, $230,774,655, total $2,078,004,170.   48 parks of 1663 acres, including Prospect, 516 acres, most beautiful in the world; 44 miles of parkways; 1,459 miles of streets.   Brooklyn is a city of homes, with 320,000 school children, yet its 5,000 factories in 1913 produced goods valued at $900,000,000.   Busiest shipping district in the world; N. Y. Dock Co., Atlantic Basin (40 acres), Erie Basin (161 acres), Bush Terminal, South Brooklyn, largest piers in the world.

Williamsburg Bridge   Broadway Ferries   Navy Yard   Wallabout Bay   Manhattan Bridge   Brooklyn Bridge   Fulton Ferry   Columbia Heights   Pierrepont Stores   Prentice Stores   N. Ger. Lloyd West Indies Line   Union Stores   Atlantic Basin   Red Hook   Erie Basin   N. Y. Bay

Fulton St. "L"   Hall of Records   Kings County Court House   Municipal Bldg., back of Borough Hall, to be replaced by $2,000,000 structure.   Polytechnic Institute   Court St.

BROOKLYN BOROUGH HALL, facing Park at Fulton and Court Sts.; City Hall prior to consolidation, 1898; white marble, 102 x 162 ft., 75 ft. high; offices of Borough President.   Brooklyn has 24,700 inhabitants to the sq. mile; its area is 77.62 sq. miles which is room for 8,875,000 people at present density of population in Manhattan.   During rush hours 100,000 people cross the East River an hour by bridges and ferries; Subway under East River capacity 24,000 an hour; another tunnel being built under East River with 124 miles of new subway and "L" tracks in borough.

Myrtle Ave.   Jay St.   Offices of Deputy Commissioner and Borough Chief.

BROOKLYN AND QUEENS FIRE HEADQUARTERS, 367-9 Jay St.; 89 engine companies, 37 hook and ladder, 22 hose companies, 2,034 men; an average of 13 fires a day; $2,125,000 high pressure service, with 1,384 hydrants in business district, 1914

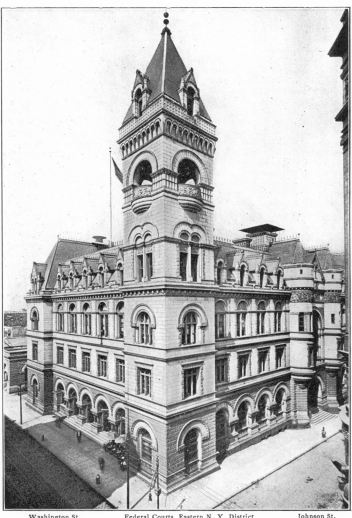

Washington St.   Federal Courts, Eastern N. Y. District   Johnson St.

BROOKLYN POST OFFICE, N. E. Cor. Washington and Johnson Sts.; completed 1892; cost $2,000,000; 21 branches; 143 sub-stations; 1,727 employees; receipts for year, $3,100,000; money order business, $14,700,000.   William E. Kelly, Postmaster.

Battleships and Cruisers at anchor in Wallabout Channel   Pile Driver   Pumping Plant for Emptying Dry Docks   Battleship "Kentucky" in Dry Dock   Naval Tug   Machine Shops   Foundry

NEW YORK NAVY YARD, Wallabout Bay, East River, between Manhattan and Williamsburg Bridges, Brooklyn; established 1803; built first steam war-vessel "Fulton" 1815; 17,666-ton steel battleship "Connecticut," 1903-6; 21,825-ton "Florida," 1909-10; 26,000-ton super-dreadnaught, "New York," 1911-14; most important of the nine American Navy Yards; 2½ miles water-front; 144 acres; four dry-docks—No. 4, 723 by 110 ft. at bottom and 35 ft. deep over sill at high water, granite, cost $2,500,000; $55,000,000 construction plant, 45 acres, employing an average of 4,000 mechanics; chief naval base; vast storehouses filled with war supplies.   Marine barracks east of Navy Yard.   Naval Y. M. C. A., 167 Sands St., built by Miss Helen M. Gould (Mrs. F. J. Shepard).   U. S. Naval Hospital, Flushing Ave., 21 acres, 500 beds.

STEINWAY & SONS' PIANO FACTORIES, Steinway, L. I., in Queens Borough; Factory No. 1, occupying ten acres on Bowery Bay, near foot of Steinway Ave., including case-making shop, foundry and machine shop, extensive drying kilns for lumber and large lumber yard, employing 500 men; Factory No. 2, assembling departments, on Ditmars Ave., 200 x 350 ft. employing 600 men; average value of output $3,000,000 yearly, not including product of factory at Hamburg, Germany; business founded in 1853 by Heinrich E. Steinway and his four sons, the path-breakers of the piano industry, who brought the pianoforte to its highest state of perfection, inventing many improvements which have made the Steinway piano the most famous musical instrument.   Executive offices, Steinway Hall, 109-111 East 14th St.   Above picture is Factory No. 2.

Queensboro Bridge   "L" extension of Steinway Tunnel line   Transfer Station   Brewster & Co.   Queensboro Corporation   "L" line to Corona   "L" line to Astoria   Sunnyside Yards

QUEENSBORO PLAZA, Long Island City; terminus of Queensboro Bridge from 59th St., Manhattan; centre from which radiate surface lines to all parts of Queens and "L" lines to Astoria and Corona. QUEENS BOROUGH, 128 sq. miles, 387,444 inhabitants, has been erecting $1,500,000 worth of new buildings a month; since incorporation into the greater city in 1898, 47,553 buildings have been completed costing $185,891,398; realty assessments have increased from $103,752,600 in 1899 to $488,686,756 in 1914. Factory output valued at $151,680,000 in 1914.

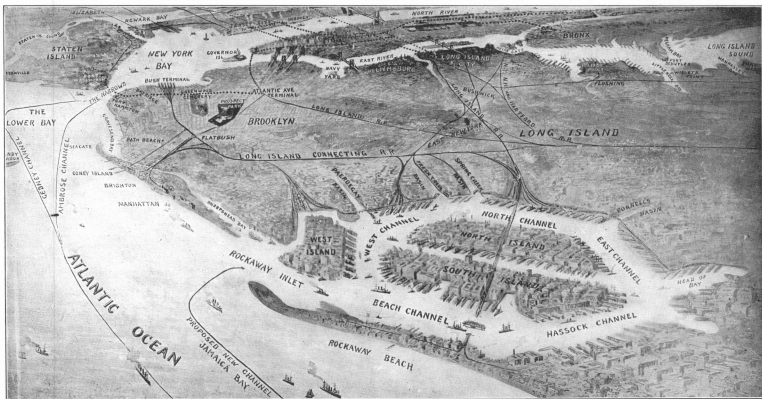

Entrance to the Port of New York   Entrance to New Harbor   Site for Piers and Warehouses   Long Island

JAMAICA BAY, proposed supplemental harbor to be created by dredging channels and building piers and warehouses where now are duck marshes. In this bay, right on the Atlantic Ocean, yet protected from the sea by a rocky rampart, is room for 150 miles of piers, with direct connection with all the transcontinental railroads through the Connecting Railway, and connection with the State Canals is proposed by a canal across Long Island to Flushing Bay on the Sound; authorized by Congress and by the City and the initial appropriations made. Estimated cost, $70,000,000.

Interior View of Luna Park   The Court of Luna

CONEY ISLAND, facing the Atlantic Ocean, in the Borough of Brooklyn, separated from the mainland by Coney Island Creek and Sheepshead Bay; the greatest seaside resort in the world, with sea bathing and unique amusements such as scenic railways, panoramic productions, merry-go-rounds, vaudeville, dancing, etc.; visited often on Saturdays and Sundays by over half a million people. LUNA PARK, Coney Island's most famous amusement resort; a hundred novel diversions; Court of Luna, Trip to the Moon, novel scenic railways, the Old Mill, etc.

Washington Ave.   Institute Park, 50 acres   Brooklyn Institute as planned by McKim, Mead & White, Architects.   Eastern Parkway   Reservoir

BROOKLYN INSTITUTE OF ARTS AND SCIENCES, near Plaza entrance to Prospect Park, Brooklyn; founded as Apprentices' Library, 1823; 12-acre site; first section of $5,000,000 group, 560 ft. sq. with four interior courts, completed '97; second section, '04; third section, '08, fourth section, '14; lectures in 29 departments; art classes, school of pedagogy, biological laboratory, (branch at Cold Spring, L. I.), museum, library of 35,000 vols; concerts and dramatic readings; Children's Museum, Bedford Park; 6,856 members; F. W. Hooper, Director; A. Augustus Healy, Pres.

STATUES AND MONUMENTS.   1. Gen. Henry W. Slocum, by MacMonnies, Eastern Parkway and Bedford Ave. Brooklyn.   2. "The Pilgrim," J. Q. A. Ward, Central Park, near E. 72d St.   3. Athletes Training Wild Horses, by MacMonnies, Ocean Parkway, Entrance, Prospect Park.   4. Alexander Hamilton's Tomb, Trinity Churchyard.   5. Martyrs' Monument, Trinity Churchyard, near Trinity Building, in honor of patriots who died in British prisons.   6. Robert Fulton's Tomb, Trinity Churchyard, near Broadway and Rector Street.   7. Gen. William Tecumseh Sherman (Augustus St. Gaudens), Plaza entrance, Central Park.   8. Henry Ward Beecher (Ward), facing Borough Hall, Brooklyn.   9. Gen. Franz Sigel, Riverside Drive.

ARMORIES. 1. Seventh Regiment, Park Ave , 66th to 67th Sts.; org. 1806; Col. Daniel Appleton. 2. 22d Regt. Engineers, '61, Ft. Washington Ave.; Col. W. B. Hotchkin. 3. Squadron A, '89, Madison Ave. & 94th; Maj. W. R. Wright. 4. 9th Coast Artillery, 14th St., 1812; Lt. Col. John J. Byrne. 5. 8th Coast Artillery, Park Ave. & 94th; Brig. Gen. E. F. Austin. 6. 71st Regiment, '52, 4th Ave. & 34th; 236 ft. high; Col. W. G. Bates. 7. 14th Regiment, '47, 8th Ave. & 15th, Brooklyn; Col. John H. Foote. 8. 69th Regiment, '51, Lexington Ave. and 25th ; Col. Louis D. Conley. 9. 1st Cavalry, Bedford Ave., Union to President Sts., Brooklyn; Col. Charles I. Debevoise. 10. 23d Regiment, '62, Bedford Avenue & Pacific Street, Brooklyn ; Col. F. H. Norton. 11. 13th Coast Artillery, Sumner and Putnam Avenues, Brooklyn ; Col. N. B. Thurston.

| Long Island City Queens Borough | Blackwell's Island in East River | Queensboro Bridge to E. 59th St. | Central Park 839.9 acres | St. Luke's Hospital | Cathedral of St. John the Divine | Brooklyn Borough | Williamsburg Bridge | Plaza Hotel | St. Patrick Cathed |

Amsterdam Ave.   Harlem (on the low ground)   Broadway   Teachers' College   Columbia University, occupying 6 city blocks   Claremont Avenue

ACROPOLIS OF AMERICA, so styled by Col. John Jacob Astor in recommending this site for the Cathedral of St. John the Divine, which, standing 250 ft. above mean tide, will rise 445 ft. above its foundation of the metropolis.   It is now the centre of learning, Columbia University and its allied institutions, Barnard College for Women, (founded 1889) and Teachers' College (1886) with their $15,000,000 groups of 140th St.; Horace Mann Schools, 120th St.; Manhattan College, 131st St. and Broadway; National Academy of Design, 109th St. and Amsterdam Ave.; Union Theological Seminary, 120th St. and Broa

nard College   Apartment Houses   Riverside Drive and Park, 140 acres   Grant's Tomb   Columbia Stadium

visible 25 miles away. By the time this $15,000,000 group is completed, giving America the finest and most splendidly located cathedral in the world, Col. Astor predicted that this will be the centre of population, crowning the plateau that is with the exception of a small plot in Washington Heights, the highest ground on Manhattan Island. The College of the City of New York is on Amsterdam Ave., 138th to Gen. Grant's Tomb commemorates his services in preserving the Union; a Water Gate is to honor Robert Fulton, whose invention of the steamboat made the commercial greatness of city and nation possible.

Broadway   Furnald Hall   Pulitzer School of Journalism   South Field   Professional Schools   Low Library   Professional Schools   Hamilton Hall   Hartley Hall   Livingston Hall

COLUMBIA UNIVERSITY, Broadway to Amsterdam Ave. W. 114th to W. 120th St.; founded in 1754 as King's College, at Broadway and Barclay St.; moved in 1857 to Madison Ave. and E. 49th St.; new site of 26 acres secured 1892 and 1902; $15,000,000 group erected 1902-1914, Library, $1,200,000 gift of Seth Low, President 1890-1901; 600,000 volumes; School of Mines, Engineering Building, Earl Hall, west of Library; Schermerhorn, Havemeyer, Kent, Philosophy and Avery Halls, north; with St. Paul's Chapel; 12 faculties, 907 instructors, 9,840 students and 5,785 in summer courses; University includes Barnard College for Women, at 119th St. founded '89; Teachers' Colle_e, 120th St. '86; College of Physicians and Surgeons, W. 59th St.; College of Pharmacy, W. 68th St.; Nicholas Murray Butler, Pres.

Wadleigh High School   Golden Gate Apartments   Cathedral Parkway   6th and 9th Ave "L"   Central Park   Columbus Ave.

HARLEM, view from southern end of Cathedral Heights, Morningside Park in the foreground, "L" road running from Columbus Ave. through W. 110th St. (Cathedral Parkway) into Eighth Ave, at height of 73 ft.; Harlem, founded in 1658, has 825,000 inhabitants; if a separate city it would rank fourth among American municipalities; bounded on north and east by the Harlem and East Rivers.

Bishop's Residence   Choir School   Crossing   Choir and Chancel   St. Saviour's   St. Colomba's Chapels   St. Luke's Hospital, fd. 1846

CATHEDRAL OF ST. JOHN THE DIVINE, 110th to 113th Sts., overlooking Morningside Park; begun 1892; choir and two of seven chapels by Heins & La Farge, consecrated April 19, 1911; cost $3,500,000. Choir School fd.'01, built by $150,000 gift of Mrs. J. J. Blodgett; $500,000 endowment by F. G. Bourne. Rev. Wm. M. Grosvenor, Dean; Rt. Rev. David H. Greer, Bishop.

W. 114th St.　　St. Luke's Hospital　　Amsterdam Avenue　　The Crossing　Old Orphan Asylum, to be removed　Bishop's Residence　　Synod Hall　　Cathedral Parkway, (W. 110th St.)

CATHEDRAL OF ST. JOHN THE DIVINE, Amsterdam Ave. side showing the Crossing, with its huge dome where the transepts will intersect the Choir and Nave; original plans provided that the completed Cathedral should be 165x520 ft., 288 ft. across transepts; central spire, 445 ft. high; twin western towers on Amsterdam Ave. front, each 245 ft. high; Nave to be begun in 1915, under direction of Ralph A. Cram, Architect, costing $1,000,000; it is proposed to finish dome with groups of small Gothic pinnacles and erect on either side twin spires over 500 ft. high.

College of the City of New York　　D. Willis James Memorial Chapel　　Convent of the Sacred Heart　　Dormitories　　Library　　Harlem　　Teachers' College

Professors' Apartments　　Claremont Ave　　Cloisters　　President's Residence　　W. 120th St.　　Administration Building　　Barnard College

UNION THEOLOGICAL SEMINARY, Claremont Ave. to Broadway, 120 to 122d St.; founded 1836 at 9 University Pl.; at Park Ave. and 70th St., 1844 1910; new group erected 1908-10 on site given by D. Willis James; value, $4,500,000; endowment, $3,500,000; 220 students; 24 instructors; buildings enclose a quadrangle 300 x 100 ft.; corner towers to be 200 ft. high; library 100,000 volumes, 56,000 pamphlets, 186 manuscripts; Presbyterian, but independent of ecclesiastical control.　Rev. Dr. Francis Brown, Pres.　William Kingsley, Pres. of Trustees.

WATER GATE, to be erected on the Hudson River at West 106th St., as a memorial to Hendrick Hudson, who discovered the river in 1609, and to Robert Fulton, who successfully inaugurated steam navigation on the Hudson in 1807; an imposing $1,000,000 structure to be used for public celebrations and as a fitting place for the landing and reception of distinguished guests; the plans drawn by H. Van Buren Magonigle contemplate in addition to the two quays and stately colonnade, two stadia, one for children's games, the other for ceremonies and pageants.

PARKS. 1. Bridge over Bronx River, Bronx Park. 2. Road in Bronx Park west of Falls. 3. Botanical Museum, Bronx Park; gardens cover 250 acres. 4. Falls, Bronx River. 5. Bird House, Zoological Park. 6. Conservatories, Bronx. 7. Flying Cage, Bronx. 8. Skating on Lake in Central Park. 9. The Dell, Central Park. 10. Bridge near the Ramble. 11. Swan Boats. 12. Terrace and Bethesda Fountain. 13. Bridle Path. 14. Sacred Ox. 15. The Mall, main promenade of Central Park, which covers 83.99 acres, valued at $200,000,000. 16. Camel Family, Betsy, Prince and Frank. 17. Reservoir. 18. Common. 19. View in heart of Central Park. 20. Leo. 21. Menagerie and Arsenal, Central Park. 22. Polar Bear. 23. Cooper Square, where 3d and 4th Aves. meet in Bowery. 24. Hudson Park, Hudson-Leroy Sts. 25. Harlem River Speedway at Washington Bridge; 100 ft. wide, extends from 155th to 208th St.

PARKS. 1. Van Cortlandt Mansion, Van Cortlandt Park. 2. Poe Park and Cottage, The Bronx. 3. Pell Oak, Pelham Bay Park. 4. Claremont Park and Zbrowski Mansion, **The Bronx.** 5. Antelopes, Zoological Park. 6. Washington Square and Arch, lower end 5th Ave. 7. Jeannette Park, Coenties Slip. 8. Buffaloes, Zoological Park. 9. Bronx River. 10. Japanese **Tea** House. 11. Soldiers' and Sailors' Arch, Plaza entrance Prospect Park, Brooklyn. 12, 13. Lullwood Bridge, and Restaurant and Shelter, Prospect Park. 15, 19. Ocean **Parkway** Entrance Prospect Park, groups of wild horses, winter and summer views. 17, 18. Boundary Walk and Bicyclists' Rest, Prospect Park. 20, 21. Sheep on Common and Boat Landing, Prospect Park. 22. Fort Greene Park. 23. Fort Hamilton. 24. Automobile Parade, Ocean Parkway. 25. Parade Ground Pavillion, Van Cortlandt Park.

HALL OF RECORDS, Centre St. entrance; statues by Philip Martiny.   CHURCH MISSIONS HOUSE, Fourth Ave., cor. 22d St.   COLLEGE OF CITY OF NEW YORK, Convent Ave., entrance.
MADISON SQUARE PRESBYTERIAN CHURCH.   CUSTOM HOUSE GROUPS, America and Europe, by Daniel C. French.   GRACE EPISCOPAL CHURCH, Broadway above 10th St.
APPELLATE COURT Wisdom, by F. W. Ruckstuhl.   CUSTOM HOUSE GROUPS, Asia and Africa, by French.   CHAMBER OF COMMERCE, main entrance, figures symbolical of Commerce.
CHAMBER OF COMMERCE, statues adorning façade; Alexander Hamilton, Financier, by Philip Martiny; Gov. DeWitt Clinton, father of the Erie Canal, by Carl Bitter; John Jay, Jurist, by Bitter.

CLUBS

CLUBS. 1. Bar Association, 42 W. 44th St., organized '69, 2,154 members. 2. American Geographical Society, Broadway & 156th St., '52, 1,200 members. 3. Harvard Club, 27 W. 44th St., '87, 3,816
4. Union League Club, Fifth Ave., & 39th St., '63, 1,800. 5. Union Club, Fifth Ave. & 51st St., '36, 1,600. 6. N. Y. Yacht Club, 37 W. 44th, '44, 2,325. 7. Metropolitan Club, Fifth Ave. &
60th, '91, 1,400. 8. N. Y. Athletic Club, Central Park South & Sixth Ave, '68, 4,300. 9. Engineers Club, 32 W. 40th '88, 1,999. United Engineering Societies, through on 39th St.
10. Elks Club, 108-114 W. 43d, '68, 408,000 members in U. S. 11. Republican Club, 54 W. 40th, '70, 1,700. 12. University Club, Fifth Ave. & 54th St, '65, 3,500.

STATUES AND MONUMENTS.　1. Admiral Farragut, N. W. cor. Madison Sq.　2. Soldiers' and Sailors Monument, columns 35 ft. high, Riverside Drive near 89th.　3. Carl Schurz, Morningside Drive, 116th.　4. Callendar Ball, Columbia University.　5. Washington Irving, Bryant Park.　6. Obelisk, 200 ton monolith, 3400 years old, brought from Egypt 1880.　7. W. H. Seward, Madison Sq.　8. William Cullen Bryant, Bryant Park.　9. Lincoln, S. W. corner Union Sq.　10. Nathan Hale, City Hall Park.　11. Washington, S. E. cor. Union Sq.　12. Verrazano, Battery Park.　13. Daniel Webster, West Drive, Central Park.　14. Chester A. Arthur, N. E. cor. Madison Sq.　15. Childrens' Fountain, Morningside Park.　16. Firemen's Memorial, Riverside Drive at 100th.　17. Washington and Lafayette, Morningside Ave. and 114th.　18. Richard M. Hunt Memorial, 5th Ave., near 70th.

The First City in the World

SINCE Greater New York was formed in 1898 by extending the municipal limits, there has been a gain of 70 per cent in the population of the consolidated city, the Health Department estimates for the five boroughs for July 1, 1914, indicating that 5,583,871 people lived in the city on that date. This is an increase of 816,988 since the Federal census of April, 1910.

London in 1913 had 4,521,000 inhabitants, and is losing population at the rate of 1,800 a year, while New York is gaining 16,180 a month.

In the 690 square miles of the London metropolitan district the population in 1914 was estimated at 7,454,440, while in the 964 square miles of New York City and its suburbs there were 7,553,662 inhabitants. Greater London in the ten years ended in 1911 gained 671,591 inhabitants, while the metropolitan district of New York gained 1,866,764 in the ten years ended April, 1910.

It is estimated that by 1920 New York, within its present limits, will have 6,651,608 inhabitants, while Greater London will have 7,978,259, and "Greatest New York" will show a population of 9,064,395.

While advancing to first place in point of population, New York already had achieved the primacy in all other respects.

The Chamber of Commerce in 1914 estimated the banking power of the city at $4,460,360,980, or 17 per cent. of the $25,712,163,599 that represents the banking power of the entire United States, and more than 10 per cent. of the banking power of the world.

The average amount of money held in the banks in New York City is half a billion dollars or about 14 per cent. of all the money in the United States.

With eleven great railroad systems and 130 steamship lines focusing at the greatest harbor in the world, goods to the value of considerably over $12,500,000,000 are borne annually upon the waters of the harbor, this huge total not including the large aggregate of freight handled by the railroads and not figuring in the harbor traffic.

Though the foreign commerce of New York ($1,916,934,800 in the year ended June 30, 1914) is but a fraction of the shipping of the port, it greatly exceeds the totals for the largest European ports—$1,791,857,641 for London, $1,674,187,176 for Hamburg, $1,637,280,476 for Liverpool, $1,121,654,799 for Antwerp. And these ports have no domestic shipping comparable to the coastwise trade.

New York's foreign trade was 45 per cent. of the total for the United States.

Unlike other great commercial cities, New York is also an industrial centre, the greatest manufacturing city in the whole world. Not only does the city trade in the products of all nations, but it produces nearly every sort of manufactured goods.

Within the limits of the city proper there are 34,000 factories and shops engaged in 350 lines of manufacture, representing an investment of $1,800,000,000, a sum nearly half the total of the money in circulation in the United States.

In these industries there are 80,000 salaried people and 682,796 wage earners, making up an army of workers outnumbering the entire population of Liverpool. The pay rolls in the year foot up to over half a billion dollars, or enough to buy the entire city of St. Louis, at the valuation put by the assessors upon that thriving hive of 800,000 people.

The cost of the materials used in New York's manufactories in a year exceed $1,275,000,000, and the estimated wholesale value of the output of the city's industries in the past year was $2,375,000,000, or four times the combined value of the manufactured goods exported in the same period by France and Germany.

With 5.18 per cent. of the population of the country, New York City produces 9.85 per cent. of all the manufactured products.

For the accommodation of the largest transient population to be found anywhere in the world, average 250,000, and the largest permanent hotel population, 150,000, New York maintains over 750 hotels, representing an investment of $265,000,000, and capable of entertaining 350,000 people without crowding. And over half a billion is spent annually in the city's 5,500 restaurants and 750 hotel dining-rooms. The annual food supply of the city is estimated at $2,000,000,000.

These big facts but begin to tell the tale of the greatness of the city that has risen since that day, three centuries ago, when Hendrik Hudson sailed up the river named after him, and saw the wigwams of the Indians on the wooded island that now holds the tallest and the largest buildings and is the centre of the greatest business interests of the world.

MOSES KING

Brooklyn 1905

Fulton St. "L"   Hall of Records   Kings County Court House   Municipal Bldg., back of Borough Hall, to be replaced by $2,000,000 structure   Polytechnic Institute   Court St.

BROOKLYN BOROUGH HALL, facing Park at Fulton and Court Sts.; City Hall prior to consolidation, 1898; white marble, 102 x 162 ft., 75 ft. high; offices of Borough President. Brooklyn has 18,374 inhabitants to the sq. mile; in 1907 8,311 buildings were erected in the borough at a cost of $63,159,176; its area is 77.62 sq. miles, which is room for 7,800,189 people at the present density of population in Manhattan. During rush hours 70,000 people cross the East River an hour by bridges and ferries; the Subway under East River has a capacity of 24,000 an hour.

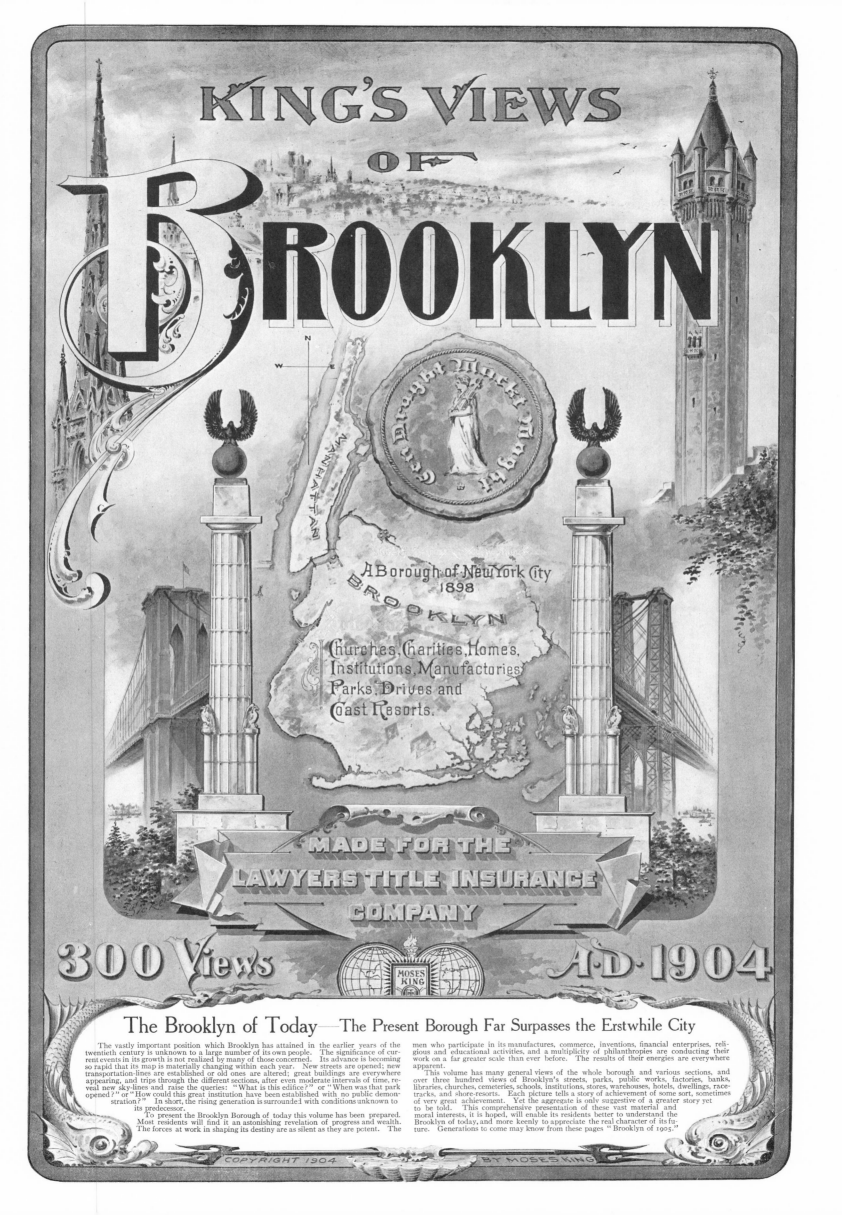

KING'S VIEWS OF BROOKLYN

A Borough of New York City
1898
BROOKLYN

Churches, Charities, Homes,
Institutions, Manufactories,
Parks, Drives and
Coast Resorts.

MADE FOR THE
LAWYERS TITLE INSURANCE
COMPANY

300 Views

A·D·1904

MOSES KING

The Brooklyn of Today—The Present Borough Far Surpasses the Erstwhile City

The vastly important position which Brooklyn has attained in the earlier years of the twentieth century is unknown to a large number of its own people. The significance of current events in its growth is not realized by many of those concerned. Its advance is becoming so rapid that its map is materially changing within each year. New streets are opened; new transportation-lines are established or old ones are altered; great buildings are everywhere appearing, and trips through the different sections, after even moderate intervals of time, reveal new sky-lines and raise the queries: "What is this edifice?" or "When was that park opened?" or "How could this great institution have been established with no public demonstration?" In short, the rising generation is surrounded with conditions unknown to its predecessor.

To present the Brooklyn Borough of today this volume has been prepared. Most residents will find it an astonishing revelation of progress and wealth. The forces at work in shaping its destiny are as silent as they are potent. The

men who participate in its manufactures, commerce, inventions, financial enterprises, religious and educational activities, and a multiplicity of philanthropies are conducting their work on a far greater scale than ever before. The results of their energies are everywhere apparent.

This volume has many general views of the whole borough and various sections, and over three hundred views of Brooklyn's streets, parks, public works, factories, banks, libraries, churches, cemeteries, schools, institutions, stores, warehouses, hotels, dwellings, race-tracks, and shore-resorts. Each picture tells a story of achievement of some sort, sometimes of very great achievement. Yet the aggregate is only suggestive of a greater story yet to be told. This comprehensive presentation of these vast material and moral interests, it is hoped, will enable its residents better to understand the Brooklyn of today, and more keenly to appreciate the real character of its future. Generations to come may know from these pages "Brooklyn of 1905."

BROOKLYN BOROUGH, FROM THE ATLANTIC OCEAN TO LONG ISLAND SOUND, showing most of its 33 miles of water front.

No city in the world possesses a greater or more varied water front than that of Brooklyn, which combines ocean, bay, river, creek, and canal.   Besides the immense facilities thus afforded for international and internal commerce, a large share of its shore space is given to manufactories, homes, parks, and pleasure resorts, which yet have pre-empted only a portion of the beaches available.

BROOKLYN

The Greatest of the five Boroughs of Greater New York

History and Prophecy by the Rev. JOHN W. CHADWICK

IT is proverbial wisdom that "a good wine needs no bush," and a book so good as this aggregation of Brooklyn Views is hardly to be bettered by any introductory word. If these views do not speak for themselves, if they are not eloquent of the immense development and promise of what was the City, and is now the Borough, of Brooklyn, no prologue, though Mark Twain should write it, would impress a mind insensible to this pictorial exhibition. When the consolidation of Brooklyn with New York was effected in 1897, the Brooklynite who did not feel that he was "a citizen of no mean city" must have been one of the duller sort. The growth of the city had increased not only by such leaps and bounds as the annexation of Williamsburg in 1855, and the outlying towns of New Lots, Flatbush, New Utrecht, and Flatlands in the last decade of the century, but by steady increments of immigration and by the course of nature under conditions highly favorable to the settlement of young people and the creation of families. Not until 1816 did the fine old Dutch farms of the region cohere into a village organization. Not until 1834 did this take on the dignity of a city government. The population at that time was but 27,854. It was close on to a million at the time of the consolidation, and since then it has been increased by at least three hundred thousand more.

But increase of population would be a sorry basis for civic gratulation if it were not accompanied with other traits equally or more significant. The civic consciousness of the Brooklynite has been nourished by a history of commanding interest. There was the idyllic stage of which we have a charming picture in the journal of those Labadists who came spying out the land in 1679, and found the ground covered with ripe fruit and the oysters at Gowanus "not less than a foot long," reminding us of those for which Thackeray felt "profoundly grateful and as if he had swallowed a small baby." There was the heroic period, marked by the Battle of Long Island and the splendid service of Colonel Glover's Marblehead regiment of fishermen. No statue of Colonel Glover will be found among these Brooklyn Views, but that is not the fault of the collector. The Colonel patiently awaits the honor due. The civic consciousness of the Brooklynite is augmented further by the fame of the most popular preacher that has ever preached in this country since Whitefield left his bones upon our shore. We have at least Beecher's monument, thoroughly characteristic, facing the City Hall, which requires looking into now and then, and Mr. Stranahan's, "in habit as he was," at the Park entrance, where the hard bronze of the Park Commissioner's effigy might well dilate with conscious joy in the adjacent beauty. For Brooklyn's Park is indeed "a thing of beauty," and it will be "a joy forever" to the inhabitants of the Borough. This, also, Brooklynites are proud of and of the splendid record that they made with their great Sanitary Fair in 1864, passing $402,943.74 to the credit of the Sanitary Commission. That noble building, the Academy of Music, was finished just in time to house the Fair. It was destroyed by fire in 1903, but the passion for good music, which has always been strongly developed in Brooklyn, will build "some new temple, nobler than the last," to which the votaries of music will come up in a joyful swarm. Add to these elements of a highly developed civic consciousness those furnished by the religious, educational, and humanitarian aspects of the community, and it should not seem strange to anyone that this consciousness should have survived the shock given to it by consolidation, and have passed from the City to the Borough without loss of force and even with some appearance of actual augmentation.

Not seldom in the history of institutions have names given derisively been adopted cheerfully and worn as a diplomat or general wears a decoration on his breast. Brooklyn has been variously named and the intention has not been always flattering. It has been called the "dormitory" and the "sleeping chamber" of New York. The implication has been that even in the day-time it is a rather sleepy place. But the Philadelphian who complained that he could not sleep in New York (in the day-time!) would find Brooklyn quite as unfavorable to a somnolent disposition. Commissioner McAdoo finds certain involutions of travel in Brooklyn more bewildering than any "death curve" in New York. The shopping throng on Fulton Street, Brooklyn, makes the similar throngs on Twenty-third and Fourteenth Streets, Manhattan, seem but thin and small. The child's dream of "Christmas all the year" seems realized. Brooklyn has also been named "a city of women," and there are many other names by which it would not smell so sweet. One sometimes reads of it as being, by day, like that island of the Ægean Sea which for a tragical period had no

male inhabitants. But the demand for menfolk must be exigent that is not satisfied by the number of them that diversify the crowds of "weaker vessels" which brighten the sunshine of the great and lesser thoroughfares every pleasant day. These humorous descriptions of Brooklyn (as a "dormitory," as a "woman's city") are more or less genial distortions of the fact that Brooklyn is preëminently a residential city. There is nothing here to its discredit. There is still less in the fact that as a residential city it is preëminently a city of young married people with moderate means and growing families, and of thrifty householders, men who own the comfortable houses in which they live. Nothing is more characteristic of Brooklyn than the multitude of such houses, but that others of a more ambitious character are not wanting on the Heights, the Park Slope, and elsewhere, this volume contains ample proof. With the facilities for rapid transit already afforded, but in the way of indefinite expansion, Brooklyn is destined to become increasingly "a city of homes," a "neighborhood city" also, where people living next door to each other know each other and share their joys and sorrows in some appreciable degree. One has only to look at a map of Greater New York, and see how much of its unoccupied territory lies on the outskirts of Brooklyn, to be persuaded that Brooklyn is destined to wear its residential honors with an ever braver heart. The "diffusion of cities" is one of the happiest results of the electrical development of local travel. It makes congestion hereafter an unnecessary evil and preventable, not to be suffered further without "contributory negligence." Not only the tenement-house but its fine neighbor, the apartment-house, will be superseded by the individualized domicile to a more pronounced degree when "the present distress" of tunnelling, etc., is over and the reign of settled peace has come.

But those who examine carefully these Views of Brooklyn will hardly need to be assured that the representation of Brooklyn as a residential city has been much overworked. Not only does the daily subsistence of so huge a population create a vast amount of business, but Brooklyn's manufacturing and commercial interests are immense. Her water-front is lined with wharves and docks from which lines of steamers radiate to foreign and domestic ports of every latitude and longitude. Especially in the Williamsburg district there are colossal manufactories of various kinds. Others are springing up everywhere in the wide space which is coterminous with the Borough of Brooklyn. The manufacturer may have his office in New York, but his goods are made by men and women who live in Brooklyn and have their work-shops there.

Brooklyn has been called the City of Churches oftener, perhaps, than by any other name. In this respect it may no longer have a proud preëminence, but it has some four hundred of one Protestant denomination or another, some of them beautiful buildings, and of Roman Catholic churches a proportionate number. These churches have had their personal associations with pastors widely known or greatly loved, Beecher, Storrs, Cuyler, Father Malone, which are more to them than piles of splendid masonry, and the new men preaching from their pulpits are not unworthy of their best traditions. If they go wrong in their theology, they are set right by Dr. McKelway, the editor of the Brooklyn *Eagle*, a Brooklyn institution of first-rate importance, having a wide range of influence, and yet always haunted by a pleasant, neighborly village air which seems a reminiscence of the time when the farmers whose hard names adorn the city's streets sat by their comfortable hearths and smoked interminable pipes and drank their home-brewed ale.

Scant space remains to speak of what is so important that if Brooklyn were called a City of Schools or an Educational City it would deserve the name. Not only is its public school system highly perfected but it has special educational institutions of great reputation, some of them of a unique excellence. Among these are the Polytechnic Institute, Adelphi College, Packer Institute, Pratt Institute, the Long Island Historical Society, and the Brooklyn Institute of Arts and Sciences which probably has furnished more valuable lectures to its patrons during the course of its later history than all the lecture-bureaus in the United States. With these institutions the Public Libraries, housed by Mr. Carnegie's munificence, work sympathetically and efficiently. It is a good sign that the circulation of books by the Brooklyn Library has been increased threefold since it became a public library, while the proportion of fiction read has not appreciably increased. Out of a hundred possible coigns of vantage from which to take a last look with my readers, I choose Brooklyn Heights, the month of December, the hour 5 P.M., when the towering office-buildings of Manhattan make for the eye a Feast of Lights, incomparably bright and fair.

FORT GREEN

NAVY YARD

WALLABOUT
CHANNEL

CITY
PARK

WILLIAMSBURG

BROADWAY FERRY

FULTON FERRY

Williamsburg Bridge   Broadway Ferries   In the Revolution the Bay was fortified, and the notorious British prison ship "Jersey" anchored here   Wallabout Bay and Navy Yard   Factories   Brooklyn Bridge   Fulton and New Jersey "Annex" Ferries
BROOKLYN BETWEEN THE BRIDGES.   THE EAST RIVER, FROM BROOKLYN BRIDGE TO WILLIAMSBURG BRIDGE.   BROOKLYN BRIDGE TO WILLIAMSBURG BRIDGE.   In this locality the last slave sale in the county took place, at the division of the estate of the widow Rappelje, in 1773.
Between two of the world's grandest bridges nestles the oldest section of Brooklyn, the first settlement having been made, in 1637, at "Rennsgackonck," in the bend of Marechkawieck," the modern Wallabout Bay.   Farming was the main industry, and tobacco the principal product.

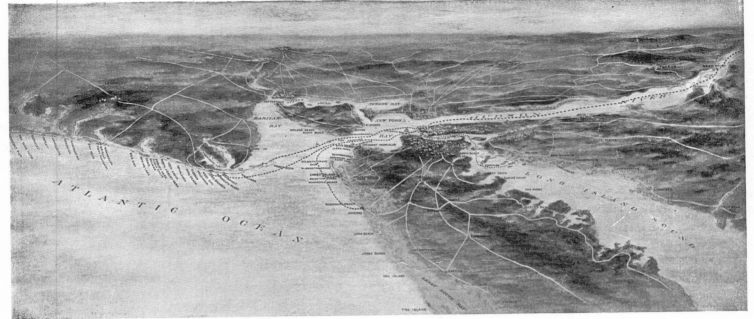

New Jersey Coast   Sandy Hook   Staten Island   Brooklyn   Long Island   Connecticut

GREATER NEW YORK, AND ITS ENVIRONS, LOOKING WESTWARD FROM THE ATLANTIC.

INDEX TO VIEWS AND TEXT

Black-face numerals indicate titles of pictures; light-face, inclusions in other views, and references

EDITOR AND PUBLISHER

THE MAKERS OF THIS BOOK

Printing by THE PLIMPTON PRESS, Norwood, Mass.
Thirty drawings and impressions by Richard Rummell.   Drawings by Henry M. Pettit and F. W. Jopling.
Title arch by American Bank Note Co.   Cover and art groupings by Charles E. Sickels.
Three hundred photographs, mainly by George P. Hall & Son ; also by Fred. A. Walter, Joseph A. Tschirhart,
    Irving Underhill, Burr W. McIntosh, Joseph Byron, and Frank E. Parshley.
Phototypes by Gill Engraving Co. and Walker Engraving Co.
Paper made by Champion-International Co. and supplied by Seymour Co.
Descriptions by Edward St. John, James E. Homans, and Miss Annie M. Buckminster.

1904

BROOKLYN

KING'S VIEWS

THREE HUNDRED ILLUSTRATIONS

Dedicated, 1892   Bas-reliefs unveiled, 1902   Cost $250,000; paid by State and private subscriptions

SOLDIERS' AND SAILORS' MEMORIAL ARCH.   Plaza Entrance to Prospect Park, junction of Flatbush, Vanderbilt, and Ninth Avenues and Eastern Parkway.   John H. Duncan, Architect.
The *Arc de Triomphe* of America.   Surmounted by bronze quadriga, designed by Frederick MacMonnies.   Bronze groups at the sides represent the Army and Navy.   Bronze equestrian bas-reliefs of
Lincoln and of Grant, designed by Maurice J. Power, are on the inner sides of the archway.   This noble monument stands upon nearly the highest land in Brooklyn, visible from many distant points.

BROOKLYN: An Historical Past, a Substantial Present, a Glorious Future.

By JAMES E. HOMANS, A.B. (Harvard).

BROOKLYN, although officially a borough of Greater New York, in reality would rank as one of the largest cities of the world. Its population and area give it fourth place among the cities of the Union. Only Chicago, New Orleans, and Philadelphia exceed it in square mileage, and only Manhattan, Chicago, and Philadelphia number more inhabitants.

This noble borough measures about eight miles in its greatest width and a little over eleven miles in its greatest length, including within its boundaries an area of nearly 50,000 acres. Common custom calls it the "City of Churches," a title well merited, with its 493 houses of worship and its 527,000 church members, as against 901 churches and 829,000 members in the boroughs of Manhattan, Bronx, Richmond, and Queens. Brooklyn also merits the equally appropriate designation of "City of Homes." With an area of about 78 square miles out of a total of 327 for the greater city, it houses 1,313,000 inhabitants, about one-third of the population in the five boroughs. Brooklyn first emerged into history as a colony of the Dutch East India Company. Its first settlers were farmers from the Walloon provinces of Holland, who about 1625 founded a hamlet known as Wallbogt (Wallabout) or Walloon's Bay, near the present Navy Yard. Later the growing settlement received the name of Breucklyn, in honor of an old Dutch city, whence many of the colonists had emigrated.

The first recorded land-deed was given by Gov. Kieft to one Abraham Rycken in 1638, and the earliest grant to Thomas Besker in 1639. A "full and ample patent" to all freeholders of the town was granted by Gov. Nicolls in 1667, and confirmed by Gov. Dongan in 1686, in consideration of the annual payment of twenty bushels of wheat as quit rent. The first church was erected at Midwout (Flatbush) in 1654, after the founders of the present "City of Churches" had for nearly thirty years crossed weekly to "Nieuw Amsterdam" to attend service.

The government of the town was originally vested in a "superintendent," whose powers were briefly those of a justice of the peace. Later a *schout* (overseer) was appointed with a secretary and assessor to assist him.

The settlement steadily increased. In 1816 it was incorporated as a village; in 1834 chartered as a city; in 1855 consolidated with the outlying districts of Williamsburgh and Bushwick, and by popular vote in 1898 became a borough of Greater New York. The personnel of the colony was Dutch at the start: then largely English. But the marked intellectual and literary atmosphere for which the city has long been noted is largely due to the fact that in later colonial and early national days many New Englanders sought homes within its borders. It seems almost as if a New England town had been transplanted bodily to the western end of Long Island, there to maintain the culture and sedate atmosphere of the old Bay State in the very heart of the greatest financial and commercial center of the world.

Brooklyn's educational institutions are unique and magnificent. Everything is done on a large and generous scale. Its Institute of Arts and Sciences is almost unparalleled, while the Pratt Institute, the Polytechnic Institute, the Packer Institute, the Adelphi College, and other institutions stand among the best in the country.

The park-system of the Borough contains 1,070 acres and over forty miles of parkways throughout the city and along the ocean front. The five miles of beach at Coney Island afford space for several immense hotels and numberless enterprises of amusement, forming one of the most extensive popular resorts in the world.

The assessed value of Brooklyn realty sums up over $850,000,000. Its personalty represents more than $100,000,000. It contains 588 miles of paved streets; 670 miles of water mains; 697 miles of sewers; and 550 miles of railways. With a total ocean and river waterfront of thirty-three miles, unusual facilities are afforded for commercial and manufacturing establishments; a goodly array of grain-elevators; ship-building establishments; private and customs warehouses, and the piers of a great navy of merchant-ships. The shores from Long Island City to Bay Ridge are dotted with foundries, oil and sugar-refineries, mills for the production of machinery, food-stuffs, chemicals, clothing, and nearly everything used by civilized man.

As a financial center Brooklyn holds an enviable record. In 1904 its sixteen savings banks reported an aggregate surplus of $21,000,000 and deposits of $182,000,000. Its trust companies reported a total surplus of nearly $10,000,000 and its eighteen national and state banks a capital and surplus of $8,250,000 and deposits of $46,500,000.

Historically, Brooklyn is famous. Here was fought the Battle of Long Island, the first strategic conflict of the Revolution, whose most tragic episode is commemorated by Battle Pass, within the limits of Prospect Park. No American city supplied a larger quota to the National forces of the Civil War, or was a scene of greater activity in the raising and forwarding of supplies. The United States Navy Yard, within its borders, was then, as now, the foremost naval station of the country.

In the number of its citizen-soldiery Brooklyn is the second city in New York, mustering 3,250 men, as against the 5,420 from Manhattan and Bronx, or the total of 14,800 for the entire State. It is the home of the famous 13th Heavy Artillery, the largest militia organization in the country, mustering at the present time 1,050 men, nearly 150 more than the famous 7th of Manhattan.

Brooklyn is only at the threshold of possibilities, the magnitude of which cannot be estimated. With the completion of its marvelous bridges and tunnels and general improvements now under way an even greater population will settle within its borders, new industrial and commercial activities will arise and thrive, and the City of Churches and homes, industries and resorts, will attain to heights of grandeur, strength and glory hitherto undreamed of, until it becomes the great center of the Earth's greatest city.

Montague Street   Minard Lefever, Architect   L. I. Historical Soc.
HOLY TRINITY PROTESTANT EPISCOPAL CHURCH, Clinton and Montague Streets.
Organized 1846. One of the most noted landmarks of the older city. Rev. J. H. Melish, Rector. Membership about 1,100. Famous for a generation for its musical services.

Erected 1892   William Ordway Partridge, Sculptor
ALEXANDER HAMILTON STATUE, Hamilton Club, Remsen and Clinton Sts.
Superb bronze statue designed for the Hamilton Club, and gracing its entrance. One of the note-
worthy architectural features of the vicinity, attracting frequent attention of appreciative observers.

Erected 1891   John Q. A. Ward, Sculptor
HENRY WARD BEECHER STATUE, facing Borough Hall.
Commemorating Mr. Beecher's notable services to the entire Union, during forty years' pastorate of
Plymouth Church (1847-1887). Inscription: "To honor the great apostle of the brotherhood of man."

Henry K. Brown, Sculptor   Flower Gardens
LINCOLN STATUE, Prospect Park, overlooking the lake.
Erected 1869 by popular subscription. On a plaza visible from all parts of the Lake, at entrance to
Flower Gardens. A noble and ornate bronze monument to the martyred President.

Frederick MacMonnies, Sculptor   Soldiers' and Sailors' Arch
JAMES S. T. STRANAHAN STATUE, Plaza Entrance, Prospect Park.
Erected 1891, during Mr. Stranahan's lifetime. Unique honor to "Brooklyn's First Citizen." Com-
memorating services as prime mover in founding Prospect Park. Suggested by Rev. Dr. R. S. Storrs.

4

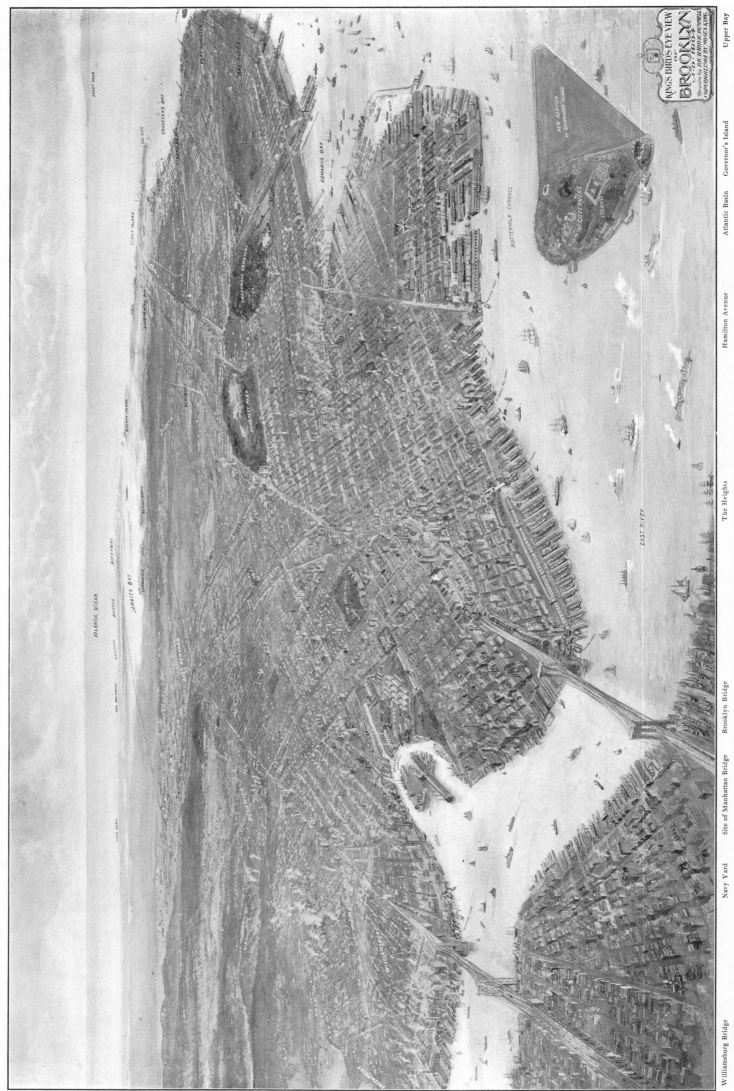

Williamsburg Bridge   Navy Yard   Site of Manhattan Bridge   Brooklyn Bridge   The Heights   Hamilton Avenue   Atlantic Basin   Governor's Island   Upper Bay

BIRD'S-EYE VIEW OF BROOKLYN BOROUGH, FROM THE EAST RIVER TO THE ATLANTIC OCEAN, SHOWING THE WHOLE BROOKLYN TERRITORY AND GOVERNOR'S ISLAND. Drawn for "King's Views" by Richard Rummell.
Greatest length represented, 11½ miles; greatest depth, 9¾ miles. Total area, 112 square miles, of which 78 lie within the boundaries of Brooklyn Borough. The two main avenues, Broadway and Fulton Street, running from the river almost to the farthest limits of the Borough, indicate the old towns of Williamsburgh and Brooklyn, consolidated in 1855. To the left (north), between the bridges, appear the U. S. Navy Yard and Reservation, founded 1801, notable as the site of Long Island's first Dutch village (Wallbogt). The view shows locations of the chief parks, hills, centers of business activity, notable buildings, thoroughfares and parkways, and includes the homes of 1,300,000 people and the probable site of the future homes of myriads. Between the two bridges shown will rise in the near future the Manhattan Bridge.

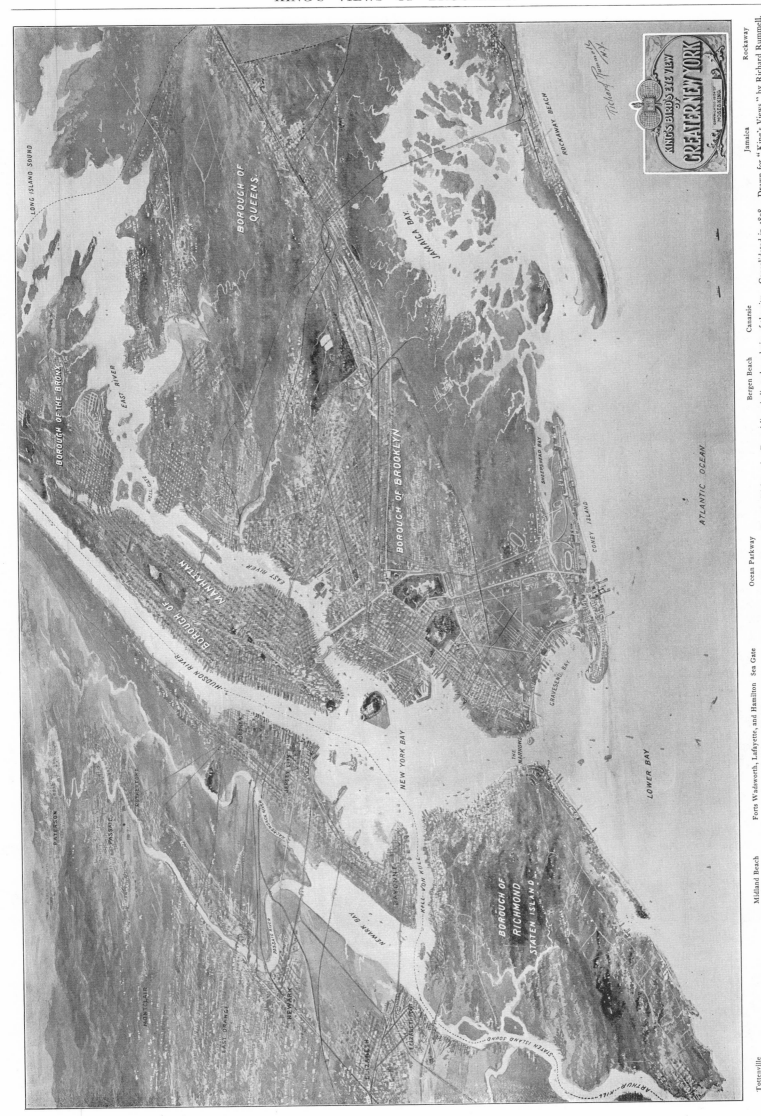

Totenville　　Midland Beach　　Forts Wadsworth, Lafayette, and Hamilton　Sea Gate　　Ocean Parkway　　Bergen Beach　Canarsie　Jamaica　Rockaway

BIRD'S-EYE VIEW OF GREATER NEW YORK (corporate title, "The City of New York"), comprising five Boroughs: Manhattan, Brooklyn, Bronx, Queens, Richmond.　Drawn for "King's Views" by Richard Rummell. Dotted lines indicate boundaries of the city.　Consolidated in 1898.　Daily water-supply, 460 New York is the largest city in the world except London.　Greatest length, 35 miles; greatest width, 18¼ miles; area, 327 square miles, or 209,000 acres.　Miles of paved streets, about 1,800; unpaved 1,100.　Railroads (single track), including elevated, 1,200 miles. million gallons. Sewers, 1,600 miles. Population, nearly 4,000,000.　Two new bridges, being built, are here shown as finished, making four in all.　The Manhattan Bridge will open a nearly direct highway from the Bowery to the seashore; the Blackwell's Island, from Central Manhattan to Queens.

"BROOKLYN"—United States Armored Cruiser.

Built 1893. 9,215 tons' displacement. Twin-screw; 18,700 horse-power engines; speed, 20 knots. 20 guns in main battery. Led American fleet in battle of Santiago, July 3, 1898, Captain Francis A. Cook, Commander.

"NEW YORK"—United States Armored Cruiser.

Built 1890. 8,200 tons' displacement. Engines 17,400 horse-power. Speed 21 knots. 18 guns in main battery. Commanded by French Ensor Chadwick during siege of Santiago and great battle of July 3, 1898.

Castle William   Fort Jay, formerly called Fort Columbus   Officers' Quarters   Buttermilk Channel

GOVERNOR'S ISLAND, Upper New York Harbor. Occupied as a defence since 1802. Looking north from the Bay, Manhattan's tall office-buildings in the distance. Reached by ferry from the Battery. Historic island at junction of Hudson and East Rivers. Now U. S. Army Headquarters, Atlantic Division, Dep't of the East, Gen. Frederick D. Grant, Commandant. Being greatly enlarged by filling in at the southeast side. Castle William, an antiquated stone fort, built in 1811, is used mainly as a military prison. Fort Jay is a modern structure. A museum of war-relics is on the east side.

Williamsburg Bridge   Broadway Ferries, beyond bridge-tower   Wallabout Bay   Brooklyn Bridge   Factories

THE EAST RIVER. Great tidal waterway dividing the Boroughs of Manhattan (on the left) and Brooklyn (on the right).

Highway of commerce between New York and the East and Canada. The daily freight and passenger traffic through this section is enormous. The swift tides demand the greatest skill of pilots. The view shows Brooklyn Bridge in nearly its entire length of more than a mile. Williamsburg Bridge in the distance, where the river curves to the north at almost a right angle and enters Long Island Sound.

East River   Grain Barges   South Brooklyn   Governor's Island   Staten Island

THE LOWER EAST RIVER, with water-front of Brooklyn from Atlantic Street (South Ferry) to Gowanus Bay. View from Hanover Square, Manhattan.

Great commercial highway to the ocean and to the northeast, and from Brooklyn to the south, west, and Hudson River, with its New Jersey docks and railroad lines. Upper Bay on the right. The Narrows (outlet to Lower Bay) in distance, over the island. Buttermilk Channel between the island and Brooklyn. Manhattan termini of South, Hamilton, and Thirty-ninth Street ferries on the right.

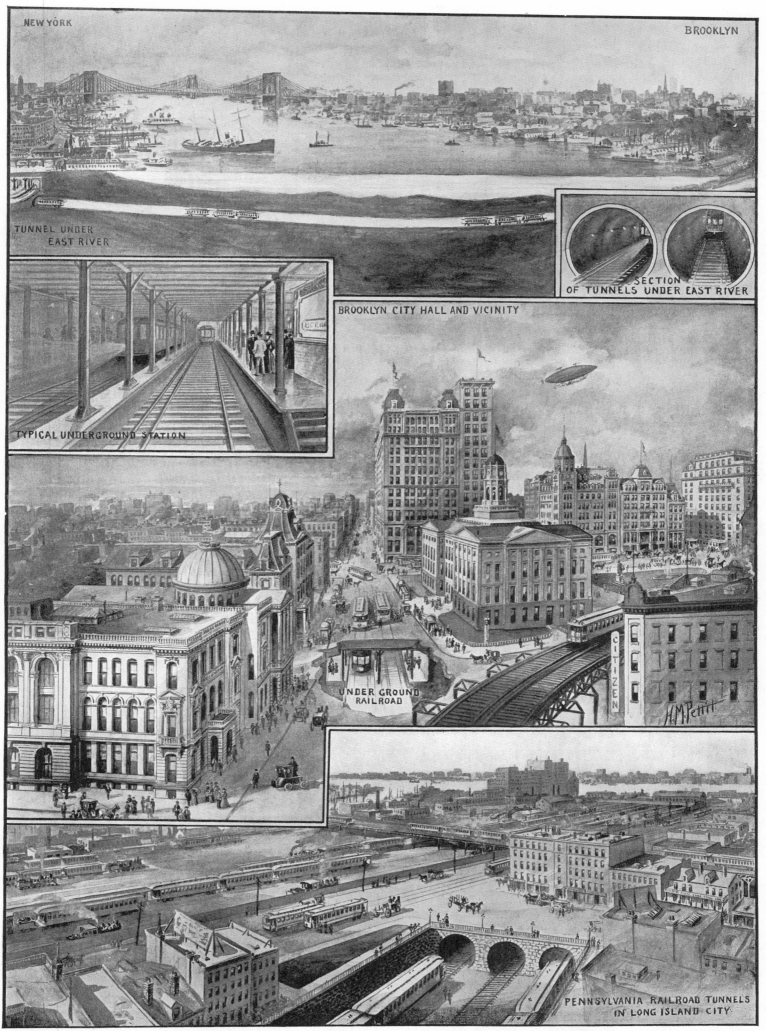

NEW YORK

BROOKLYN

TUNNEL UNDER EAST RIVER

SECTION OF TUNNELS UNDER EAST RIVER

TYPICAL UNDERGROUND STATION

BROOKLYN CITY HALL AND VICINITY

UNDER GROUND RAILROAD

CITIZEN

H.M.Pettit

PENNSYLVANIA RAILROAD TUNNELS IN LONG ISLAND CITY

TUNNEL, SURFACE, AND ELEVATED RAILROADS, indicating some of the gigantic and costly projects now well under way.

Brooklyn keeps outgrowing its transportation facilities as fast as they are provided.   The congestion of travel will soon be relieved by various improvements indicated above.   The East River Rapid Transit tunnel (consisting of two tubes) will run from Whitehall Street, Manhattan, to Joralemon Street, Brooklyn, connecting at each end with the underground railroad, which in Brooklyn will extend up Joralemon Street, Fulton Street, and Flatbush Avenue to Atlantic Avenue, at the Long Island Railroad station.   It is known as the Brooklyn Extension of the New York Rapid Transit Subway, and a single fare of five cents is to take a passenger to any station of the Manhattan–Bronx lines, — a distance of seventeen and one-half miles.   A marvelously gigantic undertaking of world-wide interest is the tunnel system of the Pennsylvania Railroad, which, passing from New Jersey under Hudson River, Manhattan Borough, and East River, will reach Long Island City near Thompson Avenue, and bring the whole of Long Island into the finest and most direct all-rail communication with the whole country.

Manhattan Tower and Approach   East River   Greenpoint   Havemeyer Sugar Refineries   Williamsburg Tower

WILLIAMSBURG BRIDGE, crossing East River from Delancey and Clinton Streets, Manhattan, to Driggs Avenue, near Broadway (Williamsburg), Brooklyn.   Cost about $10,000,000.
Combined cantilever and suspension structure.   Total length, 7264 feet; central span, 1600 feet.   Height at center, 135 feet.   Width, 118 feet.   Two roadways, two foot-paths, four trolley-car tracks, two elevated tracks.   Diameter of each of the four cables, 18¾ inches; 7696 wires in each cable.   Small parks laid out beneath the approaches.   Begun, 1896.   Roadway formally opened, Dec. 19, 1903.

Manhattan   Astoria   Fall River Boat   Blackwell's Island — Public Institutions   Long Island City.

BLACKWELL'S ISLAND BRIDGE, crossing East River from Second Avenue, near 59th Street, Manhattan, to Jane and Academy Streets, Long Island City.   To be finished 1907.
Total length, 7,636 ft.; height, 135 ft.; width, 86 ft.   Double deck.   Roadway (36 ft.) and 4 trolley-tracks on lower deck; 2 railroad tracks and 2 footpaths above.   Will open direct communication between the center of Manhattan and important towns comprised in the New York City consolidation of 1898, Astoria, Newtown, Flushing, College Point, Whitestone, Jamaica, etc.

Home Life "World"   Broadway-Chambers   Roosevelt St. Ferry   L. I. R. R. Ferry.   Brooklyn Tower

THE BROOKLYN BRIDGE, crossing the East River from City Hall, Manhattan, to Sands and Washington Streets, Brooklyn.   Begun 1870; opened May 24, 1883.   John A. Roebling, Engineer
Total length of wagon-way, about 6000 ft.; river-span, 1595 ft.; width, 85 ft.; height at center, 135 ft.   Two cable and 2 trolley-car tracks, 2 wagon-ways and a footpath.   Roebling's designing and erecting of this magnificent structure marked an era in bridge construction.   At the opening ceremonies it was stated that almost every science known to man had contributed to its accomplishment.

MANHATTAN TOWER of the Williamsburg Bridge, foot of Delancey Street.
View showing cantilever construction and strongly trussed towers, and arrangement of cables. Weight of steel in tower, 3000 tons. Height, 310 ft. above water. Masonry below water, 66 ft.

NEWTOWN CREEK BRIDGE, Manhattan Ave., Brooklyn, to Vernon Ave., L. I. City.
In process of construction. Drawbridge, of the rolling-lift pattern. This is one of numerous public improvements tending to develop a region whose advantages to commerce have been overlooked.

Brooklyn   Brooklyn Bridge   Manhattan Bridge   About 1500 feet north of Brooklyn Bridge   E. W. Bliss Co.'s Works   Manhattan

MANHATTAN BRIDGE, crossing East River from foot of Pike Street, Manhattan, to foot of Washington Street, Brooklyn. View from Brooklyn. To be finished 1906. Officially "Bridge No. 3."
Wire-cable suspension-structure. Manhattan terminus, Bowery and Canal Street; Brooklyn terminus, Myrtle Avenue and Gold Street. Length, 9,330 feet; width, 119 feet; height at centre, 135 feet.
Broad roadway, 2 foot-paths, 8 railroad-tracks. Planned by Commissioner Gustav Lindenthal as an "eye-bar bridge," changed in 1904 by Commissioner George E. Best to the cable-suspension.

Livingston St. Court Square Fulton St. County C. H.

HALL OF RECORDS, Court Square, Fulton, and Livingston Streets. Enlarged and remodeled 1904.

White marble. Classic motif. One of the best municipal buildings. Contains Offices of the Commissioner of Records, County Register, County Clerk, and Surrogate. Archives for records of realty-transactions, wills, judgments, and executions. Department for recopying old and mutilated records.

175 feet long THE "JACOB A. STAMLER." 955-ton Vessel. 50 staterooms

One of several comfortable boats, maintained by John Arbuckle, especially equipped for short sea trips for invalids and others at nominal prices.

County Court House New Municipal Building Washington Hull, Architect Court St.

NEW ADMINISTRATIVE MUNICIPAL BUILDING. To occupy site of old Municipal Building with extension to Court Street.

This eight-story Indiana-limestone structure, of late French-Renaissance architecture, will cost from $1,500,000 to $2,000,000. Of eleven competitive designs, Washington Hull's was adopted. Main entrance on Joralemon St.; another on Court St. In the centre two open courts extend to the roof.

Fulton St. County Court House Municipal Building Park

MUNICIPAL BUILDING, Joralemon Street, near Fulton Street. Erected 1876.

Occupied by the Bureaus of Highways and Sewers and other Borough offices. This familiar landmark and other buildings at the right of the park are to be removed to make room for the eight-story Municipal Building shown above, which will extend from the Court House on the left to Court Street.

One of five opened 1903–4 Axel S. Hedman, Architect

FREE PUBLIC BATH, Hicks Street, near Degraw Street.

Limestone, with marble panels. Fitted with tubs, and hot and cold showers. Known as Interior Bath, in distinction from Floating Bath.

Fulton St.　Hall of Records　County Court House　　Beecher Statue　　Borough Hall　　　Polytechnic Institute　　Court St.　　Dime Savings Bank.

CITY HALL PARK AND PUBLIC BUILDINGS, Fulton, Joralemon, and Court Streets, looking south.　Photo by George P. Hall & Son, from Mechanics' Bank.

At the centre is Borough Hall, formerly Brooklyn City Hall.　Behind it, on Joralemon Street, is the Municipal Building; next the latter, on the left (with dome) is the County Court House; next beyond is the Hall of Records, facing Court Square.　The brick building back of the Park, at the right of the Municipal Building, is the Polytechnic Institute, facing on Livingston Street.

1,200 Employees in Department.　　　　Gamewell Fire-Alarm Telegraph Co. System.

FIRE DEPARTMENT BUILDING, 367 and 369 Jay Street, near Myrtle Avenue.

Headquarters of the Fire Department for the Borough, containing offices of the Deputy Fire Commissioner and other officials, also Bureau of Combustibles, and Chief Operator of Alarm System.

Mechanics' Bank　　　Beecher Statue　　　Fulton St. Elevated Road　　　Brooklyn "Eagle"

CITY HALL PARK, Beecher Statue, and Mechanics Bank.

Court, Fulton, and Washington Sts.　View northward.　Montague St. on left.　One of Brooklyn's busiest sections.　Junction of several trolley-lines.　Great recent building activity in vicinity.

Wall St. Ferry   South Ferry   Grain Elevators   Warehouses   Hamilton Ferry   Gowanus Bay   Atlantic Basin   Yacht Clubs   Bay Ridge   Governor's Island   Staten Island

PANORAMIC VIEW OF BROOKLYN, photographed from the offices of Stephen H. P. Pell & Co., bankers and brokers, 25th (top) floor of the Wall Street Exchange, 43 Exchange Place, Manhattan. One of the grandest views of Brooklyn and environs obtainable. This impressive and magnificent panorama over East River extends (including both views on this page) from the Narrows northward to the Greenpoint section, a water-front of 10 miles. The above portion comprises South Brooklyn, from Montague Street (Wall Street Ferry) to Gowanus Bay; the Bay Ridge shore; the Narrows: Staten Island. Green-Wood Cemetery in the middle background. Opposite Governor's Island, entrance to the great Atlantic Basin, which, with the Erie Basin farther south, provides enormous wharfage, warehouse, and dry-dock facilities. Ship-building plants adjoining.

Greenpoint   Williamsburg Bridge   Sugar Refineries   Brooklyn Bridge   Navy Yard   Fulton Ferry   Warehouses   Fort Greene Park   The Heights   Office Buildings   Wall St. Ferry

PANORAMIC VIEW OF BROOKLYN (continuous with view above), from offices of Stephen H. P. Pell & Co., bankers and brokers, Wall Street Exchange, 43 Exchange Place, Manhattan. Photographed by George P. Hall & Sons, for "King's Views." From this view-point, higher than the Bridge-towers, can be seen Brooklyn's outlying districts from Flatbush to Jamaica, as well as its foreground of manufacturing and shipping industries and great hotels and apartment-houses. Prominent at the right is the residential section on the Heights, with Holy Trinity's beautiful spire; beyond, the Brooklyn Institute museum and the water-tower. Between Fulton Ferry and Greenpoint lies a great manufacturing centre; back of this, the largest residential district; beyond, the Evergreens and Cypress Hills Cemeteries and "East New York."

Joralemon St.   Union Bank   Long Island Loan & Trust Co.

TEMPLE BAR BUILDING, Court Street, N. W. corner Joralemon Street.

Tallest and most imposing office building in Brooklyn. Gray stone and light brick. Twelve stories, besides basement and towers. Two hundred offices. Completed 1901. Owned by David G. Legget.

Site of the historic Academy of Music.   Helmle, Huberty & Hudswell, Architects.

THE LAWYERS' TITLE INSURANCE CO. OF N. Y., 188–190 Montague Street.

An absolutely fire-proof, imposing, and commodious office building. This company examines and insures titles. Large force of professional experts. Capital and surplus, $8,000,000. E. W. Coggeshall, President.

Remsen Street   Nassau National Bank   Cady & Co., Architects

GARFIELD BUILDING, 26 and 28 Court Street, Corner Remsen.

Eight stories; red brick. Colonial architectural motif. Earliest of Brooklyn's great office-buildings. On main floor, Nassau National Bank. Founded 1859. Capital, $300,000. Thomas T. Barr, Pres.

Extends through block to 148 and 150 Pierrepont St.   Library   Mechanics' Bank

BROOKLYN REAL ESTATE EXCHANGE, 189 and 191 Montague Street.

Red brick building; iron bays, brown stone trimmings. Erected 1890. Real Estate Exchange, Pres., E. J. Granger; Sec., G. W. Chauncey. Hamilton Trust Co., Hon. S. B. Dutcher, Pres., on main floor.

Washington St.   Johnson St.

POST-OFFICE AND FEDERAL BUILDING, Washington Street, N. E. corner Johnson

City Post-office and Federal Courts and offices located here. Building completed 1892. Cost, $2,000,000.
Blue granite, Romanesque and modern Renaissance styles. George H. Roberts, Jr., Postmaster.

Founded 1841   Superb structure completed 1904   George L. Morse, Archt

BROOKLYN DAILY EAGLE, Washington Street, S. E. corner Johnson.

One of America's leading newspapers. Perfectly appointed. Press-room visible from street. Col. William
Hester, Pres.; W. V. Hester, Treasurer; St. Clair McKelway, Editor; Herbert L. Gunnison, Manager.

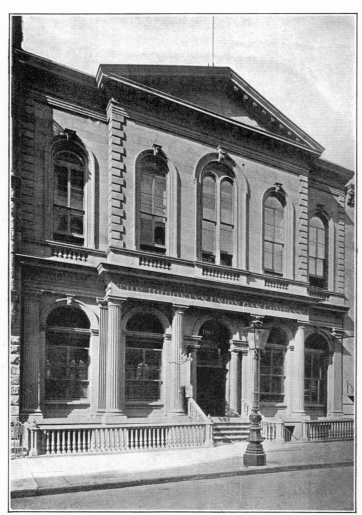

Main Office   Branches throughout the Borough

BROOKLYN UNION GAS CO.   General offices, 180 Remsen Street, near Court Street.

One of the largest manufacturing corporations in Brooklyn. Producing and supplying gas for illuminating, heating, cooking, and manufacturing purposes. James Jourdan, Pres.; Walter K. Rossiter, Sec'y.

Extension in rear to 317 Fulton St.   Leading Republican daily   Formerly at Fulton and Front Sts.

BROOKLYN STANDARD UNION, 292 to 296 Washington St., near Johnson St.

"Union" founded 1864. Later combined with "Argus" and "Standard." Evening and Sunday issues.
Many citizens identified with its history. Wm. Berri, Publisher. H. L. Bridgman, Manager.

Lawrence St.   Willoughby St.

TELEPHONE BUILDING, Willoughby, N. E. corner Lawrence Street.
The substantial and imposing headquarters of the New York and New Jersey Telephone Co. in Brooklyn.
Executive offices, "exchanges," and legal department.

Kings Co. Trust Co.   Frank Freeman, Architect

THE THOMAS JEFFERSON, Court Square, near Fulton Street.
Florid Romanesque. Brown sandstone. Copper bays in recesses between piers. Bust of Thomas
Jefferson. Home of Kings County Democracy. Headquarters of Democratic influence in Brooklyn.

BROOKLYN WAREHOUSE & STORAGE CO., 335 to 355 Schermerhorn Street.
Brick and stone. Absolutely fire-proof structure. Stores plate and valuables under guarantee; general and
household storage and safe-deposit vaults. George W. Chauncey, Pres.; H. L. Bridgman, Treas.

PIONEER WAREHOUSES, 41 and 43 Flatbush Avenue, near Fulton Street.
Imposing fire-proof building; extends to Rockwell Pl. Special and general storage; moving-vans; pack-
ing, shipping, etc. Safe-deposit and silver vaults. Louis L. Firuski, Prop. G. H. Shephard, Mgr.

Hamilton Club   Clinton St.   Franklin Trust Bldg.   Montague St.

FRANKLIN TRUST CO., Montague and Clinton Sts.   Manhattan office, 140 Broadway.
Nine-story office-building of the Franklin Trust Company.   Capital, $1,000,000.   Surplus and undivided
profits, $1,500,000.   Geo. H. Southard, Pres.   Trust and banking business.   Safes and storage-vaults.

Erected 1904–1905   Mowbray & Uffinger, Architects

THE PEOPLES TRUST CO., 181 and 183 Montague Street.   Founded 1889.
Handsome new building, to be occupied in 1905.   Branch at 1223 Bedford Ave   Capital, $1,000,000.   Sur-
plus and undivided profits, $1,600,000.   Edward Johnson, President.   Charles A. Boody, Secretary.

Bedford Ave.   Founded 1888   Broadway

NASSAU TRUST COMPANY, 136 Broadway, corner Bedford Avenue.
Five-story white sandstone building.   Branch office, 356 and 358 Fulton Street.   Capital, $500,000.
Surplus, over $500,000.   Andrew T. Sullivan, President.   Interest on deposits.   Safe-deposit vaults.

Organized 1858   Building erected 1870

KINGS COUNTY FIRE INSURANCE CO., 97 Broadway, near Berry Street.
This Company, after 46 years of business, became incorporated with the Atlas Assurance Company (Lim-
ited), of London, whose United States managers are Frank Lock and Geo. S. A. Young.

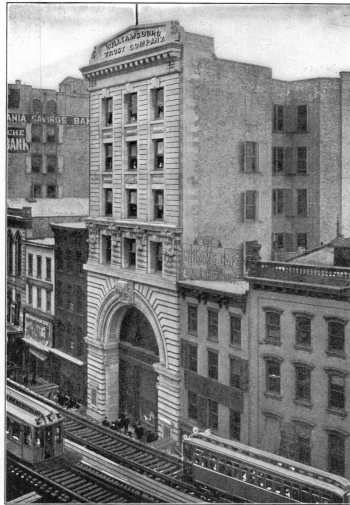

Organized 1899   Superb bank edifice, erected 1904-'5   Occupied January, 1905.
WILLIAMSBURGH TRUST COMPANY, Fulton Street, opp. Borough Hall.
Capital and surplus, $1,250,000.   Offices, Broadway and Kent Ave.; Broadway and Myrtle Ave.
John G. Jenkins, Pres.; Frank Jenkins and John W. Weber, Vice-Pres'ts.; W. Addison Field, Sec'y.

Fulton St.   Court Square
KINGS COUNTY TRUST CO., 342-346 Fulton Street, corner Court Square.
Four-story, buff sandstone office-building, in Brooklyn's financial and commercial center.   Erected 1869.
Capital, $500,000.   Surplus and undivided profits, $1,375,000.   Hon. Julian D. Fairchild, President.

WILLIAMSBURGH CITY FIRE INSURANCE CO., 13 Broadway, corner Kent Ave.
Capital, $250,000.   Reserve, $867,932.   Net surplus, $1,230,518.   Branch at 156 Montague Street.
Policies issued under Safety Fund law.   Marshall S. Driggs, President.   Frederick H. Way, Secretary.

WILLIAMSBURGH CITY FIRE INSURANCE CO., Branch, 156 Montague Street.
This branch occupies a fine old Montague Street brown-stone residence.   Besides the main office in
Williamsburg, the company owns the valuable corner, Broadway and Liberty Street, Manhattan.

Brooklyn Bank   Long Island Safe Deposit Co.

BROOKLYN BANK, Junction of Fulton and Clinton Streets, near Clark Street.

Oldest among Brooklyn banks. 1832. Capital, $300,000. Surplus and profits, $162,000. Deposits, $2,000,000. Henry E. Hutchinson, Pres. Thomas M. Halsey, Cashier. Branch at 601 Fulton St.

Red Hook Lane   Founded 1850   Fulton St.

NATIONAL CITY BANK, 350–352 Fulton Street, corner Red Hook Lane.

Six-story office building. Yellow brick and white sandstone. Sixty office suites. Capital, $300,000. Deposits, $4,000,000. Surplus and undivided profits, $600,000. Charles T. Young, President.

Berry St.   Manufacturers' National Bank   Broadway

MANUFACTURERS' NATIONAL BANK, Broadway and Berry Street, Williamsburg.

One of the largest banks in the Williamsburg District. Yellow brick and white sandstone bank and office building. Capital, $252,000. Surplus and undivided profits, $533,000. William Dick, President.

Erected 1895   Established 1888   H. Batterman Dept. Store

BROADWAY BANK, 12 Graham Avenue, Junction of Broadway.

Granite and light brick. In center of a great shopping district. Capital, $300,000. Surplus and undivided profits, $168,000. Deposits, $2,000,000. Henry Batterman, Pres't. Geo. F. Moger, Cashier.

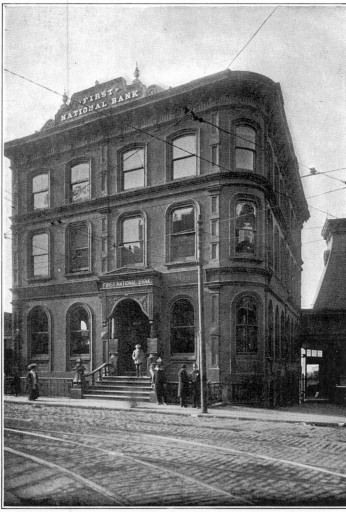

Kent Ave.   Founded 1852   Broadway Ferries
FIRST NATIONAL BANK, Broadway and Kent Avenue, Williamsburg.
Red brick building, near Broadway ferries. Capital, $300,000. Surplus and undivided profits, $574,000. President, John G. Jenkins (also President of Williamsburgh Trust Co.); W. A. Field, Cashier.

Montague St.   Mechanics' Bank and Extension proposed to Pierrepont St.   Fulton St.
MECHANICS' BANK, Junction Fulton, Court, and Montague Streets. Founded 1852.
Conspicuous building and proposed addition. Strongest State bank on Long Island. Capital, $500,000. Deposits, $9,936,970. Surplus, $465,371. Three branches. George W. Chauncey, President.

Formerly Mechanics and Traders Bank. One of fifteen branches of the largest State bank.
CORN EXCHANGE BANK, Greenpoint Branch, 144 Franklin Street, cor. Greenpoint Ave.
Main bank, William and Beaver Sts., Manhattan. Capital, $2,000,000. Deposits, $29,000,000. Surplus and undivided profits, $3,286,000. William A. Nash, President. Walter E. Frew, Vice-President.

Greene Ave.   State bank, founded 1893   Broadway
PEOPLES BANK, 1246 Broadway, corner Greene Avenue, Williamsburg.
Two-story light sandstone building. Bronze trimmings and panels. Capital, $100,000. Deposits, $1,100,000. Surplus, $166,000. George W. Spence, President. Francis I. Ketcham, Cashier.

The Touraine　Crescent Club　Clinton St.　　　　　　　　　　Brooklyn Savings Bank, founded 1827　Erected 1893　　　　Pierrepont St.

THE BROOKLYN SAVINGS BANK, Brooklyn's oldest savings-institution, Pierrepont Street, Northeast corner Clinton Street.　One of America's finest savings-banks.
Classic Roman architecture.　White granite.　Tile roof, bronze trimmings.　Former building, classic brown-stone, Fulton and Concord Sts.　This bank has had 399,000 depositors, representing $248,500,000, and has paid in interest $32,000,000.　Depositors, 63,900.　Deposits, $39,500,000.　Surplus, $5,600,000.　Bryan H. Smith, President.　Edward D. White and Crowell Hadden, Vice-Presidents.

Atlantic Ave.　　　　Established 1850, in the old Athenæum building.　　　　Clinton St.
SOUTH BROOKLYN SAVINGS INSTITUTION, Atlantic Avenue and Clinton Street.
Five-story white marble office building erected in 1870.　Deposits, $17,000,000.　Surplus, $2,400,000.
32,000 depositors.　William J. Coombs, President.　J. E. Brown, H. C. Hulbert, Vice-Presidents.

Arbuckle Bldg.　　　　　Germania Savings Bank　　　　　Park Theatre
GERMANIA SAVINGS BANK, 375 Fulton St.　Eight-story office-building, facing Borough Hall.
Modified German Gothic.　Bronze statue of "Germania" over entrance.　Assets, $7,022,929.　Deposits, $6,619,069.　Surplus, $403,859.　Hon. Charles A. Schieren, Pres't.　Julius Lehrenkrauss, Treas.

Extension, 1904–5   Popularly known as the "Temple"   Established 1851

WILLIAMSBURGH SAVINGS BANK, Broadway and Driggs Avenue.

Gray granite edifice. Classic architecture. At Williamsburg Bridge terminus. Deposits, $44,000,000; 93,000 depositors. Surplus, $8,000,000. J. V. Meserole, President. William F. Burns, Cashier.

Temple Bar   Dime Savings Bank (as proposed)   Founded 1859   The Franklin

DIME SAVINGS BANK, Court Street, S. W. corner Remsen, facing Borough Hall.

Magnificent office building, contemplated as a superstructure upon present two-story white freestone edifice, erected 1883. Deposits, $29,000,000. Surplus, $2,200,000. J. Lawrence Marcellus, President.

Bedford Ave.   Founded 1860   Broadway

KINGS COUNTY SAVINGS INSTITUTION, Broadway and Bedford Avenue.

Gray freestone building, landmark of old Williamsburg. Near terminus of Williamsburg Bridge. Deposits, $10,000,000. Surplus, $700,000. Hubert G. Taylor, Pres't; Edward McGarvey, Theo. E. Green, Vice-Pres'ts.

Boerum St.   Founded 1866   Broadway

GERMAN SAVINGS BANK OF BROOKLYN, Broadway and Boerum Street.

Three-story red brick and buff sandstone office building. Four-story extension in rear for lodge rooms. Surplus, $433,000. Deposits, $8,361,000. Charles Naeher, President. George S. Bishop, Cashier.

Machine Shops   Chain Ferry   Keel of "Connecticut," building   "Brooklyn"   "Massachusetts"   "Iowa"   Tug "Chickasaw"   Cob Dock   Receiving Ship   Chain Ferry

UNITED STATES NAVY YARD. Looking north, to the East River, along the lower end of Wallabout Channel. Williamsburg Bridge at right.

The Brooklyn (officially called the New York) Navy Yard contains immense and complete facilities for construction and repair of ships of war and accessories. The numerous buildings include foundries, machine, boiler, and plumbing shops, painting, blacksmithing, moulding, and cooperage works, storehouses, and marine barracks. Lyceum, with many captured guns and naval relics. Enormous dry docks, one of which is among the largest in America; around these, 18-foot railways for 40-ton lifting cranes, towering above all buildings and visible from long distances.

Supply ship "Culgoa"   "Newark"   "Columbia"   "Florida"   "Massachusetts," in Dry Dock No. 3   "Iowa," in Dry Dock No. 2   Tug "Powhatan"

UNITED STATES NAVY YARD. Looking northeast on Wallabout Channel. A granite sea wall of nearly 3 miles protects its extensive water front. Established, 1801, by purchase of 30 acres of land from John Jackson for $40,000. Value of entire plant now in use, about $30,000,000. The first steam war-vessel, "Fulton," was built here, 1815; among the latest, the first-class battle-ships "Maine" and "Connecticut." Admission to the Yard (8 A.M. to 5 P.M.) is by pass, obtainable by mail application to Captain of the Yard; admission to ships by additional permission from their commanding officers. Yard reached by Flushing Avenue car from Brooklyn Bridge, either end.

Scene of constant activity, thousands of men being employed.

UNITED STATES NAVY YARD, Wallabout Bay, Brooklyn, midway between Williamsburg and Brooklyn Bridges. Lower view shows hull of battleship "Connecticut," at left, then building.
1. — Floating derricks, 100-ton and 65-ton; receiving-ship "Hancock"; battleships "Illinois," "Iowa" and "Alabama." 2. — "Illinois"; overhead crane; "Alabama"; 65-ton derrick; battleship "Texas." 3. — Park and officers' quarters. 4. — Commandant's office; captured Spanish and Mexican guns; general storehouse. 5. — "Iowa"; "Hancock"; "Texas"; naval tugs; vidette boat at dock. 6. — Overhead crane; "Alabama"; battleship "Kearsarge" in distance; "Illinois." 7. — Construction railway; "Alabama." 8. — Entrance to dry-dock No. 2.

Cumberland to Raymond Sts., Myrtle to DeKalb Aves.   Fortified in 1776 and 1812.

FORT GREENE PARK ENTRANCE, Myrtle Avenue, opposite Elliott Place.   One of Brooklyn's many pleasure-grounds.

Park of thirty acres. Site of Fort Greene, of Revolutionary fame. Established 1847 as Washington Park, but popularly called Fort Greene Park. Burial-place of many of the prison-ship martyrs, whose sufferings have seldom been paralleled. Soldiers' monument by MacMonnies.

Putnam Ave.   R. L. Daus, Architect.   Sumner Ave.   Jefferson Ave.

THIRTEENTH REGIMENT ARMORY, Sumner, Putnam, and Jefferson Avenues.

Organized 1847. Served in riots, 1863, 1871; in strikes, 1877, 1892, 1895; in the Civil War, immediately upon Lincoln's call for 75,000 men, April, 1861; in the Spanish War. David E. Austen, Colonel.

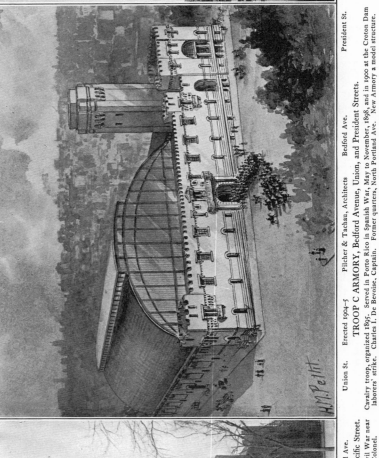

Union St.   Erected 1904-5   Pilcher & Tachau, Architects   President St.

TROOP C ARMORY, Bedford Avenue, Union, and President Streets.

Cavalry troop, organized 1895. Served in Porto Rico in Spanish War, May to November, 1898, and in 1900 at the Croton Dam laborers' strike. Charles I. De Bevoise, Captain. Former quarters, North Portland Ave. New Armory a model structure.

Pacific St.   Organized 1862.   Bedford Ave.

TWENTY-THIRD REGIMENT ARMORY, Bedford Avenue, N. W. corner Pacific Street.

Infantry Regiment. Served in draft riots, 1877, 1892, 1895, 1901. In Civil War near Gettysburg, 1863. Furnished many volunteers in Spanish War. William A. Stokes, Colonel.

Sea Gate, Coney Island, in distance.   Photo. by Enrique Muller.

FORT HAMILTON PARK, Shore Road and Fort Hamilton Parkway.   One of Brooklyn's four seaside-parks.

At southern end of Fort Hamilton Parkway, Shore Road Junction, facing the Lower Bay. Seven acres. Popular summer-resort near the United States Government reservation and harbor defences. Opposite Fort Lafayette. Beautiful view of the harbor, from Coney Island and Sandy Hook to the Narrows.

Site originally occupied by a log-fort   Built 1812–22, to command the harbor, and called Fort Diamond   Photo. by Enrique Muller

FORT LAFAYETTE. At entrance to the Narrows, on an artificial island near the Long Island shore, off Fort Hamilton. Long abandoned as to defensive purposes. Renamed in honor of the great French general who so nobly espoused the American cause in the Revolution, on occasion of his later visit to this country. Used during Civil War as a military prison, and made famous by incarceration of many prominent characters. Fire in 1868 destroyed interior. Now used for ordnance stores, etc.

15th St.   Eighth Ave.   14th St.

FOURTEENTH REGIMENT ARMORY, 8th Avenue, 14th and 15th Streets.
Regiment organized 1847. Famous service in "Orange" riots, 1871; repeatedly since. Three years in Civil War. Bull Run and 21 other battles. Five months in Spanish War. A. L. Kline, Colonel.

Popularly called Raymond Street Jail   Accommodates 250 inmates

KINGS COUNTY JAIL, Raymond Street, between Willoughby and De Kalb Avenues.
Norman architecture. Gray and white granite. For prisoners and suspects committed by city magistrates. W. H. McLaughlin, Warden. The Penitentiary is used by United States for convicted bank officers.

FIRE BOAT "DAVID A. BOODY." Berth, foot of Main Street (Catharine Ferry).
To protect water-front and shipping. Throws several powerful streams. Belongs to city Fire Department; connected with alarm system at Headquarters, 369 Jay Street. Named after ex-Mayor David A. Boody.

GAMEWELL FIRE-ALARM ROOM, in the Fire Department Headquarters, 369 Jay Street.
Equipment furnished by the Gamewell Fire-Alarm Telegraph Co., by which instant and definite notice of fire is signalled. This efficient service saves annually millions of dollars of property, and incalculable lives.

FORT HAMILTON. Military post at southwest point of land at foot of Fort Hamilton Parkway. Reached by Third and Hamilton Avenue surface cars, and by transfers from the elevated roads. On a United States Government reservation of 167 acres. Stone fort, built with casemates and earthworks front, commanding the Narrows in conjunction with Fort Wadsworth on the Staten Island shore opposite. Altitude, 47 feet. Corner stone laid June 11, 1825; first garrisoned by troops Nov. 1, 1831. Named after Alex. Hamilton. Included in Department of the East, headquarters on Governor's Island.

View of Building when completed   Corner-stone laid 1896, by Mayor Charles A. Schieren   Evolution of Apprentices' Library Association, founded 1823, and old Brooklyn Institute, 1843   First section (at right) completed May, 1897   Second section (center) in 1904   McKim, Mead & White, Architects

BROOKLYN INSTITUTE OF ARTS AND SCIENCES, Institute Park, Eastern Parkway and Washington Ave., East of Plaza entrance to Prospect Park. Next to Reservoir. Building, Indiana limestone, classic architecture. Museums, art galleries, class-rooms, laboratories   Estimated cost, $5,000,000. Brooklyn's grandest institution. Unique among American educational enterprises. Re-incorporated under present name, in 1890. General circulating library, 6,000 volumes; departmental libraries, 26,000 volumes. Academy of Arts and Sciences, 30 departments. Classes in special subjects; public lectures; facilities for original research; summer schools of fine arts and biology. Admission free, except Mondays and Tuesdays. A. Augustus Healy, President. Franklin W. Hooper, A. M., General Director. Business offices at 502 Fulton Street.

The Thrift

Main Building.—Science, Technology, and Trade Schools   Domestic Art Building

PRATT INSTITUTE, Ryerson Street, between De Kalb and Willoughby Avenues.   An institution for the promotion of art, science, industry, and technology (including trades), domestic science, domestic art, kindergarten dep'rtments.   3,500 students, 124 instructors.   Library, opposite Main Building   Spanish Cannon on the Esplanade   Founded, 1887, by Charles Pratt.   School of library science.   Children's room and library.   Museum

Industrial and fine arts, science, and technology (including trades), domestic science, domestic art, kindergarten dep'rtments.   3,500 students, 124 instructors.   Circulation nearly 200,000 annually.   Free library, 77,126 volumes;   of nature, art, and industry.   Gymnasium.   Extensive playgrounds.   "Thrift" department.   Sa ings and loan and build'ng features founded 1889;   assets, $2,325,000; encourages saving and home-building.   Charles M. Pratt, Pres't.   Frederic B. Pratt, Sec'y and Gen'l M'gr.

St. James Place   Clifton Place

ADELPHI COLLEGE, Clifton Place, St. James Place, and Lafayette Avenue.   Established 1863   Incorporated 1896

Adelphi Academy, now Preparatory School, incorporated 1869.   Science and Arts building endowed by Charles Pratt in 1888.   Adelphi College, including Normal and Fine Arts Schools, incorporated 1896.   In all departments, about 1,320 students.   Gymnasium and playing-field.   Charles H. Levermore, President,

Fourth St.   Manual Training High School   Fifth St.

MANUAL TRAINING HIGH SCHOOL, 7th Avenue, between 4th and 5th Sts.   Modern French Renaissance, 200 x 228 feet.   Fire-proof.

Chemical and physical laboratories; forge and machine shop; printing and bookbinding rooms; sewing-room; kitchen, for model-housekeeping course.   Large auditorium; lecture-room.   In basement, dining-room, gymnasium, and bicycle-room.   Cost, $500,000.   2,500 pupils.   Charles D. Larkins, Principal.

C.B.T.SNYDER·ARCH'T.

Trinity Church   Society founded 1863   Building completed 1880   George B. Post, Architect

LONG ISLAND HISTORICAL SOCIETY, corner Clinton and Pierrepont Streets.

Houses a most valuable collection of historical material, including a library of 70,860 volumes, and a museum of antiquities. Lecture-hall. Alexander E. Orr, President. John J. Pierrepont, Treasurer.

Library   Formerly the Brooklyn Library   Mechanics' Bank

BROOKLYN PUBLIC LIBRARY, Montague Branch, 197 Montague Street.

Merged into the Public Library in 1902; 164,000 volumes; 300 periodicals. The Public Library has nineteen branches; 200,000 volumes; 1,250,000 annual (free) circulation. David A. Boody, President.

Founded 1844   French Gothic brick and stone buildings   Memorial to William S. Packer

PACKER COLLEGIATE INSTITUTE, Joralemon Street, near Clinton Street.

Leading girls' school. Well equipped in all departments. Chapel seats 1000. 600 students. 50 instructors. Truman J. Backus, President of Faculty   Bryan H. Smith, President of Trustees.

Livingston Street   About 700 students   Fifty instructors   Founded 1854

POLYTECHNIC INSTITUTE OF BROOKLYN, Livingston and Court Streets.

Scientific, technical, engineering, and liberal arts departments. F. W. Atkinson, Pres't. Spicer Memorial Library, 12,000 volumes, free to students.   F. R. Lane, Principal of Preparatory School.

Erected 1887   Cost over $300,000

CENTRAL HIGH SCHOOL, Nostrand Ave., near Halsey St.

One of the best and largest Girls' High Schools in the country. Over 2300 pupils and 95 teachers. In summer beautifully surrounded with trees and flowers. Principal, Wm. L. Felter, Ph.D., LL.D.

Erected 1891   Cost over $300,000

BOYS' HIGH SCHOOL, Putnam and Marcy Avenues.

A beautiful specimen of Romanesque architecture. About 1200 students; 54 teachers, who are all college graduates. The principal is John Mickleborough.

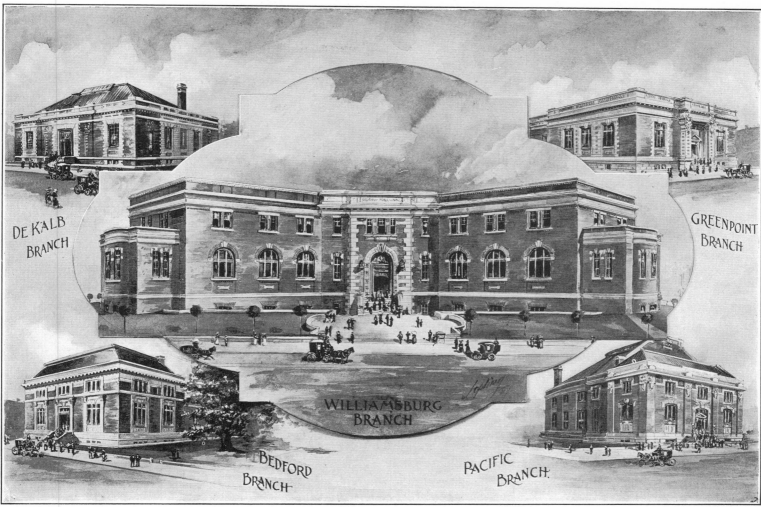

Erected 1903-1905   New Buildings of the Brooklyn Public Library system   Architects: Lord & Hewlett, W. B. Tubby & Bro., Walker & Morris, R. L. Daus, and R. F. Almirall

CARNEGIE LIBRARIES, Five Branches. Twenty are to be erected in Brooklyn.

Brooklyn derives $1,600,000, from the munificent gifts of Andrew Carnegie. The committee are D. A. Boody, D. W. McWilliams, R. R. Appleton, and J. W. Devoy. Five branches are: WILLIAMSBURG, Rodney St., Marcy and Division Aves.; DE KALB, Bushwick and De Kalb Aves.; GREENPOINT, Leonard and Norman Sts.; BEDFORD, Franklin Ave., opp. Hancock St; PACIFIC, Fourth Ave. and Pacific St.

PUBLIC SCHOOL NO. 136, Fourth Avenue, Fortieth and Forty-first Streets.

PUBLIC SCHOOL NO. 124, Fourth Avenue, Thirteenth and Fourteenth Streets.

Brooklyn abounds in modern model fire-proof school buildings, among the finest and best-appointed in the country, having large assembly halls, ventilating apparatus, heated and ventilated wardrobe rooms, rear, basement, and roof playgrounds, etc. There are 143 schools (in fourteen Districts, numbered 27 to 40), including kindergarten, elementary, high, and manual training schools, with 190,000 pupils and over 4,000 teachers. Free evening lectures.

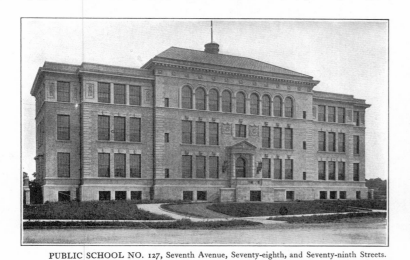

PUBLIC SCHOOL NO. 127, Seventh Avenue, Seventy-eighth, and Seventy-ninth Streets.

PUBLIC SCHOOL NO. 108, Linwood St. and Arlington Ave.

One of the first free schools founded on the American continent was established in "Breucklyn" in 1661, near present corner of Fulton and Bridge Streets, with Carl Debevoise as teacher, instruction being in Dutch until 1758; both Dutch and English until about 1830, then English only. Under English rule, free instruction was abolished, and not re-instated until after the Revolution. The Superintendent of Schools is William H. Maxwell.

AMERICAN SUGAR REFINING CO. Largest in the world. East River, Kent Avenue, between South First and South Fifth Streets, Williamsburg. Manhattan Offices, 117 Wall Street. Area, 500,000 square feet. Four city blocks on river front. Main building, ten stories, brick. Originally the "Havemeyer" and "Brooklyn," which consolidated with other refineries in 1887. Daily output capacity, 14,000 barrels of refined sugar. This company also operates several other large refineries in this and other cities, and is popularly called the "Sugar Trust." Henry O. Havemeyer, Pres't.

Twelfth Street   Seventh Avenue   Thirteenth Street

ANSONIA CLOCK COMPANY, Phelps, Dodge & Co., Seventh and Eighth Avenues, Twelfth and Thirteenth Streets. Main offices and salesrooms, Cliff and John Streets, New York. Founded 1876 at Ansonia, Conn. Removed to Brooklyn, 1877. Works occupy three entire city blocks, six and one-half acres. Largest clock-factory in the world. Ivy-covered buildings. Originally founded to manufacture inexpensive clocks. Now produces ornamental bronzes and an unlimited variety of decorative mantel-clocks of all grades. 1,500 employees. Products sold throughout the world.

Watson Stores   Hotel Margaret   Piers prominent on the water front between Fulton and Wall Street Ferries   The Heights

LAMPORT & HOLT LINE, Brazil and River Plate Steamships, Furman Street, base of Columbia Heights. Busk & Jevons, agents, 301 Produce Exchange, Manhattan.

Great freight and passenger transportation lines to South American ports. Monthly to River Plate, monthly to Brazil, and weekly to Manchester, England. 100 boats in service. From these docks begin voyages among the longest made by any vessels out of New York — 6,200 miles to Rio Janeiro, 7,100 to Montevideo, 8,000 to Buenos Ayres.

American Mfg. Co., Noble St., Greenpoint   Mollenhauer's   Brooklyn Rapid-Transit Power House

THE EASTERN DISTRICT WATER FRONT. Ships come here from all parts of the world. Commercial and manufacturing investments now here represent many millions of dollars.

Less than 100 years ago this shore consisted of farm and wooded land, with no direct connection between Greenpoint and Williamsburg, the latter comprising thirty acres. The enterprise of one man — Jeremiah Johnson — opened a river road across these lands, thus removing seventeen barred gates that had obstructed travel. Rapid commercial and manufacturing development followed.

EBERHARD FABER PENCIL COMPANY, Greenpoint Ave., Kent, and West Sts. Makers of world-famous lead pencils, penholders, rubber erasers, etc.

Extensive works of one of the largest manufacturers of lead pencils in the world. Established in New York City by Eberhard Faber in 1861. Innumerable styles, from small pocket-pencils to the long, flat carpenter's pencils, and fine stationery in endless variety, produced in enormous quantities. Manhattan salesroom, 545 Pearl Street, just east of Broadway.

THE NATIONAL SUGAR REFINING CO. OF NEW JERSEY, formerly Mollenhauer Refining Co., Kent Avenue, near South Eleventh Street, Williamsburg. Several great establishments under one management. Manhattan offices, 109 Wall Street

These buildings are among the most striking objects of Brooklyn's water front, and are in the midst of the greatest sugar-refining center of the world. In this part of old Williamsburg is barreled more than half the sugar consumed in the United States. The product comprises every grade known to commerce, from the cut cubes to the cheapest straw-colored qualities. Other industries and commodities incidentally tributary are coal, charcoal, transportation, etc., and vast cooperage plants are wholly maintained by the refinery demands. James H. Post, President. F. D. Mollenhauer, Treasurer.

Projectile Department, First Ave. and 53d St.

Main Machine Shops, Adams, John, Pearl and Plymouth Sts.

E. W. BLISS COMPANY, manufacturers of presses, dies, and special machinery for all kinds of sheet metal articles and drop forgings ; gears and pinions for street railways, gas vessels and sundry articles, etc. Offices, 17 Adams Street, near Plymouth Street, Brooklyn, N. Y.

This Company also manufactures drop forgings, armor piercings, semi-armor-piercing projectiles, common shell and shrapnel, for use of army and navy ; and also automobile submarine torpedoes, launching-tubes, etc. The views above show two of the several works of this Company, whose plant for making machinery and articles specified above is the largest in the world. The total floor-space of all the factories is about 12 acres. James W. Lane, President ; Wm. A. Porter, Vice-President ; Arthur T. Porter, Second Vice-President ; Howard C. Seaman, Secretary ; Lucien H. Gould, Treasurer.

HECLA IRON WORKS, formerly Poulson & Eger, North Eleventh and Berry Streets. Extensive plant. Architectural iron and bronze work; ornamental lamps, gates, grilles, etc. Makers of the artistic street-kiosks for subway-stations. Niels Poulson, President. All over the United States, and to foreign lands, has gone architectural metal work fabricated by this great Brooklyn manufactory. Its contracts at home have included the stores of Frederick Loeser & Co. and Abraham & Straus; Temple Bar Building; Mechanics Bank; Brooklyn Savings Bank; Union League Club; Brooklyn Bridge Terminal. Among great office-buildings in Manhattan: Standard Oil; Manhattan Life; "Park Row"; Broad Exchange; Stock Exchange; Clearing House; Hanover Bank; American Surety; University Club; Waldorf-Astoria; National Park Bank; and many others.

Water Street   Grand Union Tea Co.   Pearl Street

GRAND UNION TEA COMPANY, Pearl, Water, and Front Streets.

Six-story brick building. Largest warehouse and factory in the United States for teas, coffees, spices, flavoring extracts, baking-powders, and soaps. 200,000 square feet floor space. Fire-proof, completely appointed. Branch stores throughout the country. Frank S. Jones, President.

Ryerson Street   Jurgens Building   Flushing Avenue

WILLIAM B. A. JURGENS, Wholesale Grocer, Flushing Avenue and Ryerson Street. Established 1867. Largest wholesale grocery establishment in the Borough. Leader in the enormous trade, supplying retailers in Brooklyn, its suburbs, and the scores of towns throughout Long Island. Floor space, 55,000 square feet. Costly equipment and every modern improvement for convenience of customers and employees.

Broadway Bank   H. Batterman   Flushing Ave.

H. BATTERMAN DEPARTMENT STORE, AND BROADWAY BANK, Broadway, Graham, and Flushing Avenues.

One of Brooklyn's largest department stores. Founded 1867. Present site, 1881. Enlarged 1891 to 1896. Broadway and Ewen Street. Broadway Bank, Henry Batterman, Pres., adjoins at the left.
space. Now covers over 200,000 square feet. Business throughout Greater New York.

McLoughlin Bros. Extensions   Main Building erected 1870   Williamsburg Bridge

McLOUGHLIN BROTHERS, South 11th and Berry Streets, and buildings opposite on South 11th Street

Extensive works of a noted publishing house. Established in New York 1840 as Elton & Co. Present style adopted 1855. Specialty of children's colored
books, toys, and games, of which this firm's catalogue comprises one of the largest lists published. Salesrooms, 890 Broadway, Manhattan.

Grand Ave.   St. Mark's Ave.

KNOX HAT FACTORY, St. Mark's and Grand Avenues. One of the leading hat manufactories of the world.

Outgrowth of a hat business founded in 1840 by the late Charles Knox, and now conducted by his son, Col. Edward M. Knox. Men's and women's hats in
all styles. The Knox establishments in Manhattan are at Broadway and Fulton Street, Fifth Avenue and Fortieth Street.
Broadway and Fulton Street, Fifth Ave. Hotel, and Fifth Avenue and Fortieth Street.

Morgan Ave.   Grand St.

SACKETT & WILHELMS LITHOGRAPHING AND PRINTING CO., Grand Street and Morgan Avenue.

Four-story brick building. Completed 1903. In busiest section of Williamsburg. Equipped with the most improved machinery for color and monochrome
lithography, engraving, printing, and binding. One of the finest establishments of its kind in America. Manhattan offices, 225 Fourth Ave.

Additions 1904   130 to 140 Middleton St.

Established 1848

E. GREENFIELD'S SON & CO., Manufacturers of Confectionery and Chocolates, 101 to 111 Lorimer St., and 130 to 140 Middleton St.

Makers of the celebrated "Delatour" brand of chocolates and "chocolate sponge" and "Cupid" brand of confections. Candy especially packed for export to all countries of the world. Main office and salesroom, 44 Barclay Street, Manhattan.

Main Factory 1905

Established 1880

F. WESEL MANUFACTURING CO., 70-80 Cranberry Street, corner Henry Street.

Long-established works, recently enlarged. Makers of printing-presses, machinery, fixtures, and supplies for printers, electrotypers, stereotypers, and photo-engravers. Salesrooms: 82 and 84 Fulton St., New York, 124 South 8th St., Philadelphia, and 310 Dearborn St., Chicago. Ferdinand Wesel, President.

North 11th St.

Established 1889

Bedford Ave.

H. G. FRIEDMANN, NEW YORK MODEL BAKERY, Bedford Avenue and North 11th Street.

Uses 900 barrels of flour weekly, employing 140 men and 35 wagons. Nearly 50,000 square feet floor-space. Supplies restaurants, grocers, institutions, and shipping, throughout Manhattan, Staten Island, Yonkers, and Brooklyn and outlying towns. Modern plant, equipped for large emergency orders.

Hall St.

Park Ave.

JENNINGS LACE WORKS, Park Avenue and Hall Street.

Established 1867, in Jersey City, by Abraham G. Jennings, one of the first manufacturers of American laces on a large scale. Works moved to Brooklyn in 1871, and fitted with improved Jacquard looms and other costly and novel machinery. Manhattan salesrooms, 450 Broome Street.

Bond Street   Fulton Street Elevated Railroad   Elm Place

FREDERICK LOESER & COMPANY DEPARTMENT STORE, Fulton Street, between Elm Place and Bond Street, junction De Kalb Avenue. Covers two city blocks.
Business founded 1869, at Fulton, Tillary, and Washington Streets. Removed to present site 1887. Store enlarged to present dimensions, 1903. Total floor-space, 15 acres. Thoroughly sanitary; finely appointed. Several large warehouses. Distributing stations throughout Borough. Free delivery. Over 4,000 employees. Motto: "In every detail the leading retail establishment in Brooklyn."

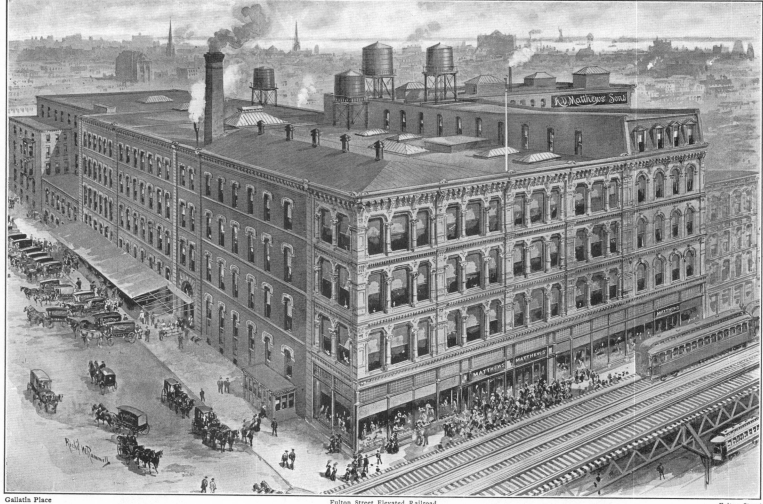

Gallatin Place   Fulton Street Elevated Railroad   Fulton Street

A. D. MATTHEWS' SONS DEPARTMENT STORE, Fulton Street, between Smith Street and Gallatin Place. Branches in Paris, Berlin, and Vienna.
Brooklyn's oldest department-store. Founded, 1837, at 93 Main Street; afterward removed to make way for approach to the Brooklyn Bridge. Removed to present site 1872. First building here, 25x100 feet. Now contains 205,500 square feet. Center of shopping district. Firm has twenty-seven agent-stations throughout Long Island for free delivery of goods. Large mail-order business.

Subway Rapid Transit   Fulton Street Elevated Road   Gallatin Place   Livingston Street

ABRAHAM & STRAUS DEPARTMENT STORE, Fulton and Livingston Streets, between Gallatin Place and Hoyt Street.

Occupies entire block to Livingston Street except small portions at the two Fulton Street corners. Storehouses at Livingston and Schermerhorn Streets connected with main building by tunnel. Founded 1865. In magnitude of business one of the largest department-stores in the United States. Modern equipment in every detail. Supplies practically everything in clothing and home furnishings.

The Montague   Remsen St.   Franklin Trust Co.   Trinity Church   Brooklyn Savings Bank   Academy of Music (rear)   Brooklyn Bridge   Real Estate Exchange

LOOKING NORTHWEST FROM THE TEMPLE BAR BUILDING, Court and Joralemon Sts. Photographed before the burning of the Academy of Music, on Montague St.

This view has especial historic value and pictures a rapidly developing section of the older city. Formerly occupied mainly by dwellings and churches; now being invaded by modern business structures and apartment houses. The Academy of Music, utilized during two generations, was burned Nov. 30, 1903. Upon a part of its site is being erected the ten-story building of the Lawyers' Title Insurance Co.

Navy Yard in background   Administration Building   150 Individual Markets   William B. Tubby, Architect

WALLABOUT MARKET, Washington, Flushing, and Clinton Avenues, on Wallabout Bay, adjoining the United States Navy Yard. Provision-center of City. Docks for fruit and provision ships in foreign trade. Second largest market-place in the world. Most picturesque and best appointed. Founded 1884 to accommodate farm-wagon traffic. Land formerly part of U. S. naval reservation, site of original Walloon settlement of 1625. Leased by City, 1884; seventeen acres purchased 1891 for $700,000; another seventy-six acres, 1894, for $1,200,000. Much of latter tract used for piers. Cars of Pennsylvania and Delaware & Lackawanna railroads landed from floats. Substantial booths, Flemish architecture, leased to market-men for five-year term. Rendezvous for farmers and retail dealers.

Site of New Crescent Club   The Mills-Platt Co.

THE MILLS-PLATT CO. BUILDING, Pierrepont Art Rooms, 44 Clinton Street.
Owned by the Mills-Platt Co., architects, builders, interior decorators, and designers of furnishings, fabrics, tapestries, porcelains, furniture. Quaint Old English architecture. Façade in wood and stucco.

MASON, AU & MAGENHEIMER, Candy Manufacturers, 22 Henry Street.
Extensive works of a leading house, for many years on Fulton Street, previous to erection of present plant, Henry and Middagh Sts. Well-known makers of high grades of confectionery in endless variety.

Park Row Building   Brooklyn Children's Aid Society   Lower Fulton St.   Tower foundation, Manhattan Bridge

GENERAL VIEW, westward across East River to Manhattan, from the Mason, Au & Magenheimer Candy Factory.   Numerous Manhattan "skyscrapers" at western end.
One of the best views obtainable of the graceful structure of the Brooklyn Bridge, its ceaseless flow of travel, and its termini in the midst of the activities of both boroughs.   The foreground shows the
literally "old" Brooklyn, the main artery of travel (via Fulton Ferry, established 1642) previous to the opening of the bridge; now changing to manufacturing and warehousing interests.

County Court House   Municipal Building   Temple Bar   Franklin Trust Company   Mechanics Bank   Brooklyn Savings Bank   Brooklyn Eagle

SKY-LINE OF SOME OF BROOKLYN'S LARGE BUILDINGS.   View west from Fire Department Headquarters, 367 Jay Street.

Beginning at the left are visible, in order: Hall of Records; tower of Polytechnic Institute; dome of Court House; (old) Municipal Building; St. Ann's P. E. Church; Williamsburgh Trust Co. (rear); Temple
Bar; Germania Savings Bank; Garfield Building; Arbuckle Building (rear); Franklin Trust Co.; Trinity spire; Mechanics Bank; Real Estate Exchange; Brooklyn Savings Bank; Touraine; "Eagle," etc.

247 to 263 Herkimer Street

1416 and 1418 Fulton Street

THE J. M. HORTON ICE CREAM CO.   Factory at 1416 and 1418 Fulton St., extending through to 247 to 263 Herkimer St.   Factories also in Manhattan, and depots throughout the city.
Brooklyn establishment of a well-known company whose products are household words.   Established in New York, 1870, its annually increasing trade long since reached every part of the city and suburbs, and the Horton
ice-creams and water ices, jellies and charlotte russes are found in dining-cars and on all river and ocean steamers leaving this port.   The entire rows shown in the views are but a part of the Horton real estate in Brooklyn.

JOHN ROGERS MAXWELL RESIDENCE, 78 Eighth Avenue, near Union Street.

Red brick and brown stone, double gable. Mr. Maxwell is senior member of Maxwell & Graves, bankers and brokers. President Atlas Portland Cement Co., Chairman Exec. Com. Central R. R. of N. J.; Director Amer. Cotton Oil Co.; American Exchange National Bank; Jersey City Water Supply Co., etc.

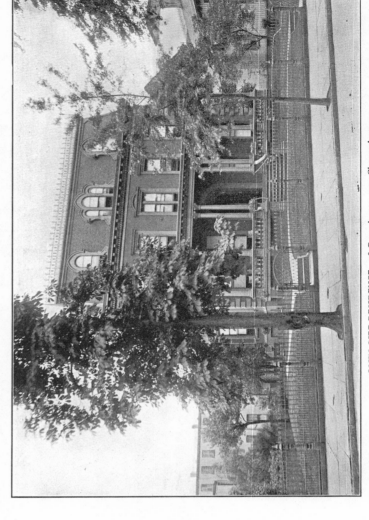

JOHN GIBB RESIDENCE, 218 Gates Avenue, near Classon Avenue.

Handsome and refined dwelling in the older residential section "on the hill." Mr. Gibb is of Scotch birth, and is one of Brooklyn's most substantial citizens. In 1865, founded house of Mills & Gibb; in 1887, acquired leading interest in firm of Frederick Loeser & Co. Trustee Adelphi College, etc.

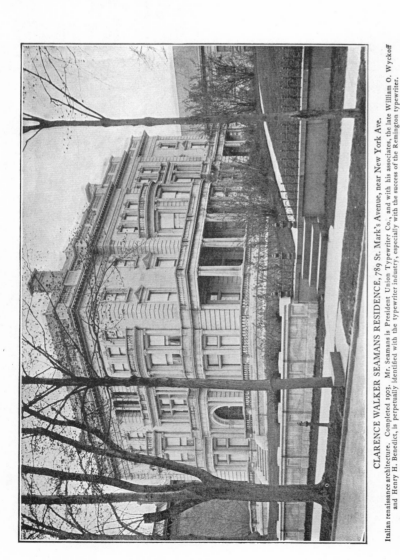

CLARENCE WALKER SEAMANS RESIDENCE, 789 St. Mark's Avenue, near New York Ave.

Italian renaissance architecture. Completed 1903. Mr. Seamans is President Union Typewriter Co., and with his associates, the late William O. Wyckoff and Henry H. Benedict, is perpetually identified with the typewriter industry, especially with the success of the Remington typewriter.

WILLIAM BERRI RESIDENCE, 467 Clinton Avenue, corner Gates Avenue.

Mr. Berri is one of Brooklyn's foremost citizens. Carpet-merchant. Former President Brooklyn Bridge. Publisher "Standard-Union." Vice-Pres. Hamilton Trust Co. Director Edison Electric Illuminating Co., National City Bank, Kings County Electric Light & Power Co., etc.

FRANK S. JONES RESIDENCE, 790 St. Mark's Avenue, corner of New York Avenue.

Of attractive design, beautifully situated on one of the finest of the city's residential avenues. Home of the President of the Grand Union Tea Co. (whose building is shown on page 33). Vice-president of the Sidney Novelty Co. Trustee of the Brooklyn Institute.

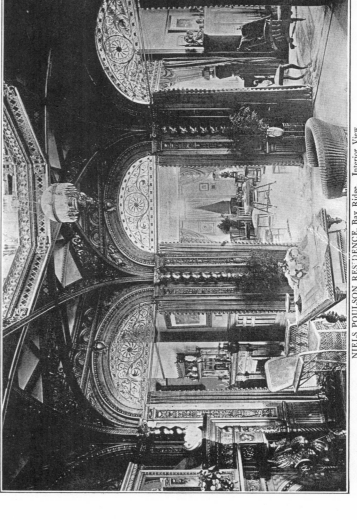

NIELS POULSON RESIDENCE, Bay Ridge. Interior View.

A magnificent interior of metal, designed and made by Mr. Poulson, to whom is due much credit for the modern advance in structural-metal adornment, in residential, business, and ornamental structures. Mr. Poulson is President of the Hecla Iron Works (illustrated on page 33).

CHARLES O. GATES RESIDENCE, 45 Plaza, opposite main entrance to Prospect Park.

Beautiful residence of the President of the Royal Baking Powder Co., whose product is known the world over in a million households. Mr. Gates is also a director of the Hale Desk Co. and other manufacturing concerns, and President of the Hoagland Laboratory.

NIELS POULSON RESIDENCE, Shore Road and Eighty-ninth Street, Bay Ridge.

A most notable structure, adorned with high art copper-bronze panels. Floors of steel and concrete. Model of fireproof construction throughout, including interior trim of metal, as seen in the adjoining photograph; a rare adaptation of architectural beauty to practical uses.

CHARLES MILLARD PRATT RESIDENCE, 241 Clinton Avenue, near Willoughby Avenue.
Mr. Pratt is a son of the late Charles Pratt, capitalist and philanthropist, and is president of Pratt Institute. He is secretary of the Standard Oil Co., and a director in the Long Island R. R. Co., Brooklyn City R. R. Co., Mechanics' National Bank of New York, Adams Express Co., etc.

GEORGE D. PRATT RESIDENCE, 245 Clinton Avenue, near Willoughby Avenue.
Elaborated colonial architecture. Red brick and white marble. Mr. Pratt is a trustee of Pratt Institute and a member of the Advisory Council of the Thrift Savings Loan and Building Fund; also treasurer of the Montauk Co. and of the Chelsea Jute Mills, etc.

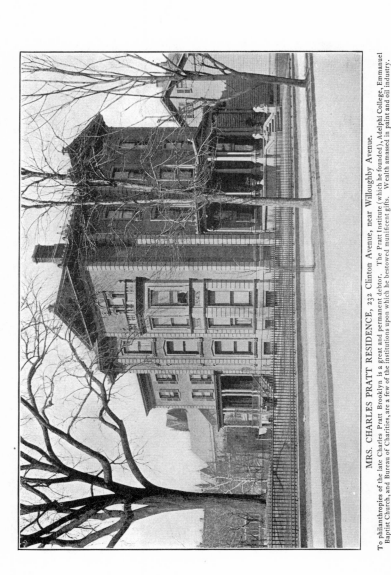

MRS. CHARLES PRATT RESIDENCE, 232 Clinton Avenue, near Willoughby Avenue.
To philanthropies of the late Charles Pratt Brooklyn is a great and permanent debtor. The Pratt Institute (which he founded), Adelphi College, Emmanuel Baptist Church, and Bureau of Charities, are a few of the institutions upon which he bestowed munificent gifts. Wealth amassed in paint and oil industry.

FREDERIC B. PRATT RESIDENCE, 229 Clinton Avenue, near Willoughby Ave.
Florentine architecture. Brick and white marble. Mr. Pratt is prominent in business and philanthropic circles. Secretary, treasurer, and manager of Pratt Institute; treasurer of Thrift Savings Fund; President of Chelsea Jute Mills; Vice-President of the Morris Building Co., etc.

RICHARD YOUNG RESIDENCE, 87 Lincoln Road, near Prospect Park.

In the modern Flatbush, noted for the refined elegance of its beautiful streets and mansions, is the home of one of Brooklyn's most devoted citizens. Ex-Park Commissioner; President Richard Young Co., leather manufacturers; Trustee East River Savings Institution; Director Mercantile National Bank, etc.

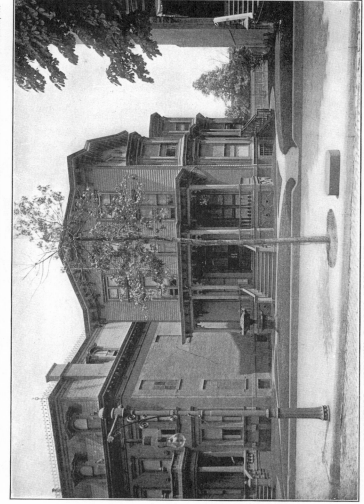

MARSHALL SYLVANUS DRIGGS RESIDENCE, 279 Washington Avenue, near De Kalb Avenue.

The home of the President of the Williamsburgh City Fire Insurance Co. As a clerk Mr. Driggs wrote the first policy issued by the company, 1853. Director of Broadway Trust Co., First National Bank of Brooklyn, Williamsburgh Trust Co., Empire State Surety Co., and other important institutions.

EDWARD H. LITCHFIELD RESIDENCE, 2 Montague Terrace, overlooking the East River.

At side of the Montague St. viaduct which, with the Ferry, makes Montague St. practically a continuation of Wall St. Vicinity long a residential center of many of New York's men of wealth. Mr. Litchfield is president of the Brooklyn Improvement Co., trustee Brooklyn Savings Bank, etc.

ABRAHAM ABRAHAM RESIDENCE, 800 St. Mark's Avenue, near New York Avenue.

Three-story red brick Queen Anne residence of one of Brooklyn's leading merchants. Mr. Abraham is senior partner in the great department-store of Abraham & Straus. Trustee Kings County Trust Co., and identified with many of the city's public and philanthropic institutions.

JAMES McMAHON RESIDENCE, 87 McDonough Street, near Tompkins Avenue.

Surrounded by grounds of half an acre, in a quiet and beautiful section. Mr. McMahon is president of the Emigrant Industrial Savings Bank, with deposits of $73,000,000 from 102,000 depositors and $10,000,000 surplus; director in other financial institutions; and connected with many philanthropies.

FRED C. COCHEU RESIDENCE, Fort Hamilton Avenue and 75th Street.

A charming villa, with extensive grounds. Mr. Cocheu is active in numerous public enterprises; President Cross Country R. R. Co.; Treasurer People's Traction Co., Vice-President New York Motor Vehicle Co., etc.

HENRY CARLTON HULBERT RESIDENCE, Prospect Park West (Ninth Avenue), corner First Street.

Gray Indiana limestone. Renaissance motif. One of the handsomest residences in the Park quarter. Mr. Hulbert is vice-president of South Brooklyn Savings Institution; director of Importers' & Traders' Nat'l Bank, Pullman Palace Car Co., Celluloid Co., Franklin Trust Co., New York Life Ins. & Trust Co., etc.

JOSEPH SILLECK CASE RESIDENCE, 276 Jefferson Avenue, near Marcy Avenue.

The residence of a veteran banker. For thirty-seven years with the Second National Bank of New York; its cashier since 1885. A native of Brooklyn, where he has resided for over sixty years.

EDWIN E. JACKSON, JR., RESIDENCE, 424 Clinton Avenue.
Granite, Indiana limestone, and brick. Mr. Jackson is a prominent New York lawyer; President Boorum
& Pease Co.; and a Director in various corporations, Merchants Exchange National Bank, etc.

CHARLES ADOLPH SCHIEREN RESIDENCE, 405 Clinton Avenue.
Superb home of a foremost citizen of Brooklyn, leading leather merchant, ex-mayor, long devoted to
public interests, political, religious, and charitable. President Germania Savings Bank, etc.

DESMOND DUNNE RESIDENCE, 25 Prospect Park West.
The spacious and tasteful home of the President of the Desmond Dunne Co., originators and controllers
of extensive advertising projects; Director Brooklyn Bank, Long Island Safe Deposit Co., etc.

GEORGE P. TANGEMAN RESIDENCE, 276 Berkeley Place, near Prospect Plaza.
Granite and brick. The home of a Brooklyn capitalist, whose fortune was largely made through Royal
and Cleveland Baking Powder Companies. Trustee of Peoples Trust Co., Hoagland Laboratory, etc.

ALBERT L. JOHNSON RESIDENCE, Shore Road and 99th St., near Fort Hamilton.

Charming brick and terra-cotta structure; wide, open verandas; extensive grounds; superb views of the Upper and Lower Bays and the Narrows. Built by the late Albert L. Johnson, who was, with his brother, the ex-Mayor of Cleveland, widely known in railroad and financial circles in New York and the West.

FREDERICK A. M. BURRELL RESIDENCE, 1409 Albemarle Road, corner Rugby Road, Prospect Park South.

One of the finest of the modern dwellings in the new exclusive section south of Prospect Park. Its owner is a member of the firm of Charles A. Schieren & Co., leather-belting manufacturers; Director Flatbush Trust Co.; Fulton Club; Vice-President Manufacturers' Association of New York, etc.

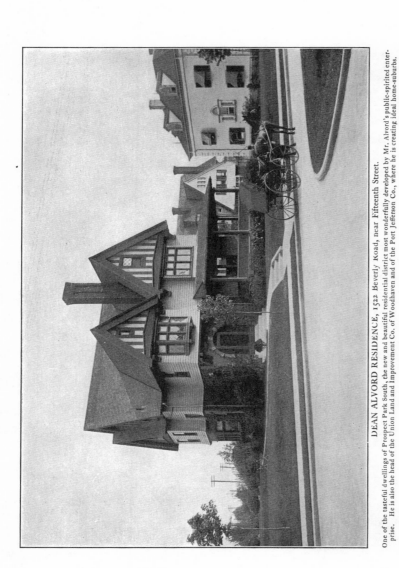

DEAN ALVORD RESIDENCE, 1532 Beverly Road, near Fifteenth Street.

One of the tasteful dwellings of Prospect Park South, the new and beautiful residential district most wonderfully developed by Mr. Alvord's public-spirited enterprise. He is also the head of the Union Land and Improvement Co. of Woodhaven and of the Port Jefferson Co., where he is creating ideal home-suburbs.

WILLIAM A. ENGEMAN RESIDENCE, 105 Buckingham Road, near Prospect Park.

In Prospect Park South, the picturesque home of the owner of the Benvenue, Augusta, and Columbia granite quarries. President of the Brighton Beach Racing Association, and large owner of Coney Island properties. Son of the pioneer in the development of the great amusement-center.

Macon St.　Halsey St.

Girls' High School occupies block opposite

ALHAMBRA APARTMENT HOUSE, Nostrand Avenue, Macon to Halsey Streets, near Fulton Street elevated railroad.

Superb structure, 200 feet front; 70 deep. Romanesque style. Octagonal towers, rock-faced stone below brick above. Open court, fountains, tennis-grounds. Public halls, 20 feet wide, with large tiled fireplace. Complete modern equipment. Electrically lighted. Erected by Louis F. Seitz.

Leased and supervised by the Park Commissioners　Accommodations for vehicles in rear

"THE SHELTER" IN PROSPECT PARK; Public Refectory and Restaurant amid the Flower Gardens.

Beautifully situated in a charming section of the Park. A popular resting-place for visitors. Close to the Terrace, facing the South Drive, where on pleasant afternoons are seated crowds of spectators of the continuous train of equipages. Popular stopping-place for coaching parties, cyclists, and equestrians.

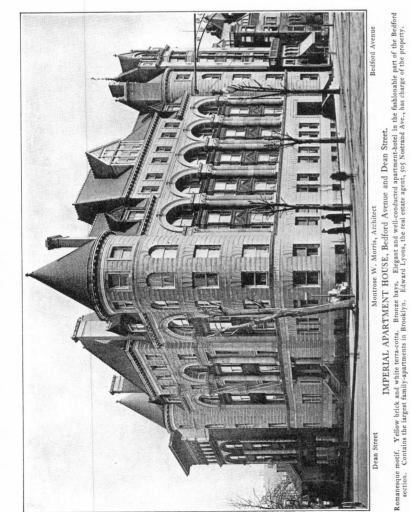

Dean Street　Bedford Avenue

Montrose W. Morris, Architect

IMPERIAL APARTMENT HOUSE, Bedford Avenue and Dean Street.

Romanesque motif. Yellow brick and white terra-cotta. Bronze bays. Elegant and well-conducted apartment-hotel in the fashionable part of the Bedford section. Contains the largest family-apartments in Brooklyn. Edward Lyons, the real estate agent, 505 Nostrand Ave., has charge of the property.

Fulton Street　Flatbush Avenue

JAMES W. EDGETT'S RESTAURANT, Fulton Street and Flatbush Avenue.

The most fashionable and most exquisite dining-place in Brooklyn. Opened in 1904 as the "Delmonico's" of the Borough. The building, erected especially for its uses, extends from 596 Fulton St., through to 13 and 13A Flatbush Ave. Frequented by the leading families during shopping and theater hours.

Hicks St.   The St. George   Clark St.

HOTEL ST. GEORGE, Clark, Hicks, and Pineapple Sts. American and European plans.
The greatest hotel in Brooklyn. A huge monument to the heroic enterprise of Capt. Wm. Tumbridge, a
retired sea-captain, who first built here in 1885; enlarged 1898 and 1903. More than 1000 rooms.

Erected 1904   Fire and noise proof

THE MOHAWK, Washington Avenue, between Greene and Lafayette Avenues.
One of the newest, most luxurious, and best-appointed apartment-houses in Brooklyn. Suites of two to five
rooms and bath. General dining-room on first floor. Built and owned by the Mohawk Realty Co.

Erected 1904   Standish Arms Realty Co., owners

STANDISH ARMS. Apartment Hotel, 167–171 Columbia Heights, near Pierrepont Street.
Select and exclusive family-hotel. Fire-proof construction. Apartments of one to three rooms and bath,
and connecting suites. Restaurant, American plan; Colonial reception-room, decorated by Christy.

Erected 1902   L. J. Horowitz, builder, and owner until 1904

THE MONTAGUE. Apartment Hotel, 103–105 Montague Street, near Hicks Street.
For those wishing small apartments in a model house on the Heights. Restaurant, private and public.
Tasteful decorations. Open nickel plumbing. No house-keeping on premises. Maid and janitor service.

Hicks St.　　　Frank S. Lowe, Architect　　　Pierrepont St.
FLORENCE COURT, Pierrepont and Hicks Streets.
Seven-story, buff sandstone and pressed brick apartment hotel. Four large apartments on each floor. Latest modern improvements. Built by Louis J. Horowitz. Brooklyn Heights Improvement Co.

Edw. H. Crandall, Mgr.　　　Frank S. Lowe, Architect　　　Crescent Athletic Club
THE TOURAINE, 21 Clinton Street, between Fulton and Pierrepont Streets.
Elegant apartment hotel. Two and three-room apartments. Let *en suite*, if desired. Restaurant. Palm garden. Brooklyn Heights Improvement Co., Charles A. Murphey, Pres.

THE ASSEMBLY (WILSON BUILDING), 153-157 Pierrepont Street.
Catering and entertainment building. Ball-rooms; restaurants; rooms for clubs, banquets, wedding receptions, etc. Important factor in social life. Assembly Catering & Supply Co.

THE MARESI CO., Confectioners, 30 Clinton Street, between Fulton and Pierrepont Sts.
Brooklyn headquarters of well-known firm of confectioners and caterers; branch also at 76 Seventh Ave. Main store in Manhattan, 719 Sixth Ave.; branches at 589 Madison Ave. and 320 Columbus Ave.

Stores: Matthews; Loeser, Abraham & Straus   DeKalb Ave.   Fulton St.   Brooklyn Bridge

JUNCTION OF FULTON STREET AND DE KALB AVENUE, looking west.

Center of the shopping district, where are located some of the largest department stores in the city.   Crowded daily, especially afternoons.   The congestion of street-car traffic along this section has been pronounced by the Railroad Commissioners greater than in any other street of equal length in the State.

F. Loeser & Co.'s store   Towers of Brooklyn Bridge   Flatbush Ave.   Hudson Ave.   Fulton St.   Williamsburg Bridge   Rockwell Place

JUNCTION OF FLATBUSH AND HUDSON AVENUES AND FULTON AND NEVINS STREETS.   View looking westward to Manhattan.   Meeting place of old and new Brooklyn.

An important locality.   Doubtless to be the leading commercial center of the Borough.   Tracks of the Fulton Street elevated railroad cross those of the Fifth Avenue elevated coming up Hudson Avenue, and running on Flatbush Avenue to and down Fifth Avenue.   Important buildings, those of Journeay & Burnham; the Cowperthwait Co.; B. G. Latimer & Sons Co.; Smith, Gray & Co.; Edgert's Restaurant; F. Loeser & Co. close by.   Tall clock-tower on Nevins Street, belonging to Fulton & Flatbush Storage Co., may be seen from all parts of the Borough.

Brooklyn Club   Brooklyn Trust Co.   Real Estate Exchange   Brooklyn Library   Mechanics Bank

MONTAGUE STREET, NORTH SIDE, Clinton to Court Streets.   Opposite stood the Academy of Music, burned in 1903.

The heart of Brooklyn's financial district.   From the Brooklyn Trust Company to Mechanics Bank are numerous banks, bankers, trust companies, and street railroad corporations, chiefly native to Brooklyn.   Main business-center of the Borough, although contiguous to an ultra-aristocratic residence district.

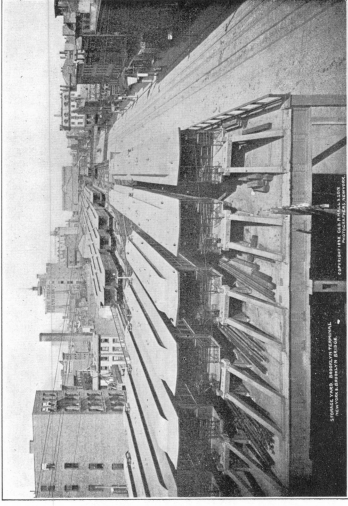

Washington St.

Tillary St.

TERMINAL AND CAR-SHEDS, BROOKLYN BRIDGE, Washington Street, from Tillary to Sands Streets.

Upon these tracks, extending nearly one-half mile from the Brooklyn tower of the Bridge, are stored the extra cars of the regular bridge-trains, when not in service for the "rush" schedule of a train a minute. Branch connections to Fulton St. elevated road, and to Myrtle and Lexington Ave. roads.

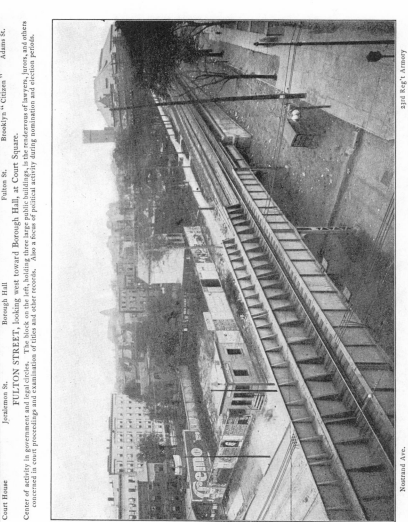

Fulton St. elevated road

Flatbush Ave.

Fifth Ave. elevated road

JUNCTION OF FLATBUSH AVENUE AND FULTON AND NEVINS STREETS. An interesting view of "L" and surface roads.

Upper end of the busy shopping-district. Two elevated roads cross one another and have stations here, over several surface-lines. From this point land is to be cleared northwestward, extending Flatbush Avenue in a direct line to the new Manhattan bridge at Myrtle Avenue and Gold Street.

Joralemon St.

Court House

Borough Hall

Fulton St.

Adams St.

Brooklyn "Citizen"

FULTON STREET, looking west toward Borough Hall, at Court Square.

Center of activity in government and legal circles. The block on the left, holding three large public buildings, is the rendezvous of lawyers, jurors, and others concerned in court proceedings and examination of titles and other records. Also a focus of political activity during nomination and election periods.

Nostrand Ave.

23rd Reg't Armory

ATLANTIC AVENUE VIADUCT, at Nostrand Avenue. Built jointly by the city and the Long Island Railroad.

The improvement of Atlantic Avenue, formerly an unsightly street abandoned to railroad uses, has been accomplished by the Commission appointed for the purpose in 1896. A combination of subway, masonry, and substantial elevated structure now reaches from Flatbush Avenue to the City line.

Sands St.   Gift of Helen M. Gould   Charles St.
BROOKLYN BRANCH OF THE NAVAL Y. M. C. A., 167 Sands Street.
Near the Navy Yard. For U. S. sailors and marines. W. L. Tisdale, Sec. Restaurant. Sleeping-rooms,
library, gymnasium, swimming pool, etc. Educational courses. Under International Y. M. C. A. Com.

Fulton St.   Erected 1885   Cost, $300,000   Bond St.
YOUNG MEN'S CHRISTIAN ASSOCIATION, 502 Fulton Street, 9–17 Bond Street.
Membership, 5,600. Average daily attendance, 3,000. Twelve branches. Library, 18,000 volumes. Read-
ing-rooms, gymnasium, large assembly-hall, 1,275 seats. Educational courses, 25 subjects. 1,000 students.

Built 1903   D. Everett Waid and R. M. Cranford, Architects
MEDICAL SOCIETY OF THE COUNTY OF KINGS, 1313 Bedford Avenue.
Organized 1822. Membership, 700. Medical and scientific reference library, of 60,000 volumes and 500
current periodicals, open to the public. John E. Sheppard, M.D., President.

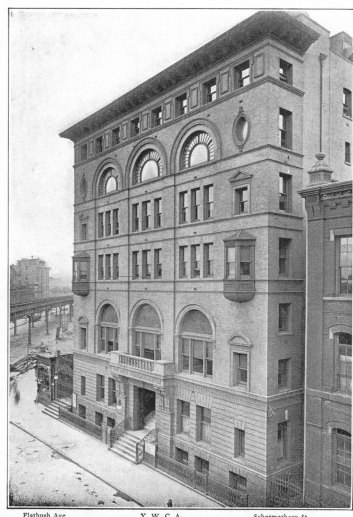

Flatbush Ave.   Y. W. C. A.   Schermerhorn St.
YOUNG WOMEN'S CHRISTIAN ASSOCIATION, Schermerhorn St. and Flatbush Ave.
Educational courses in business, domestic economy, languages, etc. Library, 11,000 volumes. Gymnasium,
with running-track. Two large halls. Boarding in Union St. for members, $2.50 to $4 per week.

SOCIETY FOR PREVENTION OF CRUELTY TO CHILDREN, 105 Schermerhorn St.
Organized 1880. For relief of neglected and abused children on Long Island. Cares for lost children.
Temporary shelter day and night. Supported by voluntary gifts. Hon. Charles A. Schieren, Pres.

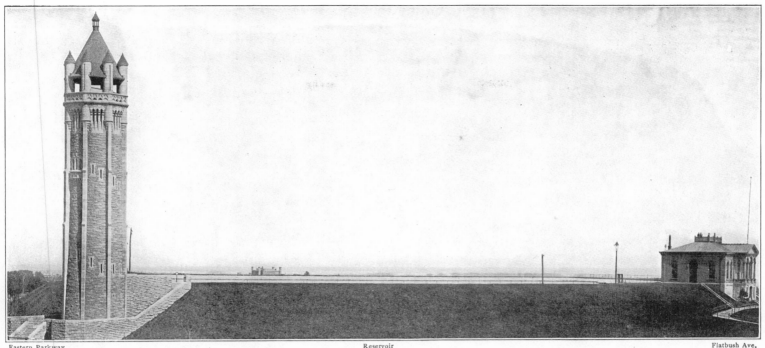

MOUNT PROSPECT WATER TOWER AND RESERVOIR, Institute Park, facing Underhill Place, junction Eastern Parkway and Flatbush Avenue, near Brooklyn Institute.

Pink syenitic granite. Romanesque tower and stand-pipe, raising water for supply of city around Prospect Park. Water raised from Ridgewood Reservoir by additional pumping station. Part of the Ridgewood, New Lots, New Utrecht, and Gravesend water-distribution system, which has a storing capacity of 1,000,000,000 gallons, and 702 miles of distributing mains.

ANNUAL PARADE OF BROOKLYN SUNDAY-SCHOOL CHILDREN. A celebration peculiar to Brooklyn. First held in 1829.

An early summer parade of its Sunday-School children. Starting from their several churches, the children, accompanied by teachers and bands of music, gather at several stated places and parade through the streets and one section of Prospect Park playgrounds. The Protestant Sunday-Schools of the Borough contain over 150,000 scholars, most of whom participate.

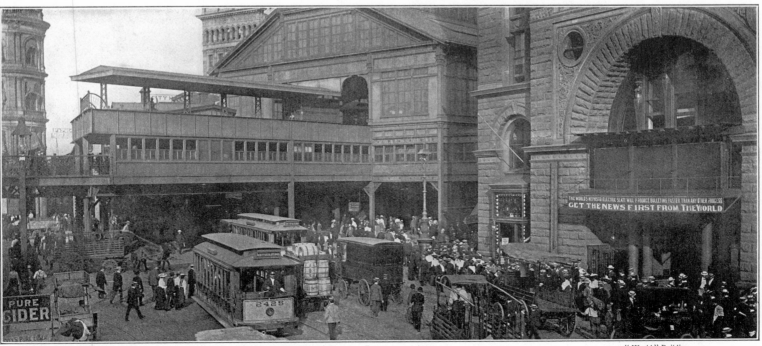

BROOKLYN BRIDGE, MANHATTAN TERMINUS, Park Row, City Hall Square, Manhattan.

Entrance to the wagon-road, foot-path, bridge-trains and trolley-cars. Southern terminus of the Third Avenue Elevated Railroad, City Hall Branch. On the right the "World" Building. On the left the "Staats Zeitung" Building, which contains the offices of the New York Corporation Counsel. Immense crowds pass this point morning and evening, coming from and returning to Brooklyn.

Coney Island Ave.   Wheelmen's Shelter   Parkside Ave.

OCEAN PARKWAY GATE, PROSPECT PARK, Parkside and Coney Island Avenues.

Like the Plaza-entrance, this southern gateway stands at the bend of a low arc-shaped wall of white granite, with a sheltered resting-place at either extremity. Imposing granite pedestals support the noble bronze groups of rearing wild horses. At this point begins the magnificent Ocean Parkway, which runs, with but one bend, five and one-half miles to Brighton Beach, Coney Island.

Coney Island Ave.   Entrance to South Drive

PROPYLON, Ocean Parkway Gate, Prospect Park.

Bronze equestrian-group, designed by Frederick MacMonnies. Pedestal by McKim, Mead & White.
View from within the driveway, looking across the Parkway-plaza down Coney Island Avenue.

Erected 1895 by Maryland Soc. Sons of Amer. Revolution   Lookout Hill

"MARYLAND" MONUMENT to Revolutionary heroes, Lookout Hill, Prospect Park.

To the memory of 400 Maryland and Delaware troops who, in a desperate engagement after the Battle of
Long Island, defended the rear of the American army with terrible loss, Aug. 27, 1776.

TENNIS.

CRICKET.

ELECTRIC FOUNTAIN & CIRCLE

MOZART

MAY DAY.

GEN. G. K. WARREN.

AT THE MAIN ENTRANCE

FLATBUSH AVE. ENTRANCE

LAKE.

PALMS & FERNS.

PUMPING STATION

SHELTER HOUSE & RESTAURANT

Planned and laid out 1860   Olmsted, Vaux & Co., Designers and Landscape Gardeners   James S. T. Stranahan, Projector

PROSPECT PARK, Brooklyn's world-famous pleasure ground. America's most beautiful park. Scene of the battle of Long Island, Aug. 27, 1776.
Area 516 acres. Seventy acres of meadow for playgrounds and field sports. The electric fountain. Soldiers' and Sailors' Arch from Plaza. Bust of Mozart erected 1897 by German Societies. Statue of Gen. G. K. Warren. Gateway Flatbush Avenue and Malbone Street. Lake, sixty-two acres area. Palm-house, Ninth Avenue and Seventh Street. Park pumping-station. Picnic-shelter.

Factories   Brooklyn Bridge   Fulton Ferry   Brooklyn Institute and Water Tower   Hotel Margaret   Holy Trinity   Temple Bar   Warehouses

FLY'S-EYE VIEW OF BROOKLYN BOROUGH. Photographed by George P. Hall & Son from a high point in Manhattan.

Water-front of Brooklyn from Catharine Ferry, Main Street, to foot of Clark Street. Columbia Heights in the foreground; Park Slope in the background. Narrowest part of the river, and always the point of greatest cross-river travel since the first ferry in 1642. Total length of river view, three-quarters of a mile. Extreme background over two miles from river. This is a most extensive view, made at one exposure on negative forty inches long. During the printing a large fly settled on the negative, thus furnishing a silent living witness to the great size of the photograph.

Half-mile stones the entire length   One mile tan-barked for speeding

OCEAN PARKWAY AND BICYCLE PATH. Famous boulevard to Coney Island. Seven parallel roads.

One of the grandest driveways in the world. The peer of the great highways of Europe. Extends, with but one turn, 5¾ miles, from Prospect Park to Coney Island. Main driveway, 150 feet from curb to curb. Two narrower roadways, two sidewalks, and two bicycle paths. Cost, $4,000,000.

Entrance   Reservoir   Observatory

HIGHLAND PARK, adjoining Ridgewood Reservoir. A beautiful outing-place of 45 acres.

One of the charming small parks developed under Commissioner Richard Young. Occupies the highest land in this district. Reached by recently finished Boulevard from Bushwick Avenue at Evergreens Cemetery. Commanding view across city and country to the ocean, Sandy Hook, and the Lower Bay.

Midget City   Tower, 300 ft   Ball room over pier   Long-distance shoot-the-chutes   Opened 1904   Realistic fire exhibition   Bathing pavilion   Leap-frog railroad

DREAMLAND, CONEY ISLAND. Great Pleasure Park at West Brighton. Latest development of collective amusements. A gigantic and artistic enterprise of State Senator William H. Reynolds. Replaced numerous pavilions and tawdry shows demolished. Broad vistas and superb views. Ablaze at night with myriads of electric lights. Canals of Venice; coasting in Switzerland; Hell Gate; big shows from St. Louis; Chilkoot Pass — huge human bagatelle board; Bostock's trained animals; circus-rings, tight-wire performers; high divers; miniature railroad; illuminated hall, restaurants, etc.

Lagoon promenades   Circus rings   Observation Galleries Entrance   Ascending merry-go-round   Chute fire-escape

LUNA PARK, CONEY ISLAND. First attempt at maintaining an immense "World's Fair" permanent assemblage of entertainments. Established 1903 by Thompson & Dundy. Enlarged, 1904. 38 acres. Popular resort at West Brighton. Most elaborate electrical illuminations on the Island. Electric fountain. Elaborate roof-garden. Endless variety of new and old attractions, including fire and flame exhibit; submarine boat; Monitor and Merrimac combat; City of Delhi, natives with elephants, zebras, camels, and spectacular Durbar ceremonies; centrifugal swings; trip to the moon, etc.

Promenade   The Oriental   Tents for Guests   Board Walk to Manhattan Beach

ORIENTAL HOTEL, Manhattan Beach, Coney Island. Looking east. In full view of the Atlantic Ocean. Erected 1880. Companion to Manhattan Beach Hotel. Oriental, on American plan, for permanent guests; Manhattan, on European, for transients. One of the choicest Atlantic Coast resorts. Summer home of many distinguished people. Largely fostered by the late Austin Corbin, who did Herculean work for Long Island.

Lou Dillon, 1:56   Sheepshead Bay Pavilion   Crescens, 1:59¾

Within the limits of Brooklyn are the courses of three famous racing associations, noted for their marvelous records and overwhelming crowds. Brighton Beach Racing Association was founded in 1879 by the late W. A. Engeman, whose son, of the same name, is now the president. The Coney Island Jockey Club has one of the finest courses in the country at Sheepshead Bay, with an immense grand-stand, splendidly equipped, club-house, paddock, and stables. The Brooklyn Jockey Club, Philip J. Dwyer, President, has a fine track at Gravesend. William K. Vanderbilt, President.

LONG ISLAND RACING SCENES. The Race Tracks and Betting Pavilion, and two of the most famous Trotters.

Atlantic Ocean   Board Walk   Music Pavilion   Hotel   L. I. R. R. Station

MANHATTAN BEACH HOTEL, Manhattan Beach, Coney Island. Looking west. One of the world's most celebrated resorts. On hot days myriads of New York's people go to Manhattan Beach to enjoy ocean breezes and the surf-bathing. Concerts day and evening, instrumental and vocal; theatricals and other entertainments. Extensive restaurants, enclosed and open; cuisine unsurpassed. Pain's world-famous fireworks.

"Marine Railway"   Bathing pavilion   Brighton Beach   Manhattan Beach   Atlantic Ocean

ALONG THE ATLANTIC OCEAN FROM BRIGHTON BEACH TO THE ORIENTAL.   Brooklyn has more coast resorts than any other city in the country.   Here myriads of people recuperate,
During the summer the coast is alive from Fort Hamilton to the Oriental.   The view shows bathing pavilions with life lines and other precautions, including constant watchers in rowboats.   At low tide,
a vast stretch of smooth and hard sand is utilized by bathers.   The beaches are illuminated at night by electric lights, and the surges of the ocean are met day and night by surges of pleasure seekers.

Music Hall   Grand Stand   Brighton Beach race course at the rear   Brighton Beach Hotel   Bathing Pavilion   Manhattan Beach

BRIGHTON BEACH HOTEL, BRIGHTON BEACH, CONEY ISLAND.   Between the Concourse and the Manhattan Beach property.   Magnificent view of the ocean and Lower Bay.
At terminus of several railroad lines from Brooklyn, connecting by transfers throughout the Borough.   European and American plans; accommodations for several hundred permanent guests.   Excellent
music by brass band during summer months.   Fine concert-hall, made famous by orchestra of Anton Seidl during his lifetime.   Spacious elevated board walk along the beach to West Brighton.

"Marine Railway"   Manhattan Beach Hotel   Music Pavilion   Bathing Pavilion   Oriental Hotel

MANHATTAN BEACH AND ORIENTAL HOTELS, Manhattan Beach, Coney Island.   Eastern limit of the improved district.   Outgrowth of the remarkable Coney Island development of 1874.
Erected to meet demand for better and more exclusive accommodations.   Access from Brighton Beach section only via "Marine Railway," one-quarter mile.   Fee for admission to grounds from other direc-
tions.   Extensive lawns and flower beds, on made ground, illuminated at night.   Manhattan Beach Hotel accommodates transient guests.   Oriental Hotel designed for permanent guests rather than excursionists.

Concourse, terminus of Ocean Parkway   Bathing Pavilion   Brighton Beach Hotel

CONEY ISLAND BATHING-BEACH, West Brighton, Coney Island.   Scene at low tide.
The beach at Coney Island is one of the most extensive on the Atlantic coast.   Its gently shelving sands afford safe and enjoyable bathing for the large crowds that congregate here every summer.
A large portion of the Brighton and Manhattan Beach water-fronts are protected by breakwaters to prevent the sea from encroaching and injuring the great hotels and pavilions there erected.

Organized 1866   Formerly at foot of 55th St.

ATLANTIC YACHT CLUB, Sea Gate (Norton's Point), Coney Island.

Brooklyn's leading yacht club. Membership, 700. A large fleet of schooners, steam yachts, large sloops, and small cabin-yachts. Club-house the headquarters for aquatic sports. Harrison B. Moore, Commodore.

Grant Monument   Organized 1889   Bedford Avenue

UNION LEAGUE CLUB, Bedford Avenue and Dean Street.

Like its Manhattan parent, a Republican stronghold, though tending more toward social lines. Gave Grant statue to city. 1896. Membership 800. Frederic E. Gunnison, Prest. Frederic P. Tuthill, Sec'y.

LINCOLN CLUB, 65–67 Putnam Avenue, near Classon Avenue.

Organized 1877. Incorporated 1879. Sixteenth Century Venetian clubhouse; R. L. Daus, architect. Social club. 200 members. James J. McCabe, Pres't.

ELKS LODGE, 123 Schermerhorn Street. Organized 1883.

Brooklyn Branch, No. 22, of the Benevolent and Protective Order of Elks. W. J. Buttling, Exalted Ruler. Headquarters at Indianapolis.

GERMANIA CLUB, 120 Schermerhorn St., near Smith St.

Org. 1860. Social intercouse and cultivation of the German language. Ball-room; theatrical hall. 250 members. A. B. Birtner, Pres't.

Eighth Avenue   Club House dedicated 1891   Francis H. Kimball, Architect   Lincoln Place

MONTAUK CLUB, Plaza Circle, Eighth Avenue, and Lincoln Place. Organized 1889.

Modified Venetian; yellow brick and pale terra cotta; modeled after Casa d'Oro, Venice. Ladies' dining-rooms. **Large ball-room. Elegantly decorated. 450 members. T. H. Troy, President.**

Clinton Street   Bronze statue of Alexander Hamilton   Remsen Street

HAMILTON CLUB, Clinton and Remsen Streets.

Brooklyn's most exclusive club. Incorporated 1882. Outgrowth of Hamilton Literary Society (1829–1882). The best club library in the Borough. 653 members. Sanford H. Steele, President.

Lafayette Ave.　　Incorporated 1880　Oldest club on "the Hill."　　S. Oxford St.

OXFORD CLUB, 109 Lafayette Avenue, corner S. Oxford Street.

For general social purposes. Exclusive and representative. Many notable citizens among its 300 members. The president, Edwin S. Marston, is president of the Farmers' Loan & Trust Co.　Theo. L. Cuyler, Jr., Sec'y.

Real Estate Exchange　　Brooklyn Club Oldest in Brooklyn, organized 1865　　St. Ann's Church

BROOKLYN CLUB, Pierrepont and Clinton Streets.

Handsome brick and brownstone front, two buildings combined, the corner one originally the Greenleaf Young Ladies' Seminary. First president, Henry E. Pierrepont. Membership, 450.　Edward M. Grout, Pres.

Flatbush Ave.　　　　　　　Park Circle

THE RIDING AND DRIVING CLUB, Vanderbilt and Flatbush Avenues.

On Prospect Park Plaza. Organized 1889. Largest private riding-ring in America, 95 x 190 feet. Spacious parlors and accommodations. Stable-room for 200 horses. Membership, 400.　Wm. N. Dykman, President.

Bay 12th St.　　　　　　　Bay 15th St.

MARINE AND FIELD CLUB, Cropsey Avenue, Bay 12th and 15th Streets.

Organized 1885. Grounds fronting Gravesend Bay, Bath Beach. Ten acres. An ideal country club. Golf links. Moorings for yachts and small boats. Membership, 400.　Edward C. Platt, President.

Founded 1889　　　　　　Membership, 100

MIDWOOD CLUB, Ocean Avenue, near Caton Avenue.

Named from Midwout, the Dutch village (Flatbush). Club-house former residence of Clarkson family. Three acres park. Scene of select social entertainments.　Hazard Lasher, Pres.　Harman S. Salt, Sec'y

Frank Freeman, Architect　　Organized 1894　　Former house nearly opposite, on Clinton St.

CRESCENT ATHLETIC CLUB, Pierrepont St., northwest corner of Clinton St.

Magnificent new city-home of this prosperous organization, now under construction. One of the finest club-houses in the country. 1,700 resident, 200 non-resident members.　Charles M. Bull, Pres.

Organized 1884　　　　　　2074 members

CRESCENT ATHLETIC CLUB, First Avenue, 83d to 85th Streets.

Country club-house, fronting the Narrows at Bay Ridge. City house 25 to 29 Clinton Street; new one under construction.　Strongest athletic club in the United States.　C. M. Bull, President.

ST. AUGUSTINE'S R. C. CHURCH, Sixth Ave. and Sterling Pl. Founded 1870. 6,000 parishoners. Thirteenth and Fourteenth Century Gothic. Most beautiful Catholic church in Brooklyn. Very Rev. E. W. McCarty, Pastor.

ST. LUKE'S P. E. CHURCH, Clinton Avenue, near Fulton Street. Memorable by long and faithful ministration of Rev. Dr. J. W. Diller. 1842-80. Rector, Rev. H. C. Swentzel, D.D. 1200 members; extensive mission work.

MARCY AVENUE BAPTIST CHURCH, Marcy and Putnam Aves. Organized 1873. A beautiful and imposing edifice. Auditorium, chapel, Sunday-School library, etc. 1858 members. Rev. W. C. P. Rhoades, D.D., Pastor.

ST. PAUL'S P. E. CHURCH, Church Avenue and St. Paul's Place. Imposing edifice of the largest and oldest Episcopal church in Flatbush. Cost, $150,000. Organized 1836. 1,200 members. Rev. T. G. Jackson, D.D., Rector.

ST. ANN'S P. E. CHURCH, Clinton and Livingston Streets. Oldest Episcopal parish in Brooklyn. Founded 1784. Present Northern Gothic edifice built 1807. 1,500 members. Rev. Reese F. Alsop, Rector.

LUTHERAN CHURCH OF THE REDEEMER, Bedford Avenue. Recently erected imposing edifice. Organized 1894. Membership, 550. Sunday-School, 500. Value of property, $115,000. Rev. R. G. Weiskotten, Pastor.

FLATBUSH REFORMED CHURCH, Flatbush Ave and Church Lane. Organized 1654. First church erected 1655; present building, 1796. Oldest Brooklyn parish, 625 members. Rev. C. L. Wells, D.D., Pastor, 1863 to 1904.

ST. MARK'S LUTHERAN CHURCH, Bushwick Ave., cor. Jefferson St. Organized 1868. Membership, 1,400. Sunday-School membership, 1,200. Church property, $200,000. Pastor, Rev. August E. Frey; installed 1871.

GRACE M. E. CHURCH, Seventh Avenue and St. John's Place. Stone, terra cotta trimmings; 13th century Gothic. Sunday-school adjoining. Built 1883; society organized 1878, 550 members. Rev. F. F. Shannon, Pastor.

ST. JAMES'S P. E. CHURCH, Lafayette Avenue and St. James Place. Organized 1868, mainly by members of St. Luke's parish, on account of removal from vicinity. 700 members. Rev. T. J. Crosby, Rector.

FIRST REFORMED CHURCH, Seventh Avenue and Carroll Street. Founded 1660. Originally at Fulton and Lawrence Sts. In 1807, Joralemon St., near Court St. 1500 members. Rev. James M. Farrar, Pastor.

LAFAYETTE AVE. PRESBYTERIAN CHURCH, at S. Oxford St. Organized 1857. Famous for long ministry of Rev, Theo. L. Cuyler. Membership 2400. Maintains two missions. Pastor, Rev. C. B. McAfee, D.D.

ALL SAINTS P. E. CHURCH, Seventh Avenue and Seventh Street. Outgrowth of a small society organized in 1867. Now 1000 members. Sunday-school 500. Property value, $100,000. Rev. W. Morrison, Rector.

SECOND CHURCH OF CHRIST, SCIENTIST, Park Place. Near Nostrand Ave. Organized 1897. Miss Bertha M. Parce, Reader, 200 members. Maintains a reading room at 1201 Bedford Ave., open daily, 10 to 5.

STS. PETER AND PAUL [R. C.], Wythe Ave., near S. Second St. Founded 1847. Famous for long pastorate of Rev. Sylvester Malone. 11,000 parishioners. Rev. John L. Belford, pastor. Important Catholic parish.

ST. EDWARD'S R. C. CHURCH, St. Edward Street and Leo Place. Erected 1903, 900 sittings. Church organized 1891. 3500 parishioners. Value of church property, $150,000. Rev. Jas. F. Mealia, Pastor.

PLYMOUTH CONGREGATIONAL CHURCH, Orange Street, near Henry Street.
Brooklyn's most widely famous church. Organized 1847. Scene of Henry Ward Beecher's memorable labors 1847 to 1887. Rev. Dr. Lyman Abbott, Pastor, 1888 to 1898, and Rev. N. D. Hillis, Pastor since 1899.

SANDS STREET MEMORIAL CHURCH, Henry and Clark Sts.   Cradle of Brooklyn Methodism.
Handsome stone edifice, erected 1889. Removal of society from Sands St. made necessary by extension of Brooklyn Bridge. Rev. George M. Brown, Pastor. Organized 1794. Sands St building erected 1848.

SECOND UNITARIAN CHURCH, Clinton and Congress Streets.   Organized 1850.
Building erected 1858, during pastorate of Rev. Samuel Longfellow, brother of the distinguished poet. Rev. John W. Chadwick, pastor from 1864 until his death, 1904. "Represents rational religion."—J. W. C.

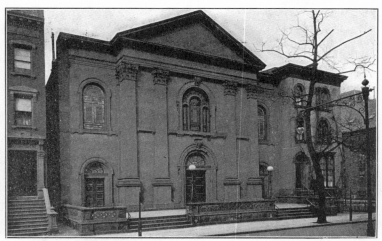

THE REFORMED CHURCH ON THE HEIGHTS, Pierrepont Street, near Henry Street.
Organized 1837. The present edifice was built in 1851, during the pastorate of Rev. George W. Bethune, D.D. Membership, 450. Rev. John Douglas Adams, D.D., Pastor.

NORWEGIAN LUTHERAN DEACONESSES' HOME AND HOSPITAL, 4th Ave. and 46th St.
Established 1883. A most useful institution, under Lutheran auspices. Supported by voluntary contributions and board paid by patients. Ambulance service. Jens Skougaard, Pres.; Bernt Berger, Treas.

HOUSE OF THE GOOD SHEPHERD, Hopkinson Avenue and Pacific Street.
Established 1868. For shelter and reformation of erring girls and women. In charge of Roman Catholic Sisters of the Good Shepherd, who also maintain St. Agnes Home. Sister M. St. Gertrude, Supt.

BROOKLYN INDUSTRIAL SCHOOL AND HOME, 217 Sterling Place.
For white Protestant children, 3 to 12 years old. Board and instruction free or partially paid. Maintains seven outside schools for poor children; supplies them warm dinners daily, and clothing. Mrs. W. H. Lyon, Pres.

ANGEL GUARDIAN HOME, Twelfth Avenue and Sixty-fourth Street.   Organized 1899.
For children of 2 to 7 years. In charge of Sisters of Mercy, 273 Willoughby Ave., who maintain also an industrial school, day schools, and a summer home and farm at Syosset, L. I. Outdoor visitors for the sick.

Pacific Street   Founded 1887 by Dr. Cornelius N. Hoagland   Henry Street

HOAGLAND LABORATORY, corner Henry and Pacific Streets.

Dutch architecture. First laboratory in America founded by private means for bacteriological, histological, and pathological research. Used by L. I. College Hospital Medical School. C. O. Gates, President.

Henry Street   Red-brown and Indiana limestone   Marshall L. Emery, Architect   Amity Street

POLHEMUS MEMORIAL CLINIC, Henry and Amity Streets. Erected 1897.

Memorial to Henry Ditmas Polhemus by his wife, Caroline H. Polhemus. 40,000 visits made by patients annually. Annual expense, $15,000. Used by L. I. College Hospital Medical School. W. B. Davenport, Pres.

Amity Street   Erected 1903   Wm. C. Hough, Architect   Henry Street

THE DUDLEY MEMORIAL, Henry and Amity Streets.

Home for nurses of the L. I. College Hospital and for students in training-school. Memorial, by Henry W. Maxwell, to the late Dr. William H. Dudley, one of the founders, and for many years president of the college.

Established 1852   For the sick poor

BROOKLYN HOMEOPATHIC HOSPITAL, Cumberland Street, near Park Avenue.

Largest homeopathic hospital in the Borough. 40,000 patients treated yearly. Training-school for nurses. Under direction of Department of Public Charities. Dr. Chas. Bowman Bacon, Superintendent.

Founded 1882   230 beds

ST. MARY'S HOSPITAL AND DISPENSARY, St. Mark's and Buffalo Avenues.

Under Roman Catholic auspices, but patients of all creeds and races received, non-contagious cases. Mechanical remedies made in orthopedic dept. Nurses' training school. Sister Stephen, Supt.

Myrtle Ave.   Founded 1878

BUSHWICK AND EAST BROOKLYN DISPENSARY, Myrtle and Lewis Avenues.

Colonial brick and white marble building. A memorial of the Henry Batterman family. 14,000 patients annually. Expenditures, $3,600. Maintained mostly by private contributions. Ira Goddard, President.

George I. Seney, founder

Raymond St.

METHODIST EPISCOPAL HOSPITAL, Seventh Avenue and Sixth Street. Founded 1881

The first and national hospital of the Methodists

2,500 patients annually in wards and rooms. Policy non-sectarian. Rev. Dr. J. M. Buckley, President. William Halle, Jr., Vice-President. Dispensary established 1895. Cares for 18,000 poor patients annually. Rev. Dr. A. S. Kavanagh, Superintendent. Maintains a training-school for nurses.

Amity Street　　　　Henry Street

LONG ISLAND COLLEGE HOSPITAL, Henry, Pacific, and Amity Streets. Established 1858

4,000 patients annually. Expenditures $90,000. Dr. R. E. Shaw, Medical Superintendent. In same building, the L. I. C. H. Dispensary; Guild for poor patients, station. Nurses' Training School; Long Island College Hospital Medical School, 404 students, four-year course. Maxwell Lester, Secretary.

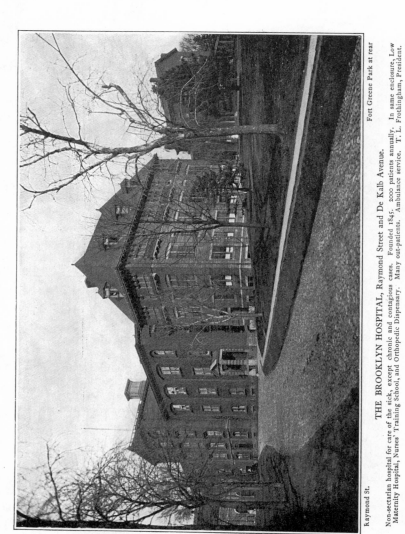

Fort Greene Park at rear

THE BROOKLYN HOSPITAL, Raymond Street and De Kalb Avenue. In same enclosure, Low

Non-sectarian hospital for care of the sick, except chronic and contagious cases. Founded 1845. 2,000 patients annually. Maternity Hospital, Nurses' Training School, and Orthopedic Dispensary. Many out-patients. Ambulance service. T. L. Frothingham, President.

Naval laboratory in same grounds

UNITED STATES NAVAL HOSPITAL, Flushing Avenue, opposite Ryerson Street. Established 1828

For sick and disabled sailors and marines. Two spacious structures. Grounds, 20 acres. 184 beds. During Civil and Spanish wars the leading naval-hospital station. Annex for contagious diseases. Naval vessels fitted out with medical and surgical supplies. Marine Director, G. E. H. Harmon, U. S. N.

Formerly Memorial Hospital Purchased in 1903
THE JEWISH HOSPITAL, Classon and St. Mark's Avenues.
Over $200,000 spent in recent improvements. For women and children.
Medical and surgical treatment. Non-sectarian. Abraham Abraham, Pres.

Warren Street Established 1864 Henry Street
ST. PETER'S HOSPITAL, Henry Street, between Warren and Congress Streets.
St. Peter's Church
Handsome brick and stone edifice. For gratuitous treatment of the sick poor. Under Roman Catholic auspices, in charge of Sisters of the Poor of St.
Francis. Accommodations for 350 patients; average cared for annually, 3,300. Property value, about $500,000. Sister Demetria, Superior.

Sunner Ave. Willoughby Ave.
ST. JOSEPH'S FEMALE ORPHAN ASYLUM, Willoughby Ave.
Brick, brown stone trimmings. Erected 1871. Chapel, playground, day school.
In charge of R. C. Orphan Society, 4 Court Square.

McCADDIN MEMORIAL, Berry Street, near South Third Street.
Gift of Mrs. Ann E. Walsh to Church of Sts. Peter and Paul, in memory of her
brother, Henry McCaddin, Jr. Library, assembly and class rooms, etc.

ST. PHŒBE'S MISSION, 125 De Kalb Ave., opp. Fort Greene Pl.
Established 1883 by A. A. Low. Aids the sick and destitute in hospitals and
tenements. Miss Sara Clapp, Sec. Miss M. S. Grider, Associate-in-charge.

CITY PARK BRANCH MISSION, 209 Concord Street.
Mission of the First Presbyterian Church. Founded 1865. Rev. G. K. Newell,
Minister. 428 members. Parish house. Neighborhood charities.

ST. JOHN'S HOSPITAL, Albany and Atlantic Avenues.
Established 1851. One of five important institutions of the Church Charity Foundation of L. I., Bishop Fred'k Burgess, Pres. For non-contagious cases.

JAMES GORDON BENNETT LOT, Green-Wood Cemetery.

Family burying-plot of the Bennett family. Marble statuary-group of angels, erected by James Gordon Bennett to the memory of his father, founder of the "New York Herald." This group is one of the most beautiful in this cemetery, widely famous for its many notable monuments.

JOHN W. MACKAY TOMB, Green-Wood Cemetery.

Magnificent tomb of John W. Mackay, the founder of the Mackay-Bennett Cable (Commercial Cable Co.) and Postal Telegraph System. His fortune was begun in Western mining-operations. The tomb is of gray granite, embellished with noteworthy bronze groups of angelic figures. On a high knoll.

JOHN ROACH LOT AND MONUMENT, Green-Wood Cemetery.

Beautiful granite shaft and statue, erected to the memory of John Roach, the famous American shipbuilder, who built many notable vessels, including several of the battleships of the United States Navy, and who was one of the greatest factors in the revival of American shipbuilding.

MARCUS DALY TOMB, Green-Wood Cemetery.

Beautiful and costly mausoleum of a remarkable man. Born in Ireland, Marcus Daly came early to America, and, beginning in Montana as a practical miner, became an expert judge of minerals and the main owner of the Anaconda copper-mine and operator in other mines and enterprises.

GREEN-WOOD CEMETERY, A WORLD-PRAISED NECROPOLIS, Fifth Avenue, 36th and 37th Streets, Fort Hamilton Parkway, Gravesend Avenue.

One of the most noted cemeteries in America; the largest in Brooklyn. Founded 1838; opened 1840. Area, 478 acres. 350,000 interments. 1.—A typical scene—chapels, tombs, shafts, and statuary. 2.—Gothic Ionic tomb. 3.—Gothic Gateway, main entrance, Fifth Ave. and 25th St. 4.—Bust and monument of Henry George, the economist. 5.—Monument to 105 victims of Brooklyn Theatre fire (1876). 6.—Henry Ward Beecher grave (square stone at right in picture). 7.—Charlotte Canda Memorial and Mausoleum of Squire P. Dewey. 8.—Grave of Elias Howe (1819-67), inventor of sewing-machine. 9.—Monument to Samuel F. B. Morse (1791-1872), inventor of the telegraph. 10.—Rear entrance, at Fort Hamilton Parkway. 11.—Monument to De Witt Clinton (1769-1828), governor of New York and father of the Erie Canal. Manhattan office of cemetery, 170 Broadway. David G. Legget, President; Samuel Carey, Comptroller; T. Hood Muir, Secretary.

CYPRESS HILLS CEMETERY, half a mile East of Ridgewood Reservoir.   Entrances on Jamaica Avenue and Myrtle Avenue.   Manhattan office, 1 Madison Avenue.
One of the oldest of the five large Brooklyn cemeteries.   400 acres.   Beautiful rural and secluded views, containing much forest-land, and several small lakes.   More than 150,000 graves, including several thousand removals from old cemeteries in Manhattan.   Large soldiers' plot, on historic Revolutionary battle-ground.   Plots of Dramatic Fund, N. Y. Press Club, and other societies.

"THE EVERGREENS" CEMETERY, in Kings and Queens Counties, adjoining Highland Park.   Main entrance, Bushwick Avenue and Conway Street.   About 300 acres.   Chartered, 1849.
Large sums expended in beautifying the grounds and preserving natural landscapes.   Terraces, lakes, and many charming vistas.   Handsome stone office-building, receiving-vaults, and many costly monuments and mausoleums.   Upon Beacon Hill the United States has erected, in a clearing visible from the sea, a monument to sailors of every nationality who died in its service.

THE SELIGMAN LOT, Salem Fields Cemetery.
One of the older mausoleums. The family tomb of Joseph, Jesse and James Seligman of the well-known firm of J. & W. Seligman & Co., bankers, whereof Isaac N. Seligman is now the head.

THE GUGGENHEIM MAUSOLEUM, Salem Fields Cemetery.
Erected in 1900 by the sons of M. Guggenheim, noted in the metal industry. Especially notable for its fine hexagonal mosaic dome and the beauty of its interior marble work. Herts & Tallant Architects.

SALEM FIELDS CEMETERY, Jamaica and Norwood Avenues, opposite Euclid Avenue.
Largest Hebrew cemetery in the City. Area, 64 acres. On a beautiful slope one-eighth mile east of Highland Park. Laid out and conducted by Congregation of Temple Emanu-El, Manhattan. Favorite burial-place for wealthy Hebrew families. Its many, beautiful, and elaborate monuments are scarcely surpassed even in Green-Wood. Octavius Hiltman, Superintendent.

THE SHEEPSHEAD BAY RACE-TRACK, The Grand Stand and the Paddock. Ocean Avenue and Voorhees Lane, half mile from Coney Island. The largest of the three racing-tracks in the Borough. Reached by the Manhattan Beach and the Brooklyn & Brighton Beach Railroads. One mile in length. Grounds over 100 acres. Owned by the Coney Island Jockey Club, Manhattan; William K. Vanderbilt, President. Upper scene is the Grand Stand at the track, seating over 5,000 people. Lower scene shows Society in the Paddock, extensive enclosure reserved for horse-owners, club members and their friends. One of the most largely attended amusement-resorts around New York. Scene of the great annual "Futurity Races." Track used also by the Sheepshead Bay Club of Brooklyn, 500 members; Frederick T. Clarke, President.

1903 1905 1911

Bank of the Metropolis   Decker Bldg.   Hartford Bldg.   "Flat-Iron"   Broadway   "Century"   Metropolitan Tower   Everett Bldg.   Fourth Ave.   Germania Life   Union Square Savings Bank

UNION SQUARE, Broadway to Fourth Ave., 14th to 17th St.; 3.48 acres set apart as a park in 1809; scene of reception to Gen. Washington, Evacuation Day, Nov. 25, 1783; Croton Water celebration, Oct. 14, 1842; Union Defence mass meeting, 1861; for a generation the heart of the hotel district; recently developed as a mercantile centre by the erection of huge loft buildings along Fourth Ave. on sites of the Everett House, at 17th St.; Hotels Clarendon, Florence and Belvedere at 18th St., Ashland at 24th St. and Putnam at 28th St.   Subway under Fourth Ave.

NEW YORK

KING'S VIEWS

FOUR HUNDRED 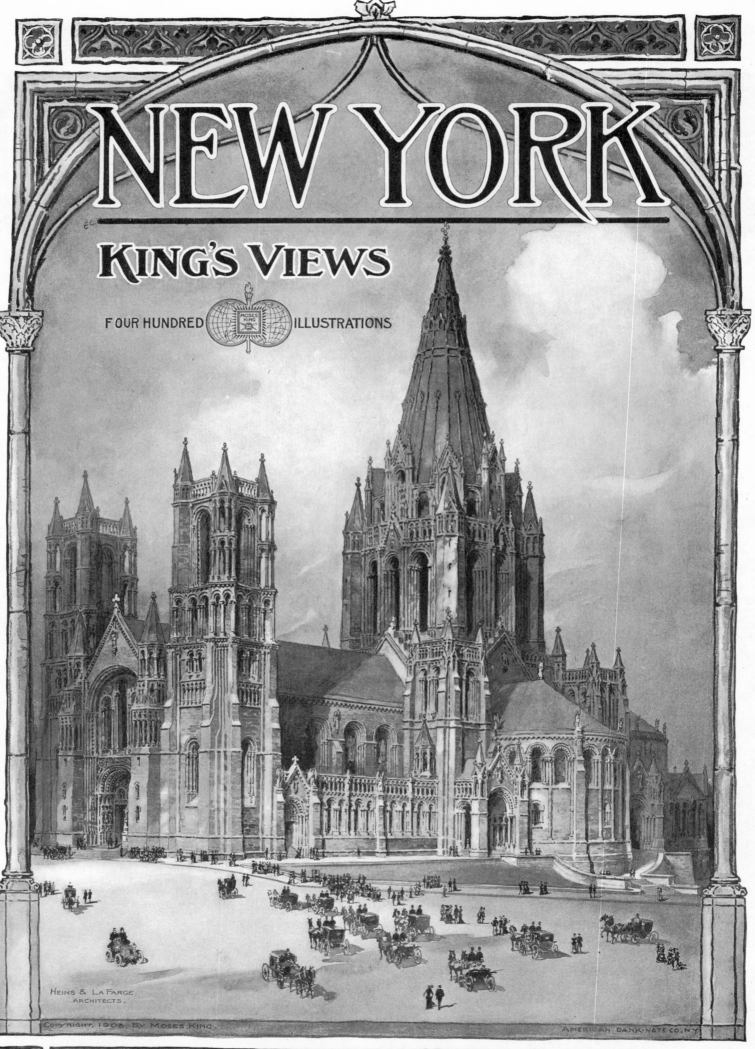 ILLUSTRATIONS

HEINS & LA FARGE
ARCHITECTS.

AMERICAN BANK-NOTE CO. N.Y

 The Protestant Episcopal Cathedral of St. John the Divine.

The year 1903 is the two hundred and fiftieth anniversary of the incorporation of New Amsterdam, the original Dutch settlement of the City of New York. The noblest local edifice in construction at this time is St. John's Cathedral, shown above, now rising on a commanding position on Morningside Heights, West 110th to 113th Streets. It is to cost over $10,000,000. Corner-stone laid Dec. 17, 1892. Services now held in crypt. Its relation to America will be virtually the same as St. Paul's to England. The Bishop of the Diocese is the Rt. Rev. Henry C. Potter, LL.D.

Stock Exchange   Trinity Church   Astor Building

TRINITY CHURCH, at Head of Wall St. View Westward from Broad and Nassau Sts.
The most valuable real estate section in the metropolis. The financial centre of America. The most famous street on the continent, the venerable Trinity Church looming up in the distance.

Geo. L. Morse, Architect   Eagle Building   Eagle Press Room

"BROOKLYN DAILY EAGLE," Washington and Johnson Streets, Brooklyn.
"The Brooklyn Eagle" is one of the leading newspapers of Greater New York, not excepting the Manhattan papers. The new plant, completed 1903, is one of America's most perfect newspaper-establishments.

Broadway   Arnold, Constable & Co.'s Retail Department   Nineteenth Street   Arnold, Constable & Co.'s Wholesale Department   Fifth Avenue

ARNOLD, CONSTABLE & CO.'S DRY-GOODS ESTABLISHMENT, Broadway and Nineteenth Street, extending to Fifth Avenue. Constable Building adjoins, on Fifth Avenue.
New York's most aristocratic dry-goods establishment. Huge, finely appointed storehouse. For three-quarters of a century a business in which New Yorkers have taken pride. Founded 1827. Comprises wholesale and retail dry-goods, carpets and upholstery. The founder, Aaron Arnold, and the late James M. Constable, were two of New York's most representative merchants.

"CHINATOWN," Pell Street, West of Chatham Square. Headquarters for the Chinese of New York, who come here from all the boroughs to worship "Joss" and obtain native supplies of food and clothing. Oriental section of the metropolis. Chinese Theatre, Chop Suey Houses, etc. A bizarre and very curious settlement. Visited at night by sightseers.

NEW YORK'S GHETTO MARKET, Seward Park, Essex, Hester, and Suffolk Streets. As the centre of the Russian and Austrian Hebrew settlements, it is a busy A characteristic and picturesque phase of metropolitan life on the East Side. Every description of merchandise is sold on these push-carts. Among the city's most interesting sights. Photograph by Byron. scene from dawn until night.

Photo. by Falk, with the Charles Mills' Panoramic Camera

Forty New Structures in 1903   Entrance   The Midway   The Theatre

CONEY ISLAND, LUNA PARK AND ITS MIDWAY. New York's Popular Pleasure-Resort. Five miles South of Prospect Park, with which it is connected by the Ocean Parkway. Reached by Trolleys, Long Island Trains, and Coney Island Boats. Coney Island in 1903 is changed from its former character. It mainly comprises a World's Fair, covering 22 acres, in Luna Park. In the centre are a heart-shaped lake and electric tower 200 feet high; before the entrance, a Court of Honor, with peristyle. Thompson & Dundy host of amusements; trip to the moon in airship Luna III; submarine journey through tropical and arctic seas; villages representing different nationalities; bombardment of Fort Hamilton; hippodrome; chutes; circus; children's theatre and playground; temples, minarets, etc. Crowds of merry bathers on the beach.

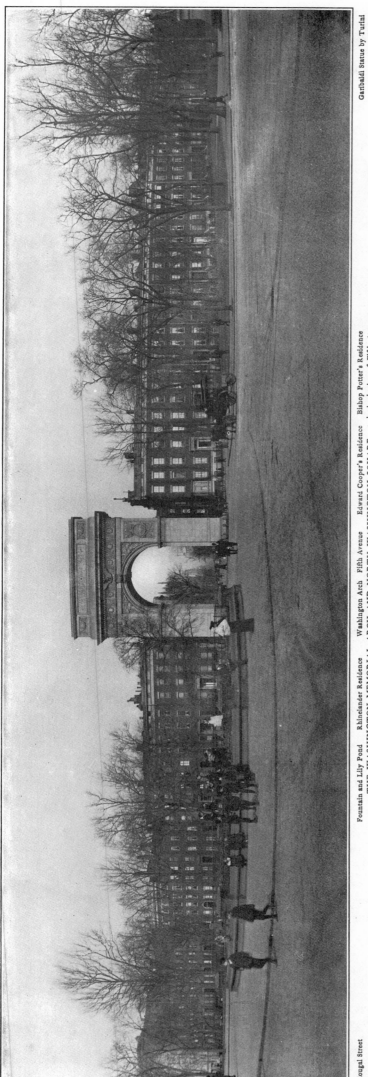

Macdougal Street   Fountain and Lily Pond   Rhinelander Residence   Washington Arch   Fifth Avenue   Edward Cooper's Residence   Bishop Potter's Residence   Garibaldi Statue by Turini

THE WASHINGTON MEMORIAL ARCH AND NORTH WASHINGTON SQUARE, at the beginning of Fifth Avenue. Originally a Potter's Field, this beautiful Park was for over half a century the chosen residential section of the Stuyvesant, Lord, Rhinelander, Potter, DePeyster, Cooper, and other esteemed New York families. These old-fashioned red brick mansions are imposing in their artistic uniformity. The stately white marble arch, designed by Stanford White, occupying the centre of this panoramic view, was erected in 1889-92 to commemorate the inauguration of General George Washington as first President of the United States. Cost $128,000, raised by subscription. Judson Memorial south side of square,

Broadway   Fourteenth Street   Lincoln Building   Brentano's—Books, Papers, etc.   Union Square   Tiffany's   Bank of the Metropolis   Lafayette Statue   Hartford Building   Flat-iron Building   Everett House   Fourth Avenue

PANORAMA OF UNION SQUARE AND VISTAS OF FOURTEENTH STREET AND FOURTH AVENUE, looking Northward and Westward from the Morton House, at Broadway and Fourteenth Street. Photo. by Burr W. McIntosh. Vivid reproduction of active metropolitan life. Great Union Defence Meeting held here in 1861 to provide New York City troops for the Civil War. The electric passenger-car is here contrasted with the horse-car, now rapidly disappearing. Lincoln statue on the left; behind it, Lincoln and Spingler Buildings, Brentano's and Tiffany's. The Bank of the Metropolis Building carries the eye toward Upper Broadway. Lafayette Statue, dedicated 1876 by French residents, in foreground. Rapid transit tunnel stations at extreme right. On the right are the Century Magazine offices and Everett House.

The Dun Building   Broadway   Where Stewart Building now stands   City Hall Park   Proposed Municipal Building on Chambers Street   New Hall of Records   City Hall

PROJECTED TWENTIETH-CENTURY MUNICIPAL BUILDING, facing Southward over City Hall Park, Broadway, Chambers, Reade and Centre Streets.   Drawn by Richard W. Rummell.   Copyright, 1903, by Moses King.

A central municipal building is a need of the city.   Among numerous plans is the above, created from suggestions by the Municipal Art Society.   It proposes to remove from City Hall Park all structures excepting the City Hall, thus providing a park as foreground, and on site of the Stewart Building to **erect a** counterpart of the new Hall of Records, and on the intervening properties (Emigrant Savings Bank, American News Co., etc.) a main structure surmounted by a lofty dome.   This plan is advocated because it provides, at minimum cost, a great structure, centrally located for all **Greater New York.** Another plan (by Gustav Lindenthal, drawings by architect Henry Hornbostel) provides for a similar structure, without dome, but extended around to Brooklyn Bridge, having at corner a gigantic tower, 45 stories, 650 feet high.   Different plans suggested by Mayor Seth Low, Andrew H. Green **and others.**

CITY HALL

CITY HALL LOOP STATION.

EAST RIVER BROOKLYN TUNNEL

VENTILATING SHAFT 104th ST

BROOKLYN BRIDGE STATION.

City Hall, with its Station below   Brooklyn Bridge and Elevated Road, Park Row and Surface Roads, and Tunnel with Subway Roads   East River and Tunnels   Ventilating Shaft

NEW YORK CITY UNDERGROUND RAPID TRANSIT SYSTEM, Connecting the Boroughs of Manhattan, Brooklyn and the Bronx. Drawn for King's Views by R. W. Rummell.

Owned by the City. Ultimate cost, $60,000,000. Inaugurated by Mayor Van Wyck, March 24, 1900. Work begun July 10, 1900. Trains will run over Manhattan Division in 1904. Brooklyn Bridge is terminal for all lines. Manhattan western line runs to Kingsbridge; eastern section, to Bronx Park. Brooklyn tunnel will pass under Broadway to South Ferry, thence under East River to Atlantic and Flatbush Avenues. Manhattan and Bronx lines will reach Yonkers and Williamsbridge. Various loop-lines and branches already projected. John B. McDonald and associates, notably August Belmont, contractors and operators. Chief Engineer William Barclay Parsons has earned New York's perpetual gratitude. Subway is rectangular, 13 feet high, 25 feet wide for 2-track sections, 50 feet wide for 4-track sections. Concrete bed, steel frame construction, concrete walls and roof, lined with asphalt and roofing-felt. Mostly near surface. 80 feet deep at Columbus Ave. and 104th St. Elevators at 169th and 181st Sts. (110 feet underground, hewn out of rock). Electricity (third rail) City Hall Park to 96th St., 13 minutes.

Hotel Cambridge   Astor Court   Thirty-third Street   The Waldorf   Waldorf-Astoria   Fifth Avenue   The Astoria   Knickerbocker Trust Co.   Brick Presbyterian Church

FIFTH AVENUE IN THE AFTERNOON.   View West on Thirty-third Street and North on Fifth Avenue.   Photograph by Burr W. McIntosh.
Typical scene on New York's most celebrated thoroughfare, famed for its hotels, clubs, homes, public buildings and churches.   Incessant cortége of vehicles, most costly-apparelled occupants, and a continuous procession of well-dressed people.   The Waldorf-Astoria occupies the centre of this picture.   Just beyond, the Knickerbocker Trust Co.'s building, approaching completion, the tall Æolian building, etc.

Fifth Avenue Bank   Collegiate Church   Windsor Arcade   Heavenly Rest Church   Fifth Avenue   Delmonico's   Forty-fourth Street

FIFTH AVENUE, FROM FORTY-FOURTH STREET TO CENTRAL PARK.   View Northward from the Fifth Avenue Bank and Delmonico's.   Photo. by Burr W. McIntosh.
An instantaneous photographic reproduction of aristocratic city life in the fashionable centre of the metropolis.   Free from railroad tracks, Fifth Avenue is an ideal carriage promenade.   On the cross streets are many of New York's most costly homes and most noted clubs: on 43d Street, the Century, Racquet, Academy of Medicine; on 44th Street, New York Yacht, Bar Association, Harvard, etc.

Plaza Hotel   Central Park   Sherman Statue   The Plaza   Metropolitan Club   Hotel Netherland   Hotel Savoy   Bolkenhayn   Fifty-eighth Street

CENTRAL PARK PLAZA, FIFTY-NINTH STREET ENTRANCE TO PARK, Fifth Avenue, Fifty-eighth and Fifty-ninth Streets.
Fashionable carriage-way to the Park and Eastern Driveway.   View taken looking north from the Cornelius Vanderbilt residence.   Shows the Netherland, Savoy and Plaza Hotels, the Metropolitan Club, Gerry residence, and beyond.   The Plaza Hotel, although a grand hotel, is to be replaced by one much grander.   The Netherland may come down for the proposed widening of Fifty-ninth Street.

Broadway   "Flat-iron"   Stern Brothers   Twenty-third Street   Stern Brothers

STERN BROTHERS, DRY-GOODS ESTABLISHMENT, West Twenty-third Street, South Side, between Fifth and Sixth Avenues. Carriage entrance also on Twenty-second Street side.
A well-established and highly esteemed house which has steadfastly devoted itself to "dry-goods only." One of the finest business establishments in New York, carrying an extensive stock of choice goods,
and enjoying a very high grade of patronage. Twenty-third Street, in the Stern Brothers locality, is an exceptionally interesting shopping-district.

Madison Avenue   Vanderbilt Avenue   Grand Central Station   Subway or Tunnel   Industrial Hall   Depew Place

NEW YORK CENTRAL & HUDSON RIVER RAILROAD, GRAND CENTRAL STATION, Forty-second to Forty-fifth Streets, Vanderbilt Avenue to Depew Place.
Metropolitan terminus of the New York Central lines—the Central Railway System of America, comprising numerous railroads operating 11,126 miles east of the Mississippi. Terminal facilities also for
New York, New Haven & Hartford Railroad and Harlem Railroad. Station built when William H. Vanderbilt was President. Remodeled 1901. A vastly enlarged and perfected station is planned, to
increase terminal facilities and connect with Rapid Transit Subway. William H. Newman, President; Hon. Chauncey M. Depew, Chairman of Board; George H. Daniels, General Passenger Agent.

NEW YORK LIFE AS IT IS. Instantaneous photographs of many subjects. Photos by Byron.

Immigrants landing at Barge Office; lemonade vender, 34th Street; immigrants at South Ferry; Staten Islanders arriving; basket-woman at market; crossing between the " Flat-iron," Fifth Avenue Hotel and Madison Square; families at Recreation Pier; lunches back of " Herald " office; Doyers Street in Chinatown; marketers in Mulberry Bend; millionaire sleighing to the Park; Free Ice for the Poor; shoe-lace merchants everywhere; vegetable woman in the market; fruit-carts at many corners; pretzel boys at Sixth Avenue and 34th Street; cabmen at Greeley Statue; newsboys playing "craps" in Greeley Square; snow-wagons at city's dumps; cars at 34th Street and Broadway, and Street Cleaners in their white garments. Fine character sketches.

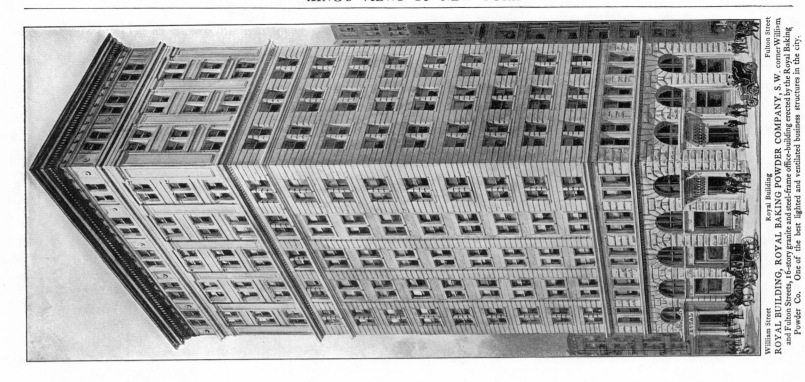

William Street   Royal Building   Fulton Street

ROYAL BUILDING, ROYAL BAKING POWDER COMPANY, S.W. corner William and Fulton Streets, 16-story granite and steel-frame office-building erected by the Royal Baking Powder Co. One of the best lighted and ventilated business structures in the city.

Royal Bldg.   Downing   "Post"   Bennett Bldg.   Market and Fulton Bank

FULTON STREET, from Gold Street, west, showing the funnels of an American liner at its North River pier. The main artery between the Jersey ferries and the Fulton St. ferries to Brooklyn. Horse-cars still hinder traffic on this busy thoroughfare.

One of the Narrowest Streets in Old New York   Nassau Street

ANN STREET, from Nassau west, looking into Vesey St, which starts at Broadway. On the right towers Park Row Building, tallest in the city; at left the Bennett and St. Paul Buildings; wing of the National Park Bank between. Push-carts and lunch-wagons at curbs.

Fifth Ave, looking North   The Cambridge   W. 33d Street   The Waldorf   The Astoria   Knickerbocker Trust Co.   Brick Presb. Church
THE WALDORF-ASTORIA, Fifth Ave, 33d to 34th Sts.   Largest, most elaborately equipped hotel in the world; 16 stories, 214 ft. high;
1,400 rooms; greatest ball-room and banquet-hall in the city; beautiful roof-garden.   Waldorf section owned by Wm. Waldorf Astor;
Astoria section by Col. J. J. Astor.   Assessed at $9,185,000.   Henry J. Hardenbergh, Architect.   George C. Boldt, Proprietor.

W. 14th Street   R. H. Macy & Co.   Broadway   Herald Sq Theatre
R. H. MACY & CO'S DEPARTMENT STORE, Herald Square, Broadway, Sixth Ave, 34th to 35th Sts, occupying a majestic model 9-story
structure with 24 acres of floor space.   Contains every personal and home necessity and adornment.   Spacious restaurant, art gallery,
exhibition hall, etc.   Founded in 1858 as the Original Department Store.   The firm consists of Isidor and Nathan Straus.

Manhattan Water-front, on North River, from Christopher to 14th Streets, in background
HAMBURG-AMERICAN LINE PIERS, at the foot of 1st and 2d Sts, Hoboken, adjoining Lackawanna Ferry.   The company's fleet of
310 vessels, of which 22 are in the New York service, has an aggregate capacity of 799,948 tons.   Regular sailings to and from Europe.
Winter and summer cruises.   50 services, to all parts of the world.   Emil L. Boas, American General Manager, 37 Broadway.

Broadway, looking south   Greeley Statue   Martinique   W. 32d Street   Imperial   Greeley Square   Union Dime Savings Institution   Sixth Avenue

GREELEY SQUARE AND UNION DIME SAVINGS INSTITUTION, at the intersection of Broadway, Sixth Ave. and 32d St; named in honor of Horace Greeley, founder of "The Tribune," whose statue, the gift of the printers of the United States, marks the Square. Under Sixth Avenue, at this point, will be the terminus of the New York & New Jersey tunnel, being built, under Pennsylvania R.R. auspices, below the Hudson River from Jersey City. The Union Dime Savings Institution, founded 1859, has 87,786 depositors; resources, $27,875,000; Charles E. Sprague, President.

Grace Church   10th Street   Wanamaker's (formerly Stewart's)   E. 9th Street   Wanamaker's New Store, Broadway Front   Astor Place, E. 8th Street   Bible House

WANAMAKER'S, occupying two blocks on Broadway, from 8th to 10th Sts, through to Fourth Ave, connected by passages under 9th St, with entrances from Astor Place Subway station. Iron building on the north, erected 1867 by Alexander T. Stewart, was then the largest store in America. John Wanamaker, the world's greatest retail merchant, with whom is associated Robert C. Ogden, in 1896 acquired the Stewart store and in 1905 erected the new Wanamaker's, a modern 14-story structure, costing $4,000,000, the greatest store in the world. D. H. Burnham & Co, Architects.

Railroad Offices   New York Central Terminal, in process of erection   St. Patrick's   Depew Place   St. Regis   To be completed 1907   U. S. Post Office

NEW YORK CENTRAL & HUDSON RIVER RAILROAD TERMINAL, East 42d St, Vanderbilt Ave. to Depew Place; magnificent edifice to replace Grand Central Station, covering 19 city blocks; 47 tracks on level below street; 15 platform tracks below for suburban trains; larger train capacity than any other station in the world; largest main concourse, 160 by 470 ft, 150 ft. high. Main entrance of three arches, each 33 ft. wide and 60 ft. high; ticket-lobby, 90 by 300 ft. Offices at left, Post Office at right. Terminal also for New York, New Haven & Hartford R. R.

Columbus Avenue   The View Shows Museum when Completed, Cady, Berg & See, Architects   Only South End is Built   Central Park Reservoirs   Eighth Avenue

AMERICAN MUSEUM OF NATURAL HISTORY, Manhattan Square, W. 77th to W. 81st Sts, Columbus Ave. to Central Park West; founded 1869; cornerstone laid by President Grant 1874; first section opened 1877; 77th St. front 710 ft. long, completed 1899; one of the largest natural-history museums in the world; many notable collections; technical library of 46,000 volumes; exhibition-halls contain 213,000 sq. ft; lecture-hall seats 1,400; over 500,000 visitors annually; conducts scientific expeditions.   Morris K. Jesup, President; Hermon C. Bumpus, Director.

NEW AMSTERDAM THEATRE, 42d St, W. of Broadway; one of the world's handsomest playhouses. Aerial Gardens. Klaw & Erlanger, Managers. Seats 1,702.

LYRIC THEATRE, 42d St, west of 7th Ave; exquisitely appointed home of musical comedy; seats 1,349. Shubert Bros, Managers.

BELASCO THEATRE, 42d St, west of 7th Ave; scene of notable triumphs; not in theatrical syndicate. David Belasco, Manager.

HAMMERSTEIN'S VICTORIA, 42d St. and 7th Ave; fine vaudeville. Paradise Roof Gardens. Owned by Oscar Hammerstein, founder New York and Criterion Theatres.

LYCEUM THEATRE, 45th St, east of Broadway; one of the most stately façades in the city; seats 958. Dan'l Frohman's chief playhouse.

FIRST NIGHT GROUP; Byron's composite gathering of dramatic critics, actors and literary celebrities between the acts discussing a new production: (1) Nat Goodwin. (2) James Hazen Hyde. (3) George Ade. (4) Carlotta Nilsson. (5) Elizabeth Tyree. (6) Marshall P. Wilder. (7) Gustav Kobbé. (8) Alan Dale. (9) Grover Cleveland (in box). (10) James Huneker. (11) Edward Fales Coward. (12) William Winter. (13) John Drew. (14) Abe. Hummel. (15) John Kendrick Bangs. (16) Henry W. Savage.

THE CASINO, Broadway, S. E. cor. 39th St; famous for its many musical burlesques; rebuilt 1905; seats 1,500. Shubert Bros, Mgrs.

SAVOY THEATRE; 34th St, west of Broadway; famous for long runs of noted productions; seats 841. Charles Frohman, Mgr.

HUDSON THEATRE, 44th St, east of B'way; one of the foremost of the city's playhouses; seats 995. Henry B. Harris, Prop. and Mgr.

GARRICK THEATRE, 35th St, east of Herald Square; scene of some of Chas. Frohman's best productions. E. R. Reynolds, Lessee.

GRAND OPERA HOUSE, 8th Ave, N.W. cor. 23d St; one of the older theatres; opened in 1868 as Pike's Opera House; afterward owned by James Fisk, and later by Jay Gould. Immense foyer and stage; scene of many triumphs; seats 2,910. Popular playhouse. John H. Springer, Mgr.

MAJESTIC THEATRE, Grand Circle, 59th St. and 8th Ave; prominent family house; seats 1,705. Col. J. S. Flaherty, Manager.

W. 46th St. New York Theatre Hotel Rector Broadway "Times" 7th Ave. Hotel Astor Astor Theatre Gaiety Theatre Cafe Madrid Globe Theatre

"TIMES" SQUARE, formerly called Longacre, formed by the intersection of Broadway and Seventh Ave., extending from the "Times" Building, at 42d St., to 47th St.; centre of the theatre and hotel district; 28 of the foremost playhouses in America within 250 yards, with seating capacity for audiences aggregating 36,000; Metropolitan Opera House two blocks below 42d St.; Hippodrome, largest playhouse in world, one block east; more people pass 42d St. and Broadway in 24 hours than any other point in world; 40 great restaurants, some of world-wide reputation, within 400 yds.

Fourtl Ave. Broadway Union Square University Pl. Fifth Ave. Sixth Ave. Retail Shopping District

NIGHT SCENE, remarkable photograph taken from the Metropolitan Life Tower at 23d St. and Madison Ave., showing the Singer Tower, at Broadway and Liberty St, 2⅓ miles to the south, near the centre of the view, and the lights of the Brooklyn Bridge, to the left; the pillars topped by electric lights, just to the right of the centre of the picture, mark Fifth Ave. illuminated for the Hudson-Fulton celebration, September, 1909, and in the right foreground are some of the great stores of the retail shopping district, while the loft buildings of Fourth Ave. fill the left foreground.

Engineering Hall   Earl Hall   Gymnasium   Seth Low Library   Schermerhorn Hall Fayerweather Hall Law School   Hamilton Hall   Hartley Hall   Livingston Hall

Subway School of Mines Broadway   Faculty Club   W. 116th St. Library Terrace   St. Paul's Chapel   South Field, devoted to athletics   W. 114th St.

COLUMBIA UNIVERSITY Broadway to Amsterdam Ave., W. 114th to 120th St.; founded as King's College, 1754, at Broadway and Barclay Sts.; moved in 1857 to Madison Ave. and 49th St.; new site of 26 acres secured 1892 and 1902; $13,000,000 group erected, 1892-1911, McKim, Mead & White, Architects; 11 faculties; 685 instructors; 6,602 students; includes Barnard College for Women at 119th St., founded 1889; Teachers' College, 120th St., 1886; College of Physicians and Surgeons, W. 59th St.; endowment, $27,000,000. Nicholas Murray Butler, Pres.

College of the City of New York   D. Willis James Memorial Chapel   Convent of the Sacred Heart   Dormitories   Library   Teachers' College   Harlem

Professors' Apartments   Claremont Ave.   Cloisters   President's Residence   W. 120th St.   Administration Building   Barnard College

UNION THEOLOGICAL SEMINARY, Claremont Ave. to Broadway, 120th to 122d St.; founded 1836 at 9 University Pl.; at Park Ave. and 70th St., 1884-1910; new group erected 1908-10 on site given by D. Willis James; value, $4,500,000; endowment, $3,500,000; 200 students; 22 instructors; buildings enclose a quadrangle 300 x 100 ft.; corner towers to be 200 ft. high; library 100,000 volumes, 56,000 pamphlets, 186 manuscripts; Presbyterian, but independent of ecclesiastical control. Rev. Dr. Francis Brown, Pres. Robert C. Odgen, Pres. of Trustees.

WATER GATE, to be erected on the Hudson River at West 106th St., as a memorial to Hendrick Hudson, who discovered the river in 1609, and to Robert Fulton, who successfully inaugurated steam navigation on the Hudson in 1807; an imposing $1,000,000 structure to be used for public celebrations and as a fitting place for the landing and reception of distinguished guests; the plans drawn by H. Van Buren Magonigle contemplate in addition to the two quays and stately colonnade, two stadia, one for children's games, the other for ceremonies and pageants.

Sacred Heart Convent   Columbia University   Grant's Tomb   Riverside Drive Viaduct   Hebrew Orphan Asylum   The Palisades   Hudson River

St. Nicholas Park and Terrace   City College, Main Bldg.   Geo. B. Post, & Sons, Arch.   Thomas Dwyer, Builder   W. 140th.St.   Gymnasium   Townsend Harris Hall   Chemistry Bldg.   Convent Ave.   Mech. Arts Bldg.

COLLEGE OF THE CITY OF NEW YORK, St. Nicholas Terrace to Amsterdam Ave., W. 140th to W. 138th St.; imposing $4,000,000 group of fieldstone and terra cotta buildings, occupied 1905; founded 1847 as free Academy; City College, 1866; four-year collegiate course, 1,228 students; three-year preparatory department, in Townsend Harris Hall, and in old college building at 23d St. and Lexington Ave., 2,200 pupils; 232 instructors. Free tuition; supported by City at annual cost of $615,000. Edward M. Shepard, Chairman. Dr. John H. Finley, Pres.

Soldiers' Monument   Apartment Houses   Belnord and Bretton Hall   The Apthorp   The Lombard   The Wellsmore

Riverside Park   Riverside Drive   W. 75th St.   Geo. H. Macy Residence   W. 74th St.   W. H. Beardsley Residence   W. 73d St.   Charles M. Schwab Residence

RIVERSIDE PARK, W. 72d St. to W. 129th, along Hudson River; 140 acres, acquired by the city 1872-1901. RIVERSIDE DRIVE, from W. 72d St. to the Soldiers' and Sailors' Monument at 89th St. This is the finest residence district in the city, where lots 100 ft. deep are worth from $1,200 to $1,600 a front foot on the Drive, from $700 to $1,100 on the adjacent side streets; Schwab residence, occupying the block from 73d to 74th Sts. through to West End Ave. is assessed at $1,700,000; other residences range in value from $200,000 to $350,000.